Legal Problem Solving

Reasoning, Research & Writing

Second Edition

Maureen F. Fitzgerald
B.Comm., LL.B., LL.M.

Butterworths

Toronto and Vancouver

Legal Problem Solving: Reasoning, Research & Writing

© Butterworths Canada Ltd. 2001
March 2001

The Butterworth Group of Companies

Canada:
Butterworths Canada Ltd.,
75 Clegg Road, MARKHAM, ONTARIO L6G 1A1
and
1732-808 Nelson St., Box 12148, VANCOUVER, B.C. V6Z 2H2

Australia:
Butterworths Pty Ltd., SYDNEY

Ireland:
Butterworths (Ireland) Ltd., DUBLIN

Malaysia:
Malayan Law Journal Sdn Bhd, KUALA LUMPUR

New Zealand:
Butterworths (New Zealand) Ltd., WELLINGTON

Singapore:
Butterworths Asia, SINGAPORE

South Africa:
Butterworth Publishers (Pty.) Ltd., DURBAN

United Kingdom:
Butterworth & Co. (Publishers) Ltd., LONDON

United States:
LEXIS Publishing, CHARLOTTESVILLE, VIRGINIA

Canadian Cataloguing in Publication Data

Fitzgerald, Maureen F.
  Legal problem solving: reasoning, research & writing

2nd ed.
Includes bibliographical references and index.
ISBN 0-433-42444-3

1. Legal research — Canada.   2. Legal research.   3. Legal composition.
I. Title.

KE250.F57 2001   340'.07'2071   C2001-930010-7
KF240.F57 2001

Printed and bound in Canada.

To Paul Clay Quinn

Preface

Legal problem solving is the most fundamental skill that lawyers possess. Lawyers practise in different areas, but they are all engaged in solving problems. Legal problem solving takes a particular form that is learned by law students in their first year at law school in a course called legal research and writing. The skill evolves throughout law school and long into practice.

This book was written to make this learning in first year more efficient, effective, and enjoyable. It was also written for non-lawyers who wish to research the law.

In 1993, I researched the ways in which legal research and writing were taught in Canadian law schools. The results indicated that the majority of law schools were struggling with the teaching of legal research and writing. Although each faculty recognized the importance of these skills, they found it difficult to find an appropriate place for them in the curriculum. Most instructors felt that students could learn the skills for legal research and writing in much more effective and efficient ways.

On the basis of my research, I adopted a problem-based, self-teaching model to teach legal research and writing, which I used to teach at the University of Victoria and the University of British Columbia. I wrote this book as the textbook for those courses. It is based on the following assumptions about learning:

- The learner should be an active participant in the learning process — students learn best by doing.
- Classroom time is best utilized for practising skills and receiving feedback on these skills.
- Peers can assist greatly in learning.
- Students learn skills best through a process of demonstration, repeated practice, and feedback.
- Basic information about the law and the location of books in the library can be self-taught through written materials.
- Responsibility for learning rests almost entirely with the student. The role of the teacher should be that of a coach or facilitator of learning.
- Problems based on real life situations have more relevance to students and therefore improve learning and make it more enjoyable.

This book consists of self-teaching materials supplemented by self-tests and exercises. Instead of teaching only how to find books in a library, this book teaches all of the skills necessary to solve a legal problem.

Who This Book Is For

This book can be used by anyone who wishes to solve a legal problem. This includes lawyers, law students, legal assistants, and the general public. It is written in a way that should be easily understandable to those who are not familiar with the law.

The Format of This Book

This book teaches the entire *process* of legal problem solving. All research begins with a set of facts or circumstances. The researcher's tasks are to analyze the facts, determine the legal issues, find relevant law, analyze the law, apply the law to the facts, and communicate the results.

Each chapter begins with a set of learning objectives and ends with a self test. This enables the reader to see quickly what is covered in each chapter and know what to expect.

Since the skills of factual analysis, issue identification, finding the law, legal reasoning, and legal writing are learned best through repeated practise, examples and problem-based exercises have been included. In addition to doing these exercises, researchers should practise the skills on their own or in small groups where skills can be simulated and feedback received.

Acknowledgements

I feel honoured to be able to write a second edition of this particular book. When I began teaching legal problem solving seven years ago, I never thought that my sometimes confused and emerging ideas would ever be shared by so many law students and law faculty. I sincerely hope that this simple tool has helped people in some way.

I again want to thank those who helped with my first edition; their impact and input was substantial. This includes: Kathleen McIsaac, the professors and students at the University of Victoria and University of British Columbia, Don Thompson, Lynn Smith, Monica and Paul Beauregard, Ron Friesen, Bill Duncan, Marion Cragg, John Fairlie, Nancy Hannum, Pat Pitsula, Pat Nelson, Sharon Samuels, Anne Morrison, Joan Honeywell, Joan Fraser, Penny Hazelton, Michael Lee, and Paul Quinn.

I would also like to thank Gayle Kiss, Michael Silverstein, Francine Drouin, Tracy Smith, Allan Dingle, Annie Rochette, Tim Perrins, Penny Hazelton, Mary Mitchell, and all of the law faculty across Canada who provided me with suggestions for this second edition.

Finally, thanks to the publishers who generously granted their permission to reproduce information contained in this book, as well as those organizations that generously provided funding for the first edition: the Legal Research Foundation, the Faculty of Law at the University of Victoria, the Office of the President at the University of Victoria, and the Law Foundation of British Columbia.

I welcome comments and feedback on the book, and can be reached via e-mail at mfitzgerald@primus.ca.

Maureen F. Fitzgerald
Vancouver, October 2000

Table of Contents

The Legal Research Process 1

The ultimate goal of legal research is to find solutions to legal problems. In simple terms, this means finding relevant statutes and cases, interpreting them, and applying them to particular situations. There is no single best way to approach a legal problem; however, all research should be approached systematically.

This book provides a basic introduction, framework, and strategy for conducting legal research. It introduces a step-by-step approach to legal research that can be utilized by newcomers to legal research. It teaches all of the skills necessary to complete any research problem from beginning to end by duplicating the entire research process that lawyers use to solve legal problems. It includes instruction on how to analyze legal problems, design a research plan, locate the law, reason legally, and present research results in an understandable way.

The skills taught here are designed to supplement other legal education and should assist students at law school, during professional legal training, and after call to the Bar. This book should be used as a springboard towards development of expert research skills.

Although the process of legal research has, herein, been broken down into distinct steps for purposes of learning, it must be recognized that legal research is complex and will be shaped by the researcher and the individual problem.

This chapter provides an overview of the entire five-step process of legal research. The remaining chapters discuss these steps in more detail.

Learning Objectives

At the end of this chapter you will be able to:

- Describe the five-step process of legal research
- Explain what is meant by factual analysis
- Explain what is meant by issue determination
- Explain what is meant by legal analysis

The Legal Research Process (FILAC)

All legal research begins with a legal problem and ends with a solution or conclusion about how the law applies to that problem. The complete process of legal research involves tasks that can be translated into the FILAC five-step approach to legal research:

    Step 1: **F**acts — Analyze the facts
    Step 2: **I**ssues — Determine the legal issues
    Step 3: **L**aw — Find the relevant law
    Step 4: **A**nalysis — Analyze the law and apply it to the facts
    Step 5: **C**ommunication — Communicate the results of the research

These five steps overlap and are repeated over and over as a researcher begins to solve a legal problem. For example, a researcher will analyze the facts initially but will continue to hone the facts as the research continues. Each of the steps is revisited periodically as the research evolves.

The following is a brief description of each step.

Step 1: Analyze the Facts — Each new legal problem will have aspects to it that are totally foreign to the legal researcher. The first task, therefore, is to make some sense of the problem by gathering the necessary facts and separating the legally relevant facts from the irrelevant ones. This is called factual analysis.

Step 2: Determine the Legal Issues — After the facts have been analyzed, the next step is to identify the legal issues raised by the facts. This involves determining the legal questions that need to be examined. This is called "issue determination" and requires reading about the law generally.

Step 3: Find the Relevant Law — After the legal issues have been identified, the researcher should visit the library, use online resources or the Internet to locate the relevant cases, statutes, and other legal sources. In order to do this, the researcher must have a basic understanding of what the law is and where it is located. The majority of your research time will be spent at this stage.

Step 4: Analyze the Law and Apply It to the Facts — Analyzing the law involves reading the relevant law, synthesizing it, and applying it to the facts. Some refer to this step as "thinking like a lawyer," legal reasoning, or legal analysis.

Step 5: Communicate the Results of the Research — The last step involves <u>communicating the results of the research to</u> the person in need of the research. The results must be communicated either orally or in writing and must be understandable, accurate, clear, and concise. This communication usually takes the form of a memorandum of law or an opinion letter.

The researcher should continually review each of the above steps and confirm the results of each as the law and the problem become clearer. Although the research process has been divided into five steps, it must be emphasized that the process is an art as opposed to a science. Researchers should feel free to develop their own techniques in addition to the basics learned here.

In the FILAC model, as with any research model, the researcher must be systematic. Research should never be approached in an *ad hoc* way. Each step should be planned and the results of the search should be recorded, as the research process sometimes extends over weeks or months.

An Example of the Research Process

The following is a simplified example of the five steps of the legal research process.

Fact Pattern
Ms. Safety Your client, Ms. Safety, is a security guard for a toy store. One night, after carefully checking the store, she inadvertently locked in Sam, a small boy, who was hiding in the building. The boy was found the next day unharmed. The boy's parents, however, are threatening a false imprisonment suit. Ms. Safety claims she had no intention to confine the boy and would like to know if the boy's parents have a basis for their threatened suit.

Facts: The relevant facts are that Ms. Safety inadvertently locked Sam inside a store. His parents suggest that this is false imprisonment.

Issues: After reading about the law you decide that the legal question to be answered is: Was the inadvertent locking of Sam in the store false imprisonment?

Law: You search the law library and online materials and find that there are no statutes that describe the law of false imprisonment, but there are a number of cases. You read these cases and synthesize them. See the example below.

Analysis: After reading the relevant cases, the researcher might synthesize this part of the law into a statement something like this:[1]

> To be found guilty of false imprisonment the person imprisoning the other must have been aware of the imprisonment. If there is no intent to imprison there cannot be false imprisonment.

Applying this law to the facts, it is likely that because Ms. Safety was not aware of the boy hiding in the store, she had no intent to imprison and therefore likely cannot be said to have falsely imprisoned Sam.

Communication: You can tell your client that it is unlikely that her inadvertent locking of Sam in the store would be considered to be false imprisonment.

Self Test

The following is a self test based on the information provided in this chapter. The answers to these questions, and the answers to all the other self test questions at the end of chapters, are found at the end of the book in the "Answers to Self Tests" section.

1. What is the five-step process of legal research?
2. What is factual analysis?
3. What is issue determination?
4. What is legal analysis?

---

[1]   This is only an example and should not be considered an accurate statement of the law.

Factual Analysis

2

The first step in the legal research process is factual analysis. Every research problem begins with a set of facts or circumstances which must be analyzed in order to determine which legal issues need to be researched. The researcher must read the facts and elicit the legally relevant facts prior to entering the library.

Every new legal problem presents new challenges to students and lawyers alike. No two situations are identical and the variety of situations that clients present to lawyers is infinite. As well, many problems involve multiple legal issues that may not be immediately obvious. It is therefore necessary to develop a method by which to break down the facts. This method may then be used on each new legal problem.

This chapter explains what factual analysis is, describes a method of analyzing facts, and provides an example of factual analysis.

Learning Objectives

At the end of this chapter you will be able to:

- Name the three steps of factual analysis
- Describe what PEC stands for
- Identify legally relevant facts
- Restate facts

What Is Factual Analysis?

Factual analysis is the task of extricating legally relevant facts from the mass of facts in a legal problem. Legally relevant facts are those with the most legal significance or that raise issues of law. These facts dictate the issues of law to be researched.

The relevant facts are those facts that the courts will take into consideration if the case proceeds to trial. Determining which facts are relevant is a judge's first task when deciding a case. Indeed, every written judgment begins with a recitation of relevant facts.

Although it is difficult to determine the legally relevant facts without some knowledge about the law, an initial attempt at sorting relevant facts from irrelevant ones can provide focus and considerably reduce the need for library research.

How to Analyze Facts

Factual analysis involves figuring out the who, what, where, and why of the problem presented; separating the relevant facts from the irrelevant ones; and restating the facts in a concise fashion. There are a number of ways to analyze facts. The method described here is a recommended systematic approach.

Although there is some skill involved in analyzing the facts of a problem, a researcher who is systematic about the process will find that it soon becomes second nature. Usually a first attempt at factual analysis will not be complete. Factual analysis should continue throughout the research process as the legal issues are defined and narrowed. The process necessitates that researchers return to the facts after looking at the law and revise your statement of the facts accordingly.

There are essentially three steps in factual analysis. They are as follows:

Step 1: Gather and organize the facts
Step 2: Identify the legally relevant facts
Step 3: Formulate the facts

The following fact pattern will be used to explain each of these steps.

Fact Pattern

Paul Quint and Melody Jones

Paul Quint and Melody Jones, after ten years of marriage, are getting divorced. They have two children, Lindsay and Wayne, and have agreed that the children will stay with Melody. However, they cannot reach an agreement as to the division of property. They own a house and a boat on Salty Island. In addition, two years ago, Melody was given a $20,000 gift from her grandmother, which she put into a separate bank account in her own name. She wants to know whether the judge will consider the gift to be a family asset when making a decision about the division of property.

Step 1: Gather and Organize the Facts

The first step in factual analysis is simply to determine what happened. This involves gathering facts and putting them in some kind of order. Researchers should select a method of gathering facts that is easy to use but comprehensive.

In law school, fact patterns are often provided to students in exercises or exams. Therefore, students are often not required to gather facts. Gathering facts, however, is an important step in legal research since the particular facts drive the research and determine the outcome.

Gathering facts usually involves speaking to people such as clients, witnesses, and experts. It also includes gathering information from books or reports and collecting physical evidence such as contracts or weapons.

Typically, fact gathering involves answering who, what, where, when, why, and how. Who is involved or affected? What happened — directly or indirectly? Where and when did it happen? Why did the situation arise? How did it occur? At this initial stage there should be little attempt to control the facts, except to enable the researcher to detect gaps or inconsistencies.

One technique that is frequently used to start thinking about facts is brainstorming. This approach simply requires that the reader think of all possible parties, events, and claims regardless of their significance, relevance, or order.

Although there are a number of ways to gather and organize facts,[1] a recommended method is called the PEC method (Parties, Events, and Claims). In every legal problem there are parties, events, and claims. In each problem presented there is a person or persons with a legal problem, events happen which lead up to the problem, and a claim is made by one or several parties. In analyzing facts, researchers should think about every potential party, every possible event, and any claim that comes to mind.

Some of the questions that should be asked under each of these headings are as follows:

Parties

- Who are the people involved in the problem?
- What are the parties' roles or occupations?
- What are the relationships between the parties?
- What are the parties' special characteristics?

---

[1] Two popular methods used for legal problems are called TAPP (Things, Acts, Persons, and Places) and PAPO (Persons, Actions, Places, and Objects). Both TAPP and PAPO provide four-step tools with which researchers can determine what legally significant events happened.

Events

- What occurred?
- When did it occur?
- Where did it occur?
- What is the nature of the location where it occurred?
- How did it occur?

Claims

- What are the parties complaining of?
- What are the parties claiming?
- What are the injuries or harm?
- What will the defence to the claim likely be?

A researcher should be able to state in non-legal terms the answers to the above questions. At this stage it is important to stay open to as many ideas as possible. There is a danger of defining a problem too narrowly, too early, and rushing into the library.

The following are the facts which were gathered and organized in the Paul Quint and Melody Jones situation:

Parties

Paul Quint: husband of Melody and father of Lindsay and Wayne
Melody Jones: wife of Paul and mother of Lindsay and Wayne
Lindsay Jones: daughter of Paul and Melody
Wayne Quint: son of Paul and Melody
Grandmother: mother of Melody

Events

Paul and Melody were married ten years ago and are now divorcing and splitting their property. Two years ago, Melody's grandmother gave her $20,000. Melody held the money in a separate bank account.

Claims

Melody: claims that the $20,000 is hers and should not be part of the family assets, which will be divided upon marriage breakdown.

Paul: claims that the $20,000 is part of the family assets and should be included in the assets to be divided upon marriage breakdown.

Step 2: Identify the Legally Relevant Facts

Once you have gathered and organized the facts, it is necessary to identify which of those facts are legally relevant and which of those facts are irrelevant. The law determines which facts are legally relevant so that is what must be looked at. The following is an example of how to identify the relevant facts in Paul and Melody's situation.

We will assume that initial research of the law pertaining to marital property disclosed that there is a provincial statute called the *Family Property Act* (fictitious). This statute applies to all residents of British Columbia and all marriages that are entered into in British Columbia. It describes particular rules for the division of property upon marriage breakdown. Sections 8–10 provide as follows:

s. 8   Upon marriage breakdown each spouse is entitled to a half interest in the family assets.

s. 9 (1) Property owned by one or both spouses and ordinarily used by a spouse or a minor child of either spouse for a family purpose is a family asset.

(2) Without restricting the generality of subsection (1), the definition of family asset includes:

(*a*) money, including inheritances or gifts, obtained while in the marriage;

(*b*) a right of a spouse under an annuity or a pension, home ownership or retirement savings plan; or

(*c*) a right, share or an interest of a spouse in a venture to which money or money's worth was, directly or indirectly, contributed by or on behalf of the other spouse.

s. 10   Where the provisions for division of property between spouses under section 8 would be unfair having regard to:

(*a*) the duration of the marriage;

(*b*) the duration of the period during which the spouses have lived separate and apart;

(*c*) the date when property was acquired or disposed of;

(*d*) the extent to which the property was acquired by one spouse through inheritance or gift;

(*e*) the needs of each spouse to become or remain economically independent and self sufficient; or (*f*) any other circumstances relating to the acquisition, preservation, maintenance, improvement or use of property or the capacity or liabilities of a spouse,

a court may order that the property covered by section 8 may be divided into shares fixed by the court.

There is only one case which discussed this statute: *Bogman v. Bregman* (B.C.C.A.) (fictitious). In February 1995 Jill Bogman petitioned for a divorce from her husband, Kevin Bregman, and asked the court to make a determination about the division of assets. The court declared that pursuant to s. 8 of the *Family Property Act* a summer cabin, a camper van, and the contents of the matrimonial home were family assets and were divided equally between Jill and Kevin. A question arose as to whether Jill's registered retirement plan was a family asset. Jill acquired the plan through a monetary gift from her mother and kept it in a separate bank account under her name.

The court held that the retirement savings plan was not to be divided equally between Jill and Kevin. Although the savings plan was automatically included within the definition of family assets under s. 9(2)(*b*) of the *Family Property Act*, the fund was a gift from her mother, not used for family purposes, and was kept in a separate bank account. Therefore, the court exercised its jurisdiction under s. 10 of the *Family Property Act*. Although the court considered the fact that the gift had been received ten years prior and was fairly entrenched in the family assets, this factor was not deemed to be as relevant as the other factors in this particular situation.

The following is a brief summary of the statute and case law:[2]

The law provides that upon marriage breakdown "family assets" must be shared equally between the marriage partners. Family assets include gifts, inheritances, and registered retirement savings plans obtained while in the marriage. However, a court may alter this division if the division would be unfair having regard to a number of factors including "the extent to which property was acquired by one spouse through inheritance or gift" pursuant to s. 10(*d*) of the *Family Property Act*.

A case that interpreted this section (*Bogman v. Bregman*) found that in determining whether the inclusion of a gift is unfair and the extent to which the property was acquired by gift the court would look at the following three factors:

- Whether the gift was kept in a separate bank account;
- Whether it was used for family purposes; and
- How long it had been in the hands of the recipient.

For each component of the law there is a matching legally relevant fact in Paul and Melody's situation. For example, the above law states

---

[2] See Chapter 4 for an explanation of case law.

that family assets include gifts. Thus, one legally relevant fact is that Melody received the money as a gift. Also relevant is the amount of time the gift was held. The following schedule helps to differentiate the legally relevant facts from the law.

The Legal Questions	The Legally Relevant Facts
1. Is the money a "family asset"?	
(a) Was the gift obtained while in the marriage?	(a) Melody received the gift while she and Paul were married.
2. Would the distribution be unfair?	
(a) What was the extent to which the property was acquired by gift?	(a) Melody received the $20,000 from her grandmother.
(*i*) Was it kept in a separate bank account?	(*i*) Melody kept the money in a separate bank account.
(*ii*) Was it used for family purposes?	(*ii*) The money was not used for family purposes.
(*iii*) How long ago was it received?	(*iii*) Melody received the money two years ago.

Since the only legal issue is whether the $20,000 gift will be considered a family asset, only those facts related to the gift are legally relevant. It is likely, therefore, that the house and the boat are not relevant. It is also likely that the children are not legally relevant. Remember that the relevance of these facts may be revised as the law and the legal issues become clearer.

Step 3: Formulate the Facts

Once you have gathered and organized the facts and determined which ones are legally relevant, it is a good idea to restate or reformulate the facts. This restatement must, of course, include all the relevant facts but will also usually include some facts that help to put the situation into context and enable a reader to understand more clearly what happened.

There are no strict rules for formulating the facts. Some prefer to list the facts chronologically, while others prefer to state a critical fact first. The following are examples of two different approaches to restating the facts in the Paul and Melody situation.

Formulated Facts A

Melody and Paul are divorcing. Melody does not want a gift of $20,000 to be included in the division of family assets. She received the gift two years ago from her grandmother and has kept it in a separate bank account in her name since.

Formulated Facts B

Melody received a gift of $20,000 two years ago from her grandmother. She placed it in a bank account separate from her husband's, under her name. Melody is now divorcing her husband, Paul, and is concerned that the $20,000 will be split equally between she and Paul as part of the division of their family property.

Tips on Reformulating Facts

When restating or reformulating the facts, the following tips should be kept in mind:

- *Often "emotional" facts are irrelevant.* For example, the fact that Melody and Paul may have had a traumatic separation is not legally relevant.

- *Try to use objective language.* Avoid using adjectives or descriptive words. These words tend to make the reading more exciting, but, at the same time, indicate subjectivity or bias. For example, it is preferable not to refer to the home as "beautifully decorated." Later, during advocacy, these words may come in handy, but not at this particular stage.

- *Put the facts in an order that is best suited for the reader.* Writers often gravitate to a chronological description, but be conscious of the fact that a reader may prefer a catchy introductory line which talks about the crux of the issue.

- *Draw attention to any missing facts and their relevance.* Clearly state any necessary assumptions in the facts. If, for example, a critical factor in determining the division of family assets was whether the children had sufficient funds, you would need to either find out about the childrens' finances or make an assumption about their financial status.

- *Do not be afraid to include facts that may not be entirely relevant, but that make the facts readable.* Often a first attempt at restating the facts will be too abbreviated. Facts that are too bald are difficult to understand. Although tabulation of the facts is acceptable, it sometimes comes across as being sterile or too cut-and-dried.

Self Test

The following is a self test based on the information provided in this chapter. The answers to these questions are found in the back of the book in the "Answers to Self Tests" section.

1. What are the three steps of factual analysis?
2. What does PEC stand for?

Sample Exercise

Do a factual analysis for the following fact pattern.

Fact Pattern

Ravi, May, and Jan

Ravi and May are being sued jointly by the Regal Bank for $30,000, which was misappropriated from the bank by Jan, their law partner. Unsure of their liability, Ravi and May have asked for your opinion as to the likelihood of successfully defending the action in court. The circumstances leading up to the action are as follows:

Jan, Ravi, and May met and became good friends while they were attending law school in the mid-1980s. They talked often about opening a small firm together some day. All three were interested in blending traditional legal practice with other forms of dispute resolution services. Jan in particular developed a keen interest in mediation while she was at law school.

After being called to the Bar, the three friends decided to form a partnership under the name "JMR Legal Services", to practise law in Toronto. Their partnership agreement included the following terms:

...

14. All profits from the law practice will be shared equally among the partners.
15. Any income or profit received by a partner from business activities, investments, or other sources not forming part of the law practice shall belong to that partner separately, and shall not be subject to sharing under paragraph 14.
16. No partner may use the firm name, letterhead, equipment, or facilities for any purpose not connected with the law practice.

...

In the beginning, the partners worked cooperatively to build their fledgling practice. While all three provided legal representation to clients on a variety of matters, Jan also took some cases as a mediator. She had to keep these roles separate, of course, or she could be in breach of the Law Society's conflict of interest rules. That is, Jan could act *either* as the lawyer for one party to a dispute *or* as a mediator between the parties, but not both.

May and Ravi soon got into the habit of referring some of their clients to Jan when they thought a dispute could be handled more fairly or efficiently through mediation, rather than through adversarial legal action. The troubles began when Jan decided that since her mediation services were separate from her traditional law practice, any profits from mediation should be hers alone to keep. In order to make this clear, Jan began to meet with her mediation clients at home, rather than at JMR's offices, and she arranged for separate bookkeeping, banking, and advertising for "Jan's Mediation Services." Jan continued to take legal clients as well, doing this work at the office and sharing any billings with her partners. Although she bent over backwards to keep the two aspects of her practice separate, Jan occasionally asked the secretary who worked at JMR to type correspondence relating to her mediation files as a personal favour.

Ravi and May were surprised and displeased by Jan's move. In their view, the mediation services were integral to the kind of law practice the three of them had envisioned. Indeed, this was one of the main attractions of going into partnership with Jan. Ravi and May wrote a letter of protest to Jan, in which they argued that mediation profits were subject to sharing under the partnership agreement.

All of this suddenly became irrelevant, however, when Jan was charged with several counts of theft, and admitted that she had misappropriated $30,000 from the Regal Bank. The bank had retained her to provide mediation services in a major dispute with one of its corporate depositors, and she was holding the money in the trust account she had opened for Jan's Mediation Services. Upon discovering that Jan had no assets, the bank sued May and Ravi as partners in the JMR firm.

Answers to Exercise

Step 1: Gather and Organize the Facts

Parties

Ravi: lawyer and partner of May and Jan
May: lawyer and partner of Ravi and Jan
Jan: lawyer and partner of May and Ravi
Bank: client of Jan for mediation services

Events

- Ravi, May, and Jan formed the law partnership of "JMR Legal Services."
- Their partnership agreement stated that all profits from the law practice were to be shared, and the firm's name and facilities were only to be used for activities related to the law practice.
- Ravi and May regularly referred clients requiring mediation work to Jan.
- Jan started "Jan's Mediation Services," set up her own book-keeping, banking, and advertising, met her mediation clients at home, and kept all the profits generated from this work. She occasionally asked the secretary at JMR Legal Services to type correspondence relating to her mediation work.
- Ravi and May wrote a protest letter to Jan stating that the mediation profits should be shared.
- Jan misappropriated $30,000 from the Regal Bank and held the money in a trust account under the name "Jan's Mediation Services."
- The bank sued Ravi and May as partners in JMR Legal Services.

Claims

- Ravi and May: claim that they do not owe the Regal Bank $30,000 since Jan was working outside the partnership.
- The Regal Bank: claims that Ravi and May owe the Regal Bank $30,000 for the fraud of their partner Jan.

Step 2: Identify the Legally Relevant Facts

The Law

Initial research of the law pertaining to legal partnership and liability of partners disclosed that there is a provincial statute called the *Partnership Act* (fictitious). This statute applies to all partnerships entered into in Ontario. It describes particular rules for the liability of partners. Section 12 of the *Partnership Act* states:

> s. 12 Where by any wrongful act or omission of any partner acting in the ordinary course of the business of the firm, or with the authority of his or her co-partners, loss or injury is caused to any person not being a partner in the firm, or any penalty is incurred, the firm is liable for that loss, injury or penalty to the same extent as the partner so acting or omitting to act.

The following two cases interpreted this section of the *Partnership Act*:

Public Trustee v. Morton (Ont. C.A.) (fictitious)

The defendant, Ms. Morton, a solicitor and partner in a law firm, acted as an executor and trustee of an estate. Morton stole money from the estate. In the course of administering the estate, Morton used the staff and facilities of her law firm. Specifically, Morton used a junior solicitor and the firm's staff for the typing and bookkeeping work on the estate. The executor's fees were included in the firm's revenues. The court found the defendant's partners liable for Morton's wrongful acts because she was acting within the ordinary course of the firm's business. The court outlined several *indicia* as possible ways to separate a partner's activities as an executor of an estate from the ordinary course of the firm's business:

> There would probably be an agreement between the partners to that effect, and one might expect to find that the partner would not charge the estate on an account issued in the firm's name, would personally keep any fees and compensation paid, rather than treat them as revenues of the firm, would keep the funds of the estate in an account separate from her firm's trust account, and would keep a set of accounting records from the estate separate from those of his firm. If she wanted to be careful to make it clear that his work as an executor was not part of the firm's business, she would not use the firm letterhead when writing as an executor.

Kozy v. Pierre (S.C.C.) (fictitious)

Mr. Kozy, a solicitor in a law firm, entered into a business agreement with two clients to form a company and serve as one of its directors. When the company went bankrupt he did not contribute his share of the financing, nor did he help his two clients settle the debts. The court, applying the *Partnership Act*, found Kozy's partners liable for Kozy's wrongful acts because he was acting in the ordinary course of the business of the firm. Kozy acted as the solicitor to the company and, by extension, the directors. He also spent several years working for both clients prior to the company's formation. In addition, all meetings of the company's directors were held in Kozy's law offices. Although there were no profits *per se*, the firm benefited by having Mr. Kozy act as a director of such a prestigious company.

Summary of Statute and Case Law

From the statute and these two cases, the factors that indicate when a partner is acting in the ordinary course of business of a law firm are whether:

- There is an agreement excluding the activity from the firm's business;

- The firm's staff (including lawyers, secretaries, and bookkeepers), facilities (including accounts and offices), and name (including letterhead) are used; and
- The profits from the activity are shared.

The law and the corresponding legally relevant facts could be set out in a diagram as below:

The Law	The Legally Relevant Facts
Words in Statute	
Was the partner acting in the ordinary course of business of the firm?	Ravi, Jan, and Mary carried on business in a partnership called JMR Legal Services to provide legal and mediation services.
Factors from Cases	
1. Is there an agreement excluding the activity from the firm's business?	There is a partnership agreement. It does not exclude mediation from JMR's business, but it states that "all profits from the law practice will be shared equally" and "no partners may use the firm name, letterhead, equipment, or facilities for any purpose not connected with the law practice."
2. Did the partner use the firm's staff (including lawyers, secretaries, and bookkeepers), facilities (including accounts and offices), and name (including letterhead)?	Jan "occasionally" asked the secretary who worked at JMR to type correspondence relating to her mediation files "as a personal favour." Jan kept banking and bookkeeping separate and met mediation clients at her home.
3. Were the profits from the activity shared between the partners?	Jan kept her mediation profits to herself but Ravi and Mary disputed this.

Step 3: Formulate the Facts

The following is a restatement of the facts:

> Ravi, May, and Jan formed the law partnership of "JMR Legal Services" (JMR) to provide traditional legal and mediation services. Their partnership agreement stated that all profits from the law practice were to be shared, and that the firm's name and facilities were only to be used for activities related to the law practice.
>
> In building their practice, Ravi and May regularly referred clients requiring mediation work to Jan. However, Jan eventually decided that since her mediation work was separate from the traditional law practice, she would keep the profits generated from this work. Consequently, she started "Jan's Mediation Services" (JMS), set up her own bookkeeping, banking, and advertising, and met her mediation clients at home. Although Jan tried to keep the two areas of her practice separate, she occasionally asked the secretary at JMR to type correspondence relating to her mediation work "as a favour." It is assumed that the secretary did not use JMR letterhead.
>
> Viewing the mediation services as integral to the firm's practice, Ravi and May wrote a protest letter to Jan stating that the mediation profits should be shared. However, before this dispute was resolved, Jan was charged with theft for misappropriating $30,000 from the Regal Bank, which had retained Jan to provide mediation services. During the mediation process, Jan had held the money in a trust account under the JMS name. Since Jan had no assets, the bank sued Ravi and May as partners in JMR. It is assumed that there was no previous relationship between Regal Bank and JMR, and that the bank did not know that Jan was a lawyer.

Note that a few assumptions were made, such as the assumption that the secretary did not use JMR letterhead. Note as well that certain important facts were placed in quotations, indicating their importance.

Issue Determination

3

After you have analyzed the facts, you are in a position to determine the legal issues.

Issue determination involves eliciting relevant legal issues from a set of facts. This takes some skill and an understanding of the law. Defining the legal issues is central to the research process. If you are clear about the issues and ask the correct questions your research will be direct and efficient. Time spent at this stage saves significant time later in the research process.

This chapter explains how to identify legal issues, describes how to formulate legal issues, and provides an example of issue determination.

Learning Objectives

At the end of this chapter you will be able to:

- Name the three steps in determining legal issues
- Name a few techniques to assist in thinking about applicable areas of law
- Name two library sources that might help in defining legal issues
- Distinguish between a legal issue and factual issues

How to Determine Legal Issues

Issue determination involves translating facts into legal issues. The goal of issue determination is to ask yourself: What are the legal questions that must be answered in order to solve this legal problem?

Since researchers are rarely familiar with all areas of law, they must devise an efficient and effective way to determine the legal issues. A recommended way to do this is to think generally about the areas of law that are likely to apply to the facts, read the law generally in relevant areas, and formulate the legal issues.

Step 1: Determine Applicable Areas of Law

There are some techniques that can help get researchers started in thinking about which areas of law might apply to a set of facts. The methods suggested below are: using the subjects of law courses; brainstorming and word association; and using library sources.

Using Subjects of Law Courses

When determining what the legal issues are, researchers are most likely to attempt to fit the facts into a framework with which they are familiar. Some have past experiences with law and recognize a few areas of law (*e.g.*, criminal or family law). Most, however, have limited experience in law courses. For example, first-year law students typically try to fit issues into the framework of one of their first-year law courses (*e.g.*, torts, contracts, property, etc.).

Using the subjects of law courses to define legal issues may be helpful in situations where the problem fits clearly within the subject area. However, there are two problems with this approach. First, law school courses do not cover the ambit of the law. Second, legal problems rarely fit neatly into these particular divisions. It is important to recognize that law courses are divided into particular subjects for teaching purposes. These divisions are not always helpful when analyzing problems with several dimensions. For example, a situation involving divorce may involve issues of property, contract, tax law, and custody, among others. Therefore, if a researcher categorizes the divorce as involving only an issue of property, other areas of the law may be overlooked.

Brainstorming and Word Association

Brainstorming is another way to start thinking about areas of law that might apply. Brainstorming is a process whereby a few people sit in a group and freely share random ideas about the facts and potential legal issues. Brainstorming results in a list of words or phrases that helps describe possible legal issues. This method is particularly helpful if the people involved have a reasonably good understanding of the law.

Word association is a process similar to brainstorming. Word association involves listing words from the facts presented and creatively thinking of synonyms, antonyms, related words, and categories. This method assists in breaking down pre-established frameworks and assumptions, which can be barriers to creative thinking. Word association enables researchers to think of the issues from different perspectives and avoid narrowing the issues too early in the research process.

As a general rule, when determining issues, researchers should work from the general to the specific: think about broader categories of law first, while working towards narrower subcategories of law. The following is the result of an actual brainstorming session:

Scenario

Mr. Red and Ms. Green

Mr. Red and Ms. Green had a birthday party for a close friend and served drinks to most of their guests. Later that night, one of the guests who had been drinking drove into a telephone pole and injured a passenger in the vehicle. Are the hosts liable for the injury?

Results of Brainstorming and Word Association

Hosts, guests, liable, property, alcohol, invitations, driving, drinking, consumption, risk, harm, responsibility, duty to take care, joint liability, driver's responsibility, negligence, parties, friends, drunk, inebriated, passenger's responsibility, contributory negligence.

Using Library Sources

A final way to think about potentially applicable areas of law is by using sources in the law library. Books that describe the law organize it into various compartments. Each author or publisher organizes legal concepts into different categories. The following are three library sources that have highly developed categorizations of law and are most helpful in determining applicable areas of law. Each of these are called "secondary materials" and are discussed in more detail later in this book.

The Canadian Encyclopedic Digest

The *Canadian Encyclopedic Digest* (CED) is a comprehensive encyclopedia of Canadian law. It is published in three different formats: in loose-leaf multi-volume set in most law libraries, on CD-ROM (from Carswell), and online from *e*Carswell. It is not available on the Internet. The CED divides Canadian law into approximately 150 different categories, headings, and subheadings. This division is found in the library in the *Key*, which is in the first volume of the paper version of the CED. If you have access to the CD-ROM version you can scan the table of contents for relevant subject areas.

Textbooks

Every law library has a collection of legal textbooks. Very few of these textbooks are available online or on the Internet just yet. These books include summaries of the law in a number of areas. They can be located by using a card or computer catalogue and conducting a search by subject.

Almost all legal textbooks have tables of contents and subject indices. Both provide examples of the ways in which authors categorize a particular subject. For example, a textbook on employment law might have one chapter on unionized employees and one chapter on non-unionized employees. By perusing a table of contents or subject index, researchers can gain ideas about the divisions and categories of the law, which will help determine applicable areas of law.

Periodical Indexes

Legal periodical indexes are published to assist researchers in finding journal articles and other legal sources such as book reviews and reports. These indexes list legal journal articles and other legal sources by subject and author. They therefore have extensive subject categories. These subject categories are extremely well-developed divisions of legal concepts. A researcher can go to the library equipped only with a factual analysis and a list of key words and after perusing these indexes have a good idea about the area of law that might apply and how it is categorized.

Each of these three secondary sources categorizes the law in very different ways, so it is best to use them in combination. For example, in the Melody and Paul situation (in Chapter 2), the issue of division of family assets was labelled in the following ways in the three sources:

- CED: Family Law (general); Family Law (divorce)
- Textbook on Family Law: Financial Problems; Proprietary Rights in Matrimonial Property
- Periodical Index: Marriage Law; Marital Property

All of these sources are fairly easy to find and, as you will see, are the first sources that you should look at when you begin to look for the law.

Researchers should be careful to keep open minds about potentially applicable areas of law. It is wise to look at as many areas of law as possible to avoid overlooking relevant areas. Do not delve too deeply into the text of the library sources until you have perused a few. Just look at the indexes of each source until you have a better idea about the specific areas of law that may be relevant. Beware of going off on tangents into areas of law that may be irrelevant.

Step 2: Identify the General Legal Issues

Once you have an idea about the general areas of law that might apply, you can go into the library, read about these areas generally, and identify the legal issues.

In order to identify the legal issues, you must know about the law. Although the process of issue determination is ongoing, you should attempt to identify the broader legal issues early in the research process. This will help you focus your research.

Reading about the subject generally will enable you to formulate the general issues and arrange them in a logical pattern, which will form an outline for your research. For example, if you read about family law, you will learn that there are statutes in most provinces that determine how property is divided upon marriage breakdown. These statutes may then form the starting point for your research.

As you read about the law in more depth you will be able to formulate the legal issues.

Try This Example

Jill's Will

Jill died last night and her daughter, Madeline, found a handwritten will under Jill's bed. Madeline has come to you to find out if the will is valid.

Assume that you read about the law generally and found that there is a provincial statute that regulates the making of wills. You find out as well that in order for a will to be effective it must be in writing and must be witnessed. This is described in case law.

The first question you will likely want to answer is: Is Jill's will valid? This is a broad legal issue. The next question you might ask is: Did Jill's will have all the necessary requirements of a will? More specifically: Is Jill's handwritten, unwitnessed will valid? These last two questions are more focused legal issues which emerge as you read about the law. This focusing of issues is ongoing throughout the research process.

The more you learn about your particular area, the better you become at drafting legal issues.

Step 3: Formulate the Specific Legal Issues

Only after you have a fairly clear idea about the law will you be able to formulate the specific legal issues. A legal issue is a question arising from the facts that demands an answer in law. The following is an example of a well-drafted legal issue based on the Paul and Melody situation (Chapter 2):

Will the $20,000 gift that Melody received from her grandmother two years ago, which she kept in a separate bank account in her name, form part of the family assets to be divided upon marriage breakdown?

Because each and every situation is different, each situation has a legal question specific to its particular circumstances. Legal issues should, ideally, include enough information to enable a researcher to go into the library and find the answer to the problem.

Factual Issues vs. Legal Issues

Legal issues combine facts and law into questions. The legal issue must be put into the context of the facts. Without some facts, the issue is incomplete.

The object in drafting issues is to include just enough facts to make the question answerable in that particular situation and no other. Sometimes beginners at research confuse factual issues and legal issues. Factual issues demand a factual answer and can be answered without referring to the law. They do not contain questions about the law. The following are examples of factual issues:

- Why did Melody's grandmother give her the money?
- In whose bank account was the money placed?
- Did Paul know about the money?
- When did Jill write the will?
- Was the will signed?
- Did anyone witness the will?

Sub-Issues

There may be more than one issue or one large issue and several sub-issues. Sub-issues emerge through the identification of the larger issues. They usually take the form of necessary components of the larger issues. For example, there are two sub-components of every crime: *mens rea* (intent) and *actus rea* (act). These sub-components will often be the sub-issues of the larger issue of whether the accused is guilty of a crime.

Try This Example

Nancy and Steve

Nancy slipped and fell on Steve's icy driveway today and broke her wrist. Steve had been away on a business trip for a week and there had been a major snow fall over the last three days. Steve was too tired last night to shovel the driveway when he got in from the airport and he was hoping it would warm up overnight and the snow would melt.

Summary of the Law

Negligence law provides that every person has a duty to take reasonable care to prevent foreseeable harm. The duty owed by homeowners to the public is that of the reasonable homeowner in a similar situation (*i.e.*, standard of care).

Possible Main Issue

Is Steve liable for Nancy's fall and broken wrist for failing to clear his driveway of snow for three days?

Possible Sub-Issues

1. Did Steve owe a duty of care to Nancy to clear the driveway? Was it reasonably foreseeable that Steve's failure to shovel the driveway would result in Nancy's slip and fall?
2. Did Steve meet the standard of care required of a reasonable homeowner when he failed to shovel the driveway?
3. Did Steve's failure to shovel the driveway cause Nancy's broken wrist?

Often the sub-issues are elements of a cause of action. For example, the three sub-issues above are the three elements you must prove in a negligence action: duty of care, standard of care, and causation. Each sub-issue should be able to stand on its own as a distinct question of law.

Defining the issues sets the stage for the eventual organization required to write the results of research. Often the logic arising from the formulation of the issues is good logic to follow when explaining the law later.

Although defining the legal issues is important, researchers should not become too concerned about the specific wording of the legal issues too early in the research. It is best to err on the side of defining legal issues too broadly. As the research evolves, these issues will become clearer and more defined. It is wise to review the issues periodically to ensure they are complete and accurate. Often this may not be accomplished until the research is near completion.

Self Test

The following is a self test based on the information provided in this chapter. The answers to these questions are found at the end of the book in the "Answers to Self Tests" section.

1. List three steps in determining legal issues.

2. Name a few methods that might assist you in thinking about possible areas of law that might apply to legal problems.
3. What library sources might assist you in determining legal issues?
4. Do correctly formulated legal issues include just facts, just law, or a combination of facts and law?
5. Should legal issues be drafted as questions?

Sample Exercise

Instructions

Assume you are given the following fact pattern and you know nothing about this area of law. Do a factual analysis; then go through the three steps for determining legal issues and attempt to formulate the legal issues.

Fact Pattern

Homes and Watson

Sherly Homes asked Mr. Watson, a trusted friend, to assist her in purchasing an automobile. She specified the type and price of automobile Mr. Watson was to search for and stipulated that he was to consult her prior to concluding a deal.

A few weeks later, Mr. Watson found a car suitable for Homes. Unfortunately, he forgot to obtain her prior approval of the vehicle and concluded a deal to purchase the automobile by signing the sale papers in her name.

Before Mr. Watson was able to inform Homes of the purchase, the vendor telephoned him and stated the "the deal is off." Mr. Watson then advised Homes of the automobile purchase and the vendor's telephone call. Homes approved Watson's purchase of the automobile.

Ms. Homes wants to know if she gets to keep the car.

Answers to Exercise

Factual Analysis

The following is a restatement of the facts:

Sherly Homes asked Mr. Watson to help her buy a car. She specified the type and price of automobile and stipulated that he was to consult her before concluding a deal.

A few weeks later Mr. Watson found a car and, before obtaining Ms. Homes' approval, signed the papers of sale in her name. Before Mr. Watson told Ms. Homes of the purchase, the vendor telephoned him and stated the "the deal is off." Mr. Watson then advised Ms. Homes of the automobile purchase and the vendor's telephone call. Ms. Homes approved Mr. Watson's purchase of the automobile.

Issue Determination

Step 1: Think about possible areas of law that might apply.

- *Law Courses* — Two law courses that could potentially be relevant are contract and property law. A review of contracts course materials indicates that these facts may fall into the categories of offer, acceptance, and ratification.

- *Brainstorming and Word Association* — Some words that might come to mind during a brainstorm are: contract, car, automobile, ratification, offer, acceptance, agent, principal, on behalf of, authority, apparent authority, and ostensible authority.

- *Library Sources* — There are several textbooks on contracts. Some of the indexes of these texts have chapters devoted to offer and acceptance. The *Canadian Encyclopedic Digest* has a section devoted to contract law.

Step 2: Identify the legal issues by reading the law in more depth; read generally at first. The following three cases describe the relevant law in this area.

Monty's Insurance Co. v. McGill (Alta. C.A.) (fictitious)

An employee of the plaintiff insurance company accepted a promissory note as payment for a policy of insurance. He then entered a notation of the policy on the company's record book. The promissory note was subsequently dishonoured, although no attempt to return the note or to change the notation in the book regarding the policy was made. Several months later, the policy-holder's premises were destroyed by fire. The insurance company refused to honour the insurance policy because the employee did not have authority to accept a promissory note as payment for the policy. The court stated:

> For it cannot be doubted that an agent may bind his principal by acts done within the scope of his general and ostensible authority, although those acts may exceed his actual authority as between himself and his principal; the private instructions which limit that authority, and the circumstances that his acts are in excess of it, being unknown to the person with whom he is dealing.

The court held that by accepting the promissory note, the employee acted outside his scope of authority, as promissory notes were not a recognized method of payment for a policy of insurance. Therefore, the employee did not bind the company to a contract of insurance.

Tillman v. Leader (Sask. C.A.) (fictitious)

Mr. Jones, purporting to act as agent for Mr. Tillman (the plaintiff), contracted with Mr. Leader (the defendant) in the name of Mr. Tillman. Mr. Jones was actually contracting on his own behalf and with fraudulent intent. When the defendant discovered the identity of the agent, he refused to complete the contract. Mr. Tillman, however, then ratified the act of Mr. Jones. The court held that the ratification was valid and stated:

> ... we think that the contracts could be validly ratified by the person in whose name they purported to be made, even although they were in fact made without his actual authority, and although the agent had in his mind some fraudulent intent. ... They were, therefore, contracts which not only purported to be made by him, but which he had the means to carry out. ... It is not found that Tillman the principal was guilty of any fraud. If there was such a finding, the question would be altogether different. ...

Bilder v. Lampton (B.C.C.A.) (fictitious)

The defendant, Lampton, made an offer to the agent of the plaintiff, Bilder, which was accepted by the agent, although the agent had no authority to bind his principal to a contract. The defendant subsequently withdrew the offer. The plaintiff then ratified the acceptance made by his agent. The court held that the contract was binding, and that the ratification went to the date of the acceptance. The court stated:

> The rule as to ratification by a principal of acts done by an assumed agent is that the ratification is thrown back to the date of the act done, and that the agent is put in the same position as if he had authority to do the act at the time the act was done by him.

Step 3: Attempt to articulate the legal issues.

The legal issues appear to be:

Issue 1: Did Mr. Watson have authority to bind Ms. Homes to the purchase of the automobile?

Issue 2: Did Ms. Homes' retroactive ratification of the purchase make the contract binding?

Appendix A: Summary of Steps of Issue Determination

The following is a summary of the steps of issue determination:

Step 1: Use the following techniques to think about possible areas of law that might apply to the facts:

    a. Use law school course subjects (*e.g.*, tort or contract);
    b. Brainstorm or word associate; and
    c. Use library sources (*e.g.*, *Canadian Encyclopedic Digest* or textbooks).

Step 2: Identify the general legal issues by reading the law generally in the relevant areas. The *Canadian Encyclopedic Digests* or textbooks are frequently used at this stage.

Step 3: Formulate the specific legal issues. Read the law in more detail and attempt to articulate the legal issues into questions of law and facts. Remember to continually hone the legal issues as you progress in your research.

Introduction to Law and Legal Materials

4

In order to conduct legal research, you must have a basic understanding of what the law is and how it is made. You must also know about other legal resources, sometimes called secondary materials, and their importance to finding and learning about the law.

This chapter provides a basic introduction to legal systems, the law, and the law-making process. It describes both primary sources such as statutes and cases and secondary materials such as journals and textbooks. This chapter also describes what regulations and municipal bylaws are and how they are made.

Chapter 5 explains how these legal materials are typically organized in law libraries, on CD-ROMs, and online.

Learning Objectives

At the end of the chapter you will be able to:

- Explain the difference between civil and common law systems of law
- Understand the relationship between statutes and cases
- Define what is meant by "the Constitution"
- Describe the law making process
- Describe some secondary materials

Systems of Law

An understanding of legal systems and the way that laws are made is critical to legal research. It assists you in recognizing the relationship between legislation and cases and in understanding why and how law is put in written form, published, and categorized.

There are two types of legal systems that prevail in Canada: the civil law system that applies in Quebec and the common law system that applies in all other provinces and territories. In addition, there is an international system of law that governs the relationship between Canada and other countries in the world.

The Civil Law System

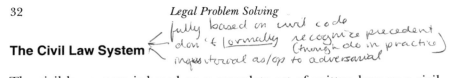

fully based on civil code
don't formally recognize precedent
(though do in practice)
inquisitorial as/op to adversarial

The civil law system is <u>based on a complete set</u> of written laws or a civil code. Unlike the common law system, <u>judge-made cases simply interpret</u> <u>that code and need not be treated as precedents.</u> In practise, however, judges <u>informally recognize precedent</u> and, when cases are appealed, higher courts will not forget what they have said in prior cares. Another feature of the civil law system is that the <u>actual cases are inquisitorial as</u> <u>opposed to adversarial.</u> This means that civil law judges play an active role in eliciting information. They are even permitted to call witnesses and order investigations.

The Common Law System

Canada (with the exception of Quebec) inherited a system of "common law" <u>that originated with travelling courts in England.</u> Because there were few written laws in England, English judges developed a system whereby prior decisions from one area of the country were applied to other areas of the country. These decisions were based on the "common custom" as the judges saw it. These decisions slowly became uniform across the country and were referred to as the "common law".

The common law is, therefore, law made by judges and found in decided cases. Each decided case modifies the law slightly as it is applied to a particular set of circumstances; this system of precedents is called case law. By applying prior case law and interpreting statutes, the courts build upon and revise the law. They clarify ambiguities and elaborate upon the intentions of Parliament as they see them.

Another type of case law is found in the decisions of administrative tribunals. In order to better administer the law, governments create administrative bodies. Governments delegate to these bodies the authority to make decisions but not to pass laws. Although these decisions also form part of the law, they have not been fully integrated into the common law. This is partially because administrative law is not made by judges and, therefore, judges are not compelled to follow it as precedent.

International System of Law

Various international laws also affect Canadians and cannot be over-looked in legal research. These laws include international treaties and covenants, which are agreements signed by the Government of Canada and other countries. The government is ultimately bound by these agreements and Canadians are required to act in accordance with them. These treaties and covenants are sometimes interpreted by Canadian courts and administrative bodies.

What Is the Law?

There are essentially two types of written law in Canada: case law and legislation. Case law is judge-made law and legislation is government-made law. Cases and legislation form the law in Canada and are called "primary sources" of law.

Case Law

As described above, case law or court decisions are the written decisions of judges and tribunals. Therefore case law consists of cases from all levels of courts from all jurisdictions, from various provincial courts to international tribunals. The next chapter explains how these cases are published and filed in libraries and databases. Chapter 10, on legal analysis, explains the hierarchy of these cases and how they are interpreted.

Legislation

Legislation is that part of the law that is made by elected members of parliament. Legislation is made by each level of government: federal, provincial, and municipal. Federal and provincial legislation is usually in the form of statutes and regulations, whereas municipal legislation is manifested as bylaws.

The main products of legislatures are statutes and regulations. The government is constantly introducing or repealing statutes and thereby creating new law. Although statutes are new law, they are often codifications of case law and are created to clarify case law. In 1993, for example, the federal government passed 74 statutes and the government of British Columbia passed 48 statutes. There are approximately 1,100 federal statutes.

Legislation is introduced primarily to create new laws or to clarify or amend case law. There is rarely a legal problem that is not touched in some way by legislation. Although Canada has a common law legal system based on the rule of precedent or decided cases, it seems that, with the increased creation of statutes, Canada is moving towards a more legislative legal system.

Statutes are published by the federal government and each provincial government. These governments also publish research aids such as indexes of statutes, although many of the tools researchers use to locate statutes are published by commercial publishers.

Statute-Making Authority

In Canada, the federal government and provincial governments share governing and, therefore, have separate spheres of law-making powers. This division between federal and provincial powers is described in ss. 91 and 92 of the *Constitution Act, 1867*.[1] Essentially, the provincial governments regulate provincial matters (*e.g.*, education and property) and the federal government regulates matters that extend across Canada (*e.g.*, banking, national defence, and postal services).

There is often overlap between these two spheres and, therefore, legislation affecting certain matters sometimes appears in both federal and provincial laws. For example, there are both federal statutes and provincial statutes dealing with employment and labour law. As a general rule, the federal laws apply to employees in businesses that cross provincial boundaries and provincial laws apply to employees of businesses of a local or provincial nature; however, this distinction is not always clear. A good researcher will look at both federal and provincial statutes to determine what they cover.

It is a good idea to review ss. 91 and 92 periodically to recall the fundamental divisions and the differing law-making powers.

Regulations and Municipal Bylaws

Because the day-to-day administration of statutes can be time consuming, Parliament often delegates some of its law-making authority to other government bodies. These more detailed laws, which deal with the implementation of statutes, are called regulations or rules and have as much force in law as statutes.

Regulations and municipal bylaws are laws created by a delegated authority and are called subordinate or delegated legislation. Elected representatives delegate their law-making power to other authorities who, in turn, make laws on their behalf.

Regulations describe the day-to-day administration of a statute. They "put meat on the bones" of statutes. For example, while the British Columbia *Name Act*[2] sets out the basic law permitting British Columbians to change their names, the regulations under the *Name Act* describe the process involved in changing names and the cost of doing so. Federal regulations are called statutory instruments (SI) or statutory orders and regulations (SOR).

---

[1] R.S.C. 1985, Appendix II, No. 5.
[2] R.S.B.C. 1996, c. 328.

The Constitution

The most important piece of legislation in Canada is the Constitution. The Constitution will almost always have some effect on a legal problem and thus usually plays a role in research.

The Constitution is the highest law in Canada. <u>All other laws must be consistent with the Constitution or they</u> can be struck down and declared invalid by the courts. Section 52 of the *Constitution Act, 1982*[3] states:

> The Constitution of Canada is the supreme law of Canada, and any law that is inconsistent with the provisions of the Constitution is, to the extent of the inconsistency, of no force or effect.

In simple terms the Constitution describes the rules about how a country governs itself. It specifically describes:

- who can make laws (legislative power);
- who will enforce the laws (executive powers); and
- who interprets the laws (judicial powers).

The Constitution <u>also defines the rights and freedoms</u> of Canadians in the *Canadian Charter of Rights and Freedoms* (the *Charter*).[4] Specifically, it restricts governments from interfering with certain basic rights of individuals. Indeed, there are few areas of law that are not affected in some way by the *Charter*. It protects fundamental freedoms (*e.g.*, speech and religion), democratic rights (*e.g.*, voting), mobility rights (*e.g.*, travel), language rights, equality rights, and legal rights (*e.g.*, consulting a lawyer).

The Constitution of Canada originated as a statute of the United Kingdom entitled the *British North America Act, 1867* (*B.N.A. Act*) (see the *Constitution Act, 1867*). This statute includes ss. 91 and 92, which describe the powers of Parliament and the courts. It established Ontario, Quebec, Nova Scotia, and New Brunswick as the first provinces of Canada. The remaining provinces joined Canada afterwards. Because the *B.N.A. Act* was a statute of the United Kingdom, only the United Kingdom could amend it.

In 1982, that statute was patriated. The United Kingdom introduced the *Canada Act, 1982 (U.K.)* and its schedule, the new *Constitution Act, 1982*. The *Canada Act, 1982* renamed the *B.N.A. Act* to the *Constitution Act, 1867* and contains the amending formula. It gives Canadians sole power over their own constitution and includes the *Charter*. The Act also states that the United Kingdom will not pass any laws affecting Canada.

---

[3] R.S.C. 1985, Appendix II, No. 44.
[4] R.S.C. 1985, Appendix II, No. 44, Sched. B.

Therefore, the Constitution consists of a number of documents: the *Canada Act, 1982 (U.K.)*, the *Constitution Act, 1982*[5] and the acts listed in the schedules to the *Constitution Act*. Part I of the *Constitution Act, 1982* is the *Canadian Charter of Rights and Freedoms* and one of the schedules is the *Constitution Act, 1867*. The constitutional documents can be found in the Appendices volume of Revised Statutes of Canada, 1985.

The Constitution is important to legal research for two fundamental reasons: it defines the limits of legislative authority and defines the rights and freedoms of Canadian citizens.

The Law-Making Process

As described above, statutes and cases combine to form the law of Canada. The law-making process looks something like this:

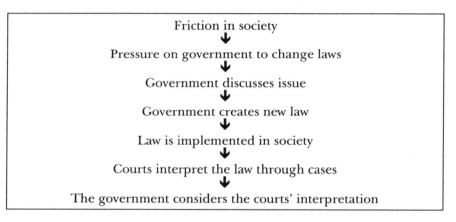

Friction in society
↓
Pressure on government to change laws
↓
Government discusses issue
↓
Government creates new law
↓
Law is implemented in society
↓
Courts interpret the law through cases
↓
The government considers the courts' interpretation

If friction exists in society, groups or individuals will often pressure the government for change (e.g., through lobbying). The government will often investigate the issue by setting up commissions or committees. If, after an investigation, the government believes that the conflict can be resolved by creating a new law, it will introduce legislation (e.g., a statute). Eventually, that legislation will be implemented in society. If there is a dispute about the law, it can be challenged in court. If the court finds that the new law is inconsistent with existing law, it will make a decision stating this. Courts interpret the legislation. Each case that is decided affects prior cases and legislation. The following fictional example assists in describing the law-making process.

---

[5] R.S.C. 1985, Appendix II, No. 44.

Example
In 1998, research was conducted indicating that the taking of vitamin BX7 prolongs life and general happiness. Activists for preventive medicine pressured the Canadian government to introduce legislation making the use of BX7 mandatory. In 1999, the federal government created a Vitamin Commission, which traveled across Canada gathering data and opinions about the use and effect of BX7. The results were astounding. All those people who had taken BX7 were much happier and appeared to live longer. As a result of this investigation, the government passed legislation, the *Vitamin Act*, requiring that all Canadians take BX7 three times a day. The penalty for non-compliance was ten years in prison. An administrative body was set up to enforce the statute.
Mr. Beauregard, a resident of Vancouver, refused to take BX7 and was imprisoned. He hired a lawyer who brought an action in the courts arguing that Mr. Beauregard's rights and freedoms were violated. The court hearing the case agreed with Mr. Beauregard and stated in its decision that the *Vitamin Act* was inconsistent with Mr. Beauregard's constitutional rights and, therefore, was of no effect. When the government of the day heard about the court decision it decided to repeal the law and remove it from the statute books.

It is important to recognize the interplay between legislation and case law. In Canadian law, neither stands alone and research will always involve a search of both types of law.

It is also important to keep in mind the entire legislative process when researching legislation. Since statutes are only the final product of a long process of consultation and debate, researchers should be aware of documents such as reports of government commissions, which can assist in interpreting statutes or understanding the policy reasons for their introduction.

Secondary Materials

Other types of legal materials are sometimes considered to be part of the law. These are called "secondary materials." They are, however, only aids in interpreting and finding the law; they are not the law. Secondary materials include such things as textbooks and journal articles. They assist legal researchers in two ways: in understanding the law and in locating the law. For example, encyclopedias and textbooks summarize the law and, in doing so, provide references (*i.e.*, citations) to cases and statutes. These cases and statutes form a basis for further case and statute research.

Secondary materials provide researchers with summaries and overviews of the law, which enable researchers to quickly become familiar with legal subject areas. They are most frequently used at the beginning of the research process, primarily to gain an understanding of a particular area of law. For example, in Chapter 3, the *Canadian Encyclopedic Digest* and textbooks were used to help determine legal issues. Remember that they are not the law.

Secondary materials take many forms. Those that aid in understanding the law include textbooks, encyclopedias, and journal articles. There are two main secondary sources used to locate the law. Both are huge multi-volume sets. The first is called the *Canadian Abridgment* and the second is called the *Canadian Encyclopedic Digest* (CED). Both are published by Carswell and are available in electronic form. Chapter 5 explains in detail how to locate and use secondary materials.

Self Test

The following is a self test based on the information provided in this chapter. The answers to these questions are found at the end of the book in the "Answers to Self Tests" section.

1. What are the two types of law in Canada?
2. Where does the term "common law" originate?
3. What is legislation?
4. Describe the law-making process.
5. What is the difference between primary sources and secondary materials?

Law Libraries, Disks, and Databases 5

The law and legal resources are often available in both paper and electronic form. The paper version is printed and published in books and stored in law libraries. The electronic form is stored on disks or databases, readable by computer. All research involves making appropriate use of both paper and electronic resources.

This chapter explains how information is sorted in libraries and databases and where these legal materials are typically located in a paper-based library. It describes the difference between CD-ROMs, commercial online services, and public access Internet sites, as well as their strengths and weaknesses. Because computers are being used simply as data retrieval devices, researchers must know what information is available electronically, who owns and provides this information, and how this information can be accessed most effectively and efficiently. Researchers must also be able to use the language of the database software in order to instruct the computer to conduct a search. This chapter will instruct researchers to do all of these things while focusing on the key providers of online services in Canada: Quicklaw, *e*Carswell and LEXIS.

Learning Objectives

At the end of the chapter you will be able to:

- Describe the "four doors" of access to the law library
- Describe some of the pros and cons of using electronic research
- Name three companies that provide online Canadian legal services
- Describe the four steps of electronic legal research
- Construct word searches using Boolean logic

Law Library Basics

Whether you are using a law library or an electronic library, you must always ask yourself three questions:

- What information do you need?

- Where is it likely located?
- Where can you find this information most effectively and efficiently?

For example, if you are looking for cases, you will find them in law libraries, on CD-ROM, online through various service providers, and on the Internet. You must decide which is the most cost- and time-effective for your particular search. You should be able to answer the first question about what you need after completing the first few chapters of this book. Your choices will likely be cases, statutes, secondary sources, or all of the above. Then, unless you have a very clear idea about the exact item you need and where it is located, you will begin your search in the library by reading broadly and narrowing your focus as you refine your problem. In order to continue to stay on track you must continually ask yourself the three questions above as you move along.

Why Learn about Paper-Based Libraries?

Although many beginners at research think electronic sources simply replace law libraries, for now libraries are still necessary for most research. The most important reason to learn library skills is that in some situations you may not have access to the materials in electronic format. The database you have access to may not include a particular resource, or you may not have access to the necessary service or CD-ROM. As well, some courts are slow to accept electronic versions of cases or statutes because there is still a lack of confidence that the electronic version is completely accurate.

Another reason to learn the skills of library research is that they are very similar to the skills of electronic research. Many of the companies who publish laws and legal materials in paper form are also the publishers who provide the information in electronic form. These publishers collect and organize their paper and electronic publications in the same manner. They each develop specially designed tools for use in both the law library and for the electronic version. You may also prefer to turn to a paper-based library because, for the time being, most electronic research is much more expensive than law library research.

Information Sorting Basics

Each law library sorts its books on the shelves in a particular manner and many create their own search tools. At the same time, publishers publish materials in a certain manner and create their own search tools to be used with their own publications. Electronic libraries contain similar information to paper-based libraries and the information is often sorted in a similar manner.

In a public library, books are sorted by topic and by author. This makes sense because most people who are looking for a book are searching for a book on a particular subject or author. Books on a similar subject are placed in proximity to each other to make subject searches easier. In order to sort by subject, librarians use a national system of classification and each book is assigned a corresponding call number. These call numbers, subjects, authors names, etc., are placed in a computer database. This database can then be searched in a variety of ways.

Journals and periodicals are sorted in libraries by the title of the journal. Comprehensive indexes are compiled to assist researchers in locating articles by subject, author, or title of the article. These indexes are available in print or CD-ROM, and some are now are available online.

A law library is simply a storehouse of the law and other sources relating to the law. Like other libraries, law libraries contain books and articles about a variety of subjects written by various authors. Unlike other libraries, law libraries contain the written laws and specialized tools to assist researchers in both finding and interpreting the law. For example, most governments publish consolidated lists of statutes to enable researchers to find the citation (location) of the statute and any revisions to statutes by looking at just one resource.

Books and periodicals are filed in law libraries in the same way they are filed in public libraries. Textbooks and other treatises are filed by subject and call number and periodicals are filed by the title of the journal. The way to find these sources is through a library computer catalogue for locating books and periodical indexes for locating periodical articles.

However, legal researchers also need to locate the law itself: cases and legislation. The specific research tools for locating legislation and cases are described in later chapters. Cases, statutes and regulations are kept in distinct places in a law library and are not sorted by subject. Tools have been developed to help researchers locate this law.

In a law library there are four access points: one for general materials such as textbooks; one for journals and periodicals indexes; one for cases; and one for legislation. I refer to access points as the "four doors" to the law library. All four doors should be used for comprehensive legal research.

The Four Doors to the Law Library

Door	What You Are Looking For	Where It Is Shelved	How To Find It	Example
1.	Textbooks	By subject and classification number (*e.g.*, KF505.S9 1992)	Computer catalogue	Search the law library computer catalogue for the words "family law" to locate textbooks on family law.

Door	What You Are Looking For	Where It Is Shelved	How To Find It	Example
2.	Journals and periodical indexes	By the title of the periodical or journal	Periodical indexes	Search a periodical index on CD-ROM by subject for an article on matrimonial law.
3.	Legislation	By jurisdiction (federal and each province)	The relevant federal or provincial statute index.	Look in the Federal *Table of Public Statutes* under the letter "L" for the Labour Code.
4.	Cases	By the title of the case reporter (*e.g.*, Dominion Law Reports)	Case indexes or case digests.	Look in *Case Digests* under the subject "family law" to locate digested cases on that topic.

Novice legal researchers will almost always enter the library first through the first door: the library computer catalogue, which provides access to most general sources. Only after gaining a general understanding of the law will a researcher use the two doors leading to the cases and legislation. Since each law library has its own particular filing scheme, it is best to always look at the floor plan of a library before beginning research.

Electronic Library Basics

There are three generations of electronic law products. The first generation is computer disks and CD-ROMs, the second is online access to commercial database services, and the third is public access to data on the Internet.

Generation 1: CD-ROM

CD-ROM stands for Compact Disc-Read Only Memory. "Read only" means the information on the disk can be read but not altered. These computer discs store a significant amount of information and contain more than just printed words. For example, the newer CD-ROMs contain video and audio. A standard CD-ROM holds about 250,000 typed pages or 2,000 computer floppy disks. A laser beam reads the information on the disc very quickly. These discs often contain information identical to that found in books or other resources. The three main benefits to CD-ROMs is that they can contain more information than books, are easier to store, and the information is easier to search. CD-ROMs also contain hyperlinks that enable a researcher to quickly move between data. This is particularly useful when relating statutes and cases.

Generation 2: Commercial Online Providers

The second generation of products was created by companies that collect law and other information in databases and provide access to individuals with computers for a fee over telephone lines. Over time, more publishers have begun to make their publications available in electronic form. Recently, several of these providers have merged so that there are only a few key online service providers, in competition with each other. Initially the differences between these providers was in content, particularly case law, but this is slowly changing because many cases are now provided free in electronic form by the courts. Now the main differences are in the historic information, privately held information like textbooks, and the research tools, search engines, and user supports that make searching easier.

In Canada there are three main online legal research service providers: Quicklaw (through Quicklaw Inc.), *e*Carswell (through Carswell), and LEXIS (through Butterworths). Each provider maintains its own legal information system and provides a variety of services. Keep in mind that the information in databanks changes daily and the information collected by these service providers changes on a regular basis. Always check with the service provider to confirm specific content and services. Also see the list of drawbacks of electronic research below.

Quicklaw

The first Canadian online legal research service provider was Quicklaw Inc., based in Kingston, Ontario. Since 1973 this corporation has been gathering cases, legislation, and other legal sources and compiling this information into a system. Researchers can request this information from Quicklaw over Quicklaw's private network or on the Internet. Most law students have free access while at law school.

Quicklaw has over 2,300 databases of Canadian cases, statutes, and regulations. Since 1986 Quicklaw has obtained full texts of the decisions directly from the Supreme Court of Canada and all common law provincial superior courts (*i.e.*, courts of appeal and supreme courts). It also provides business information, news, and social science information. Quicklaw recently added a collection of American legal information including the United States Code, Code of Federal Regulations, federal and state case law, and state statutes and regulations.

Quicklaw initially negotiated contracts with a number of Canadian publishers to obtain their databases, which included digests, headnotes, and some full texts of cases. As a result, many of the cases in the

Quicklaw databases are identical to the published versions in both form and content. For example, the Quicklaw database titled DLR contains a fully searchable version of the case reporter *Dominion Law Reports*. Quicklaw also offers an online citator with access to parallel citations, case histories, and judicial treatments for Canadian cases.

The most important tool for the first time user is the *Quicklaw Database Directory*, which is available in paper version and on the Internet. It lists all databases and their contents. It is best to scan the paper version and identify the particular databases that are likely to contain the information you are looking for. It is equally important to note the years covered in a particular database. Many collections of cases only go back to about 1984, and some of the statute databases are not up to date. Quicklaw offers access to more than 290,000 case law digests in the Canadian Case Summaries (CCS) database with links to the full text of decisions made since 1984. Many federal statutes databases are updated regularly by Quicklaw editorial staff and are very current. Some provincial statutes are available but are not updated regularly. A sample Quicklaw search can be found in Appendix B to this chapter.

eCarswell

Carswell, Canada's largest legal publisher, provides an online, web-based service called *e*Carswell. It provides access to most Canadian cases and statutes, and regulations in specialty areas. It provides the following four products:

family.pro	for family law practitioners
insolvency.pro	for insolvency law practitioners
securities.pro	for securities law practitioners
law.pro	for all lawyers and legal researchers

The first three services are designed specifically for practitioners in the areas of family law, insolvency law, and securities law. They are very similar to Carswell's CD-ROM products and include all of the information a busy practitioner might need including books, loose-leaf services, cases, and legislation on a particular subject, all hypertext linked. These services also provide weekly newsletters, published only electronically. In 2001 another specialty service, criminal.pro, will be launched.

Law.pro, however, is an extremely comprehensive collection of Canadian case law. At launch it included almost all of the original Carswell legal publications, including the digest and citator services, that is, the original *Canadian Abridgment*, *Canadian Case Digests*, and *Canadian Case Citations*. You will see in Chapter 9 that these two sources are the main tools for case law research in a library. Law.pro also enables researchers to search for cases by using the *Canadian Abridgment* subject classification scheme. In 2001 law.pro content will be enhanced by the addition of a collection of Canadian statutes and rules including legislative citators, the *Canadian Encyclopedic Digest*, and the *Index to Canadian Legal Literature*. A sample *e*Carswell search can be found in Appendix C to this chapter.

LEXIS

LEXIS-NEXIS is a full-text online service providing access to an extensive collection of legal information from Canada and other jurisdictions, such as the United States and Commonwealth countries. Each jurisdiction, including Canada, maintains a separate group of databases to streamline research. Canadian legal information is acces-sible on the Internet at www.lexis.com, as well as through proprietary software. Users have a choice of Boolean and natural language when searching. Federal, Ontario, British Columbia, and Alberta statutes and regulations can be retrieved in full text or by section.

Reported and unreported federal and provincial cases, including decisions of administrative tribunals, are available. Access to Shepard's Citations Service, the established tool for updating American judgments, will soon include coverage of Canadian judicial decisions.

Law reviews and journals, legal news, and other non-legislative materials such as property tax assessment records are also available.

In addition to the legal information available through LEXIS-NEXIS, the NEXIS division offers access to news and business information services.

A sample LEXIS search can be found in Appendix D to this chapter.

Generation 3: Public Access Internet Sites

The third generation is the Internet. The Internet is simply a system of links to other computers. It enables access to a number of systems and is also a means of information exchange. When "on the Net" you are connected to millions of other networked computers and billions of information sources.

To date, the main free providers of legal material on the Internet are universities and, more recently, governments who continually place materials on their websites. The only information that you will not find on these sites is information that is owned by publishers or authors. So, for example, textbooks are rarely found on the Internet. As the Internet evolves, these materials will be accessible on the Internet. Eventually you will be able to do most of your research from your desk.

Drawbacks to Using Electronic Resources

Computers can be used as tools to assist legal researchers in accessing legal sources from automated libraries. In many situations, computers can access more legal information and can access it faster than a library search. This is because computer databases often contain information that is not available in libraries, and computers are able to search through vast quantities of information at very high speeds. However, there are some drawbacks.

1. Information can be incomplete. Often databases only go back to a certain date. When initially loading information into databases, service providers made certain decisions about what information to put into electronic form. In some cases information only goes back to the 1980s and some information is not yet available.

Like legal publishers, service providers do not necessarily report all information. Publishers may decide to only publish digests of cases, as opposed to the full text. Some electronic cases do not include summaries or headnotes. Other examples of information that may not be found in electronic form are unreported cases, cases from outside Canada, decisions of administrative tribunals, and statutes from other countries.

2. Information can be inaccurate. Until recently, there was some question about the accuracy of information from computer databases. Until a few years ago, courts lacked confidence in computer versions of cases or statutes and were hesitant to accept them. As the quality of automated reporting increases, courts are more inclined to accept online versions.

3. The ability of the researcher is critical. Computer searches are limited by the skill of the researcher. Since computers search literally, researchers must be well versed in the terminology connected with a problem. Just as in a print search, the results of research are only as good as the questions asked or the search conducted. For example, if you search all cases on "cars" you may end up wading through thousands of cases and also have missed several that referred only to "automobiles." This is discussed in detail below.

4. Costs can be high. The cost of computer research can be high if researchers are not skilled at computer research. Online service providers charge either by use or at a flat rate. An hour-long search can cost hundreds of dollars at the hourly rate. CD-ROMs are very expensive. For example, the *Canada Statute Service* by Canada Law Book costs about $900 a year.

Electronic Research in Four Steps

To retrieve electronic information, a researcher must instruct the computer to find that information. This is done by conducting a word search. A researcher asks the computer to search for a word or words and the computer simply scans all of the information in the databases for the words requested. This is called a literal search. It then provides the researcher with the documents containing those words.

There are four stages to any electronic research. Here are the questions you will want to ask at each stage:

1. Plan the research.

- What kind of information do you need?
- Is the information available in electronic form?
- Could the information be found more efficiently in a library?
- What are the issues or concepts to be researched?
- How much time and money do you have?

2. Select a data source: CD-ROM, or commercial or public access sites?

- What information you are looking for?
- Which sources are available for your use?
- Which source is most effective and most efficient for your situation?

3. Select a database.

- Which database has the information you are looking for?
- Do the databases provide full text, digests, or indexes?
- Which databases include headnotes, summaries, or annotations?

4. Formulate a word search.

- What words do you want the computer to locate?
- How should the command be structured (*e.g.*, how should the words be grouped)?
- What connectors will you use?
- Do you want to limit the search by dates?
- How do you want your results to be presented (*e.g.*, chronologically)?

Step 1: Plan Your Research

Planning is particularly important for computer-assisted research since computers do only as instructed. If a search is conducted in the wrong database or if it is constructed improperly, the results will be wrong. If the problem is defined too narrowly, the information retrieved will be incomplete. If defined too broadly, too much information will be provided.

As with library research, a researcher must narrow down each problem by analyzing the facts and determining the legal issues before heading to the computer.

What Kind of Information Do You Need?

Different types of information are located in different automated libraries or information systems. Therefore, researchers should know in as much detail as possible what they are searching for. A proper search depends on the information needed. For example, journals and statutes can be found both on CD-ROM and on the Internet. A choice must be made about where and how to search. Some questions to ask are:

- Are you looking for cases, legislation, or secondary materials?
- Is the information needed from a specific jurisdiction (*e.g.*, Canada, a province, the United States)?
- If you are looking for a case, is the case from a specific court (*e.g.*, Supreme Court of Canada or British Columbia Court of Appeal)?
- Is the information from a specific period of time?

Researchers should read generally about the law to determine what specific legal materials are needed.

Is the Information Available in Electronic Form?

Not all hard-copy information in libraries is available in automated form. Information is collected and placed on computers or discs at the will of the information providers. Researchers must know what information is available and who provides this information before beginning a computer search. Most service providers provide lists of the information that they have in their databases. It is very important to look at these databases to ensure that they have what you want.

Could the Information Be Found More Efficiently in a Library?

Your decision about whether to use the library will usually be based on the amount of time and money you have, since library searches tend to take more time and computer searches tend to require more money.

As a rule of thumb, the more information you have about the location of the information, the more efficient electronic research will be. For example, if you have the complete citation of a case or statute, it is fairly easy to find the case by going directly to the case or statute databases.

You would not want to use electronic sources if you were just beginning to learn about a topic. Even if secondary materials are available in electronic form, at this time they are not in sufficient quantity or quality to enable a beginning researcher to learn about an area of law. If you try to do a word search of electronic cases without a clear direction, you will sink into the huge number of cases. The other more significant problem is that you will never know what you do not find. A main advantage of library sources is that they tend to be easier to read and scan than electronic sources. Researchers can quickly view the whole case or statute instead of just one page at a time.

What Are the Topics or Concepts to Be Researched?

A researcher should have a general idea about the law and the particular legal issues raised in a problem before going into the library or the computer. Although it is easy to request a word search on the computer, the computer search is only as good as the researcher's knowledge and skill at using computers. Unless you know exactly what you are looking for, it is best to do some manual research prior to electronic research, in order to narrow down the issues and learn about the proper terminology. This is discussed further below.

Step 2: Select a Data Source

Once you have planned your research you must decide where you are going to look for the information: in the library, on CD-ROM, or on the Internet. The main question you must ask is: What are you looking for? Is it cases, statutes, books, journals? Then you must ask which sources are available for your use and which are most effective and efficient. For example, if searching for a federal statute, you could look in a library, on CD-ROM, or online on a government website or through a service provider. There is no best source. When looking for cases you could look at any of the following:

Cases	Sample locations
SCC	Supreme Court of Canada website
Federal	Federal government website
Provincial	Online through Quicklaw, *e*Carswell, or LEXIS
Topical	Online through Quicklaw, *e*Carswell, or LEXIS
Unreported	ACWS (All Canada Weekly Summaries) database on Quicklaw or LEXIS

Which Sources Are Available for Your Use?

Because access to computer information can be expensive, law libraries and law firms do not necessarily subscribe to all of the information available. A decision is often made to only maintain access through CD-ROMs or through one service provider. Some of the questions you may ask when deciding where to look for information are:

1. Do you have access to a CD-ROM, commercial service provider, or a public access Internet site?
2. What will it cost?
3. Do you have the necessary software and hardware?
4. Is it available in a library? For free?
5. Do you know how to search effectively?

Which System Is Most Effective and Most Efficient?

Effectiveness and efficiency are driven by a host of factors, such as your particular problem, your access to the source, and your skill at searching. Never assume that one system is better than others for all purposes. At this stage you must look not just at the financial and time costs. You must also look at the likelihood that your research will be accurate and complete. If, for example, you are not skilled at constructing word searches then you might be better off starting in the library or perhaps confirming your computer research in a library afterwards. At the end of the day you may decide to go to the library and speak to a librarian. Sometimes this is most efficient.

Step 3: Select a Database

If you are using a CD-ROM, you may not have to take this step because many CD-ROMs have only one "database." Your choice will be to select that part of that data that contains what you are looking for. Online searches, however, usually require that you select a specific database to search.

Each online service provider has its own system that contains a number of databases. Like the shelves in a library, each database contains different information. Not all the information is in one database. After choosing the appropriate source, a researcher must select a database that is likely to contain the needed information. For example, if you are looking for an Ontario case, a search through the Alberta reports database will not prove fruitful.

Selecting a database requires an understanding of what exactly it contains. Each service provider provides a comprehensive list of its databases and their contents. Usually these are available online, but print copies are also available. Researchers should always look at the list of databases to find out what each includes. Every database includes information relating to specific jurisdictions, topics, and time spans.

Although each provider has its own set of databases, there are essentially three types of legal databases for three types of legal information: cases, legislation, and secondary sources. For example, there is a separate database on Quicklaw for Canadian Criminal Cases (db CCC), British Columbia Statutes (db RSBC), and law jounals (db JOUR). Note that sometimes supplements are in additional databases. So, for example, the statute database may contain only the original consolidated set. To find updates to the statute, you may have to look in other databases.

Databases of cases are in either full text or digest form. They are sometimes organized in a similar way to the paper case reports: by court, jurisdiction, and subject. For example, there is a database on Quicklaw called the Supreme Court of Canada Judgments (SCJ), which includes only Supreme Court of Canada cases. The corresponding paper case report is called the *Supreme Court Reports* (S.C.R.), which includes only Supreme Court of Canada decisions. Statutes and regulations have also recently become available online.

Some companies combine databases to make research easier. These combined databases are called global databases. Often, a computer will provide you with a description of the contents of the database after it has been selected or just before you enter the database.

Step 4: Formulate Your Search

In order to conduct an effective search you must understand the basics of the software used to store and retrieve information and must be able to construct a word search. Here are some basics about searching CD-ROMs and online databases and some basics on constructing word searches.

CD-ROM Search Basics

A CD-ROM must be installed in your computer or on a network and you must have appropriate software and hardware. The person who sells you the CD-ROM will tell you what these requirements are. Once the disk is loaded on your computer, you simply click on the menu where the CD-ROM is located. A screen will open that will list all of the contents of the CD-ROM. You then just click on the information you need.

Most CD-ROMs will instruct you about the contents of the disk and how to search for information. Most searches are based on Boolean logic, described below under How to Construct a Word Search. Most legal CD-ROMs use FolioViews search software. This is powerful software that essentially enables you to search for information in two main ways:

- *By browsing the table of contents*: Since information on disks is typically stored in levels, you can scan though the table just as you would through a file manager, opening and closing levels as you need. This is a good place to familiarize yourself with the contents of the disk.

- *Through specially designed templates*: The publishers of CD-ROMs develop templates to help researchers construct queries. For example, the template will ask you the words you are looking for and which Boolean connectors you wish to use (such as "and" or "not"), and will allow you to restrict your search to a particular date or time. You simply have to fill in the blanks.

Since CD-ROMs are usually in a "window" format you will first see such things as menu bars and lists of possible commands. Even though templates are enticing, keep in mind that they are simply Boolean word searches. This means that you need to understand how the computer is searching by way of Boolean logic to ensure your results are accurate. Most experienced librarians try a number of different combinations of searches and often look at the results critically to ensure that something was not overlooked in the search.

Commercial Service Basics

To search an online service you will need certain software and hardware. Your online service provider will tell you what you need and will give you explicit written instructions about how to sign on from your computer so you can access data.

The following are some basic first steps:

- Phone the service provider (or publisher) to obtain access and a password.
- Purchase the CD-ROM or get access through the Internet from the provider's web page.
- Scan the front page to get a sense about your choices.
- Scan the directory of databases to learn about the available data.

Most of the online providers use a web-based interface. This means that commands can be completed by easy point-and-click options. They also have embedded hyperlinks. On the first page you will see a list of the services that the online company provides. For example, because lawyers often know the citation of the case they are looking for, Quicklaw has an option on the front page to search by case citation. New interfaces are created regularly to meet the ever-expanding needs of lawyers, so always take your time on the first page.

In most situations you will need to select the particular database that contains the information that you need. This is because information is divided into distinct databases. For that reason you must know what information is included in each. It is always a good idea to review the contents of the various databases.

Each provider has its own search software so it is important to understand how the tools work. For example, many systems search words on the basis of Boolean logic. This means that the computer simply searches for words in different permutations and combinations, explained further in the section below on constructing searches.

Public Access Website Search Basics

To be able to use the Internet you need to have a computer (or access to one), an Internet Service Provider (ISP), and a browser (such as Netscape Navigator or Microsoft Explorer). Then you have access to the largest library on Earth.

Because of the overwhelming amount of information available on the Internet, software programs or search engines have been developed to sort needed information.

Internet websites can be accessed one of two ways:

- If you know of a law-related website you can type that address (the URL or http://) of the site in the address bar in your web browser and then press **Enter**; or
- If you want to search for multiple web sites, select a search engine (such as Google), insert the words you wish to search for, and press **Enter**.

Because of the huge amount of information available on the Internet, the first method is by far the most efficient. In most cases, if you begin with a legal website that has many hyperlinks, the only step you may ever need to think about is which site to go to first. This site will lead to a chain of other sites. These sites are usually maintained by legal experts or librarians who have selected and sorted legal information in wonderful ways.

If you decide to do a search on the Internet it is best to consult books that help you understand how the search engines work and how to obtain the best search results. Be sure to make use of meta-search engines such as Metacrawler or Google. For example, if you want to search a particular website and that site does not have a search engine you may use your own browser's search engine.

How to Construct a Word Search

The success of your electronic search depends entirely on your ability to construct a proper search. As mentioned above, this in turn depends on your understanding about what the computer is doing with your request and what information it is searching through.

You must articulate your search in a way that a computer will understand. The skill is in identifying words or phrases from a legal problem and arranging them in a way that will direct the computer to the specific information you need. Therefore, like manual research, it is necessary to analyze the facts and determine the legal issues before beginning a search — not only to gain an understanding of the subject matter and determine what information you need, but also to learn the proper terminology. Because computer searches are conducted through words or phrases, a researcher must select words or phrases that best reflect the legal problem.

Most electronic libraries now use a web-based interface. This means that you will likely be familiar with the look of the screens and will be able to transfer the skills you have developed in searching websites to your legal research. Until a few years ago, researchers needed to have special skills in constructing complex word combinations to ensure that the computer would looks for a particular source or topic. Even today you cannot simply insert words and hope for the best. You must understand Boolean logic and how to use connectors between words to narrow or broaden a search.

What Are You Looking For?

The formulation of the search depends on what you are looking for. Careful thought goes into constructing a search. Sometimes it is helpful to think of the document you wish to retrieve. For example, you may imagine a superior court case involving a child who was hit by a train within a municipality where a provincial statute dealing with public land is in effect. Since most search engines do not understand natural language, a researcher must translate a request into the databases's terminology. This request is called a query or search. The skill in formulating a search is in arranging the words in a particular way so that the search will be broad enough to include all relevant information and narrow enough to exclude irrelevant information.

Although companies have developed software to assist in the construction of queries, you will constantly be surprised by what turns up from a search that you thought was very straightforward. Individual commands vary from system to system, but there are also many similarities. Essentially, a search will be either for a single word, alternate words, or multiple words.

Searching for a Single Word

A single word search involves asking a computer to search for a single word within a database. Because computers will only search for the exact word requested, if a word is spelled incorrectly, the computer will search for that misspelled word. Consequently, a researcher should be careful of the following:

- Is the word singular or plural?
- Could the word have different prefixes or suffixes?
- Could the word contain a hyphen, parentheses, or other punctuation?

Search engines have remedies specifically designed to combat these potential problems. Many computer systems automatically search for the plural of each word selected. If not, most have a "wild card" or universal character command that instructs the computer to search for *any* letters where a wild card is placed in a query. In many systems the wild card is an asterisk (*). So, since practice can be spelled two ways — with a "c" or an "s" — a single word search might look like this: practi*e.

Most search engines also allow for the "truncation" of a word. Truncation is a technique used to search for words with the same root. For example, employment, employee, employed all have the same root: employ. In many systems an exclamation mark (!) placed at the end of the word directs a computer to search all words with that root. Therefore, a search for employ! would retrieve sources that include words such as employee, employment and employer.

Searching for Alternate Words

Usually searches will involve words that can be expressed in more than one way (*e.g.*, "car" or "automobile"). Your search depends on selecting the right alternatives or synonyms for that word.

Multiple Word Search

In order not to retrieve too much information, researchers can control or limit searches by combining several words together or doing multiple word searches.

For example, a search for cases with the word "doctor" in them would result in a phenomenal number of cases, whereas a search for cases with the words "doctor" and "cancer" would result in fewer cases being selected. Multiple-word searches involve the use of "connectors" or "proximity indicators."

Connectors

In multiple-word searches, connectors are used between each word. The connectors used are "or," "and," and "but not." They are linked to the software's system of logic, which is called Boolean logic, described below. This is a system which defines the relationship between concepts by symbols. The example provided is a search for cases dealing with wife assault.

Illustration 5.1
A Picture Description of Boolean Logic

Picture Description	What You Type	Connector
⊛⊛	wife assault	OR
⊙⊙	wife and assault	AND
⊛◯	wife % assault	BUT NOT

Although computers have language that describes each of these scenarios, often the words "or," "and," and "but not" are used for this purpose. Many systems make "or" implicit. For example, "dog food" would be read the same as "dog" *or* "food." The following describes the three connectors seen in the illustration:

- "Or" searches for "wife" *or* "assault." It locates all cases containing either the word "wife" or all cases including the word "assault."
- "And" searches for "wife" *and* "assault." It locates cases containing both the word "wife" and the word "assault."
- "But not" (often represented by a percent sign) searches for "wife" *but not* "assault." It locates cases containing the word "wife" but not the word "assault."

Proximity Indicators

Other connectors placed between words will limit a search even further. Researchers can search for specific phrases or for words that are part of a sentence or paragraph. By placing "proximity indicators" between words, researchers can request those cases where a word is found within a certain distance of another word. These searches involve searching for one word and another word within a certain number of words or within the same paragraph of that word. The following are some examples of proximity indicators.

Request	Boolean Search
Within the same paragraph	wife /p assault
Within one word of another word	wife /1 assault
Within a certain number of words (*e.g.*, five) of another word	wife /5 assault

Request	Boolean Search
Within a certain number of words and in a particular order (*e.g.*, appears within the following three words)	wife +3 assault
A phrase	"wife assault"

Appendix A to this chapter contains examples of common word searches using Boolean commands.

Field Search

Searches can also be narrowed down to a specific location with a document. For example, researchers can direct a computer to restrict a search to a particular part of a case such as the title or the court. This saves time.

Cases are stored in databases in much the same format as they appear in the published hard copy in the case reports. For example, the title of a case is usually the first item found in an electronic case, followed by a headnote and the full text of the decision.

The following is a sample of the first part of a case from a computer printout. Each segment of the reported case is called a "field" and each field is numbered consecutively for purposes of searching. In the example below, the first field contains the style of cause. So if a researcher is searching for a case by the names of the parties in the action, it would be most efficient to search only that particular field for this information. Most case law databases print out in a similar format.

Ranking

Computers allow you to ask that your results be displayed in a particular order. A "rank method" determines the order in which your retrieved information will appear. Most information systems automatically call up the most relevant documents first. These are those documents that contain the most occurrences of your search term. This ranking is based on the assumption that those documents with the most occurrences of the search term will be most useful. You can choose chronological (in order by date) or statistical (with the most occurrences of the term searched). The four choices are essentially as follows:

- Chronological: Oldest document first
- Reverse Chronological: Most recent document first
- Statistical: Most occurrences of term first, oldest documents first if equal occurrences
- Statistical: Most occurrences of term first, most recent documents first if equal occurrences

Many systems default to the last method for cases: most occurrences and most recent cases first.

After completing the search, a researcher may wish to save the results. Most databases have commands that enable you to print the results of your search or save them to a floppy disk or the hard drive within your computer terminal. This is called downloading. The specific procedure or commands for downloading information will vary with each company and the capabilities of your computer terminal and printer. Be careful when printing, since often what you see is not exactly what will appear in print. It is best to use a print preview function if available.

Self Test

The following is a self test based on the information provided in this chapter. The answers to these questions are found at the end of the book in the "Answers to Self Tests" section.

1. Describe the "four doors" to the law library.
2. List two benefits and three limitations of using computers to assist research.
3. Name two online legal research service providers in Canada and their corresponding information systems.
4. Describe the steps of computer-assisted legal research.
5. Describe what is meant by a "literal" search.

Appendix A: Summary of Steps in Electronic Legal Research

There are four stages to any electronic research. Here are the questions you will want to ask at each stage:

1. Plan the research.

- What kind of information do you need?
- Is the information available in electronic form?
- Could the information be found more efficiently in a library?
- What are the issues or concepts to be researched?
- How much time and money do you have?

2. Select a data source: CD-ROM, commercial, or public access sites?

- What information you are looking for?
- Which sources are available for your use?
- Which source is most effective and most efficient for your situation?

3. Select a database.

- Which database has the information you are looking for?
- Do the databases provide full text, digests, or indexes?
- Which databases include headnotes, summaries, or annotations?

4. Formulate a word search.

- What words do you want the computer to locate?
- How should the command be structured (*e.g.*, how should the words be grouped)?
- What connectors will you use?
- Do you want to limit the search by dates?
- How do you want your results to be presented (*e.g.*, chronologically)?

Appendix B: Sample Word Searches Using Boolean Connectors

Locating Cases

By Subject

To locate cases by subject, it is generally necessary to do some preliminary reading about the subject area in order to narrow down the issues to be researched and to confirm the terminology. A search by subject will typically involve a one- or two-word search, searching for words that are most representative of the legal problem confronted. For example:

spous! wife /8 assault! abuse!

By Name of Parties

To locate a specific case by name or citation, do a word search for one of the names of the parties. This search can be narrowed down by only searching that particular segment or field in which the name of the parties are located. In many systems the title of the cases is contained in Field 2. Therefore, a search would look somewhat like the following:

@2 bank /2 montreal & xerox

By Citation

Similar to locating a case by name, locating a case by citation can be narrowed down to a specific segment or field. In many systems the citation of a case is found in Field 3. So, if you are looking for a case with the citation (1989), 67 O.R. (2d) 536, your search would look as follows:

@3 67 +1 O.R. +2 536

By Judge/Court/Jurisdiction

To locate a case by judge, court, or jurisdiction, locate the segment or field in which this information is contained. For example, in Quicklaw it is located in Field 4. The following is a search for a case decided by Judge MacDonald from the British Columbia Supreme Court:

@4 macdonald & columbia & supreme

Updating or Noting-Up a Case

Because most service providers and CD-ROMs have specially designed citators, researchers merely have to enter a specific command such as "CITE" and the history of that case and a list of cases in which that particular case was judicially considered will be called up. Another way to conduct a search for cases judicially considered is by searching for the particular name of your case by doing a word search in other databases. For example, if searching a database for cases that considered *Teno v. Arnold*, your request might look like this:

teno /10 arnold

Locating Statutes

By Subject

To locate a statute by subject, it is best to read generally about the subject area in order to clarify the terminology used and determine whether the legislation is federal or provincial. Then you can select the appropriate database, do a single- or multiple-word search for words most likely to appear in the statute. For example, if searching for statutes on refugees, you might search for words such as:

immigration or human /1 rights.

By Title

To find a statute by title, do a word search for the most descriptive word in the title. This search can be narrowed down by searching only that particular segment or field in which the title is located. In many systems the title of a statute is contained in Field 1. Therefore, a search for a British Columbia statute would look like the following:

db sbc (statutes of British Columbia database)

@1 hazardous /1 waste

By Citation

Like locating a statute by title, locating a statute by citation can be narrowed down by a segment or field. In Quicklaw the chapter number of a statute is contained in Field 2. If looking for a statute with the citation of R.S.C. (Revised Statutes of Canada) 1985, c. L-1, the search might look like this:

db rscc (consolidated revised statutes of Canada database)

@2 L-1

Judicially Considered

To find cases that have considered statutes, you can use a statute citator if there is one or you can conduct a search in the case law databases for the name of the particular statute. For example, if you are looking for cases that considered s. 13(*i*) of the *Canadian Human Rights Act*, your search might look like this:

Canadian /1 human /1 rights /20 13(i)

Appendix C: A Sample Quicklaw Search

Step 1: Phone Quicklaw to obtain access, a password, and free user materials, then go to www.Quicklaw.com. Always read the first few pages in detail. This is what the Main Menu looks like:

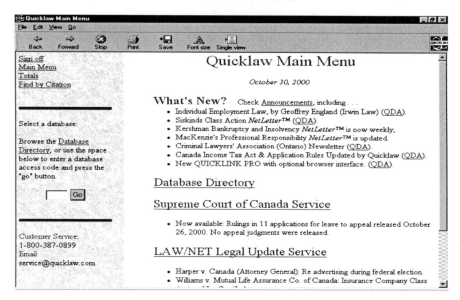

Step 2: If you are looking for a case by citation, you can make a request from the Main Menu. On the left panel (above) you can click on **Find by Citation**. You will then be shown the following template:

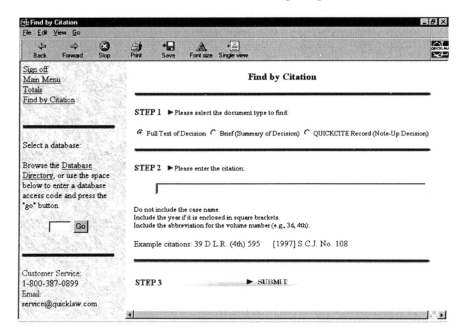

Select from the three options: full text, a summary, or the QUICKCITE history and treatment of the case. Enter the citation in the box and click **SUBMIT**. Quicklaw will search the relevant database for your case.

Step 3: If you are looking for cases by subject or for other information such as statutes or journals you must first select a database. Look through the paper or computer version of the Quicklaw Database Directory. To begin your search you must either click on **Database Directory** on the left panel or **Main Menu**, or enter a specific database in the box on the left panel and click **Go**. In the Directory you will be given a choice of countries and if you click **Canada** you will see the following screen:

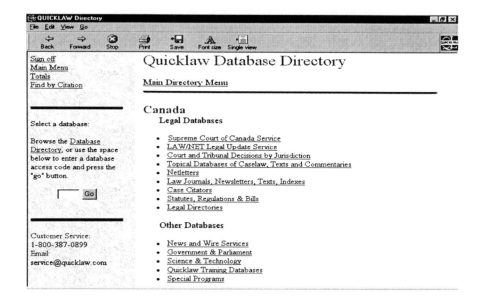

Click the links in the Directory menus until you find the appropriate database.

Step 4: Once you have selected a database you can perform a search using a search template similar to the following:

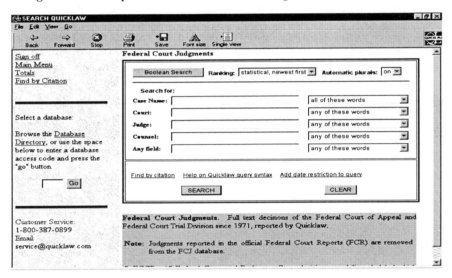

You have a choice of using the template or clicking the **Boolean Search** button to go to a Boolean search template. Refer to the text of Chapter 5 for information on how to formulate your search. In the template shown you can do any of the following:

- Select a rank method by clicking the arrow-down button in the **Ranking** box.
- Select the appropriate choice in the **Automatic plurals** box.
- Enter the information about your case in the boxes provided.
- From the drop-down menu beside each box in which you have entered information, select the way in which you would like Quicklaw to search for your terms (*e.g.*, **all of these words**).
- If you want to limit the search by date click the **Add Date Restriction to Query** button and enter the appropriate information in the box that appears.

Step 5: Click the **SEARCH** button. Once the search results appear on the left panel, click the appropriate case name or citation to view a case. This is what a case looks like:

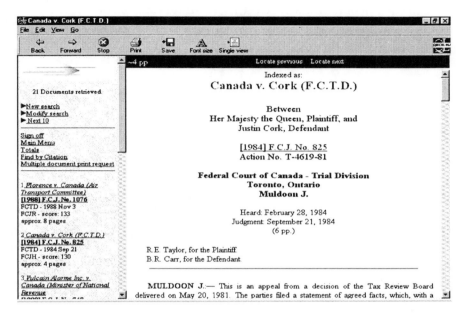

From this page you can do any of the following:

- Modify your search by clicking **Modify search** on the left panel.
- Start a new search by clicking **New search** on the left panel.
- Note up the case by clicking the **Note Up with QUICKCITE** option on the horizontal green bar at the top of your screen.
- Find a summary or digest of the case by clicking **DRS Summary** on the horizontal green bar at the top of your screen.

Step 6: If you are looking for statutes go to the **Database Directory**, click **Canada**, then **Statutes, Regulations & Bills**, then the appropriate jurisdiction and then the appropriate database code. For example, to search for a federal statute, select database **db RSC** and then, from the menu that appears, select database **db RSCT**. The following search template will appear:

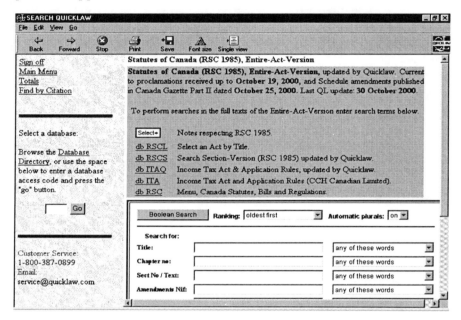

Enter the appropriate information in the search template and click the **SEARCH** button.

If you are looking for cases that have considered statutes, because Quicklaw does not have a statute citator, you must search case law databases for keywords from the statute. Quicklaw will retrieve cases that refer to this statute.

Step 7: If you are looking for journals or other secondary materials go to the **Database Directory**, click **Canada**, and then click the links in the Directory menus until you find the database you wish to search. For example, to search for commentary and analysis on criminal law, select **Netletters** from the Canada collection and then choose one of the databases under **Criminal Law**. Quicklaw will display a status message and search template that looks like the following:

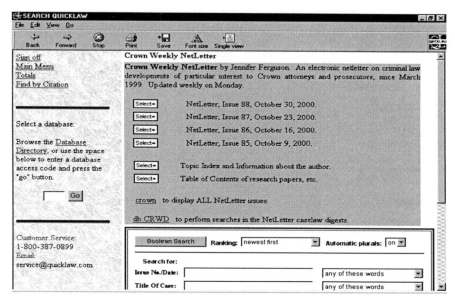

You can select a recent issue of the *NetLetter*™ from the status message or use the search template to perform a search.

All illustrations in this appendix reproduced with kind permission from Quicklaw Inc.

Appendix D: A Sample *eCarswell* Search

Step 1: Phone Carswell to obtain a password then go to the windows interface at www.ecarswell.com. From there, click on the **law.pro** option and you will see this home page. Always read this first page in detail.

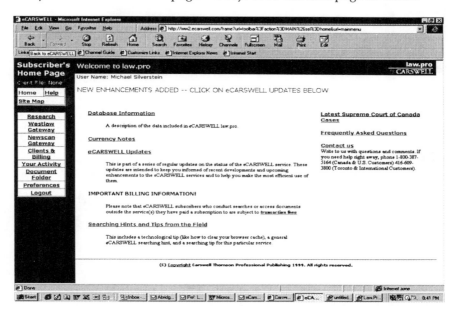

As you can see, you have several choices. Click on **Database Information** to find out precisely what is contained in the law.pro databases. Then click on your browser's back button to return to the home page.

Step 2: Click on the **Research** button in the left frame to select the data you want to search.

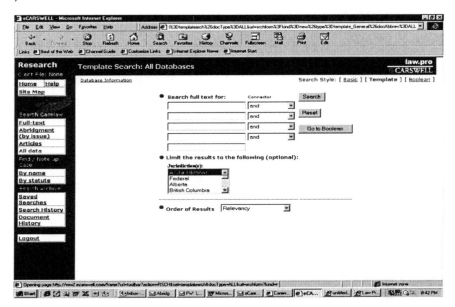

As you can see, the panel on the left prompts you to select from the following search options:

Search Caselaw

- **Full-text:** If you want the full text of a case
- **Abridgment (by issue):** If you want a digest of a case
- **Articles:** If you want an article published in a Carswell law report
- **All data:** All of the above if you have no idea what you are looking for

Find/Note Up Case

- **By name**: Case citator; if you want to find a particular case or find judicial considerations of a case
- **By statute**: Statute citator; if you want to find cases that have considered a particular statute

Step 3: After selecting a database you must select a search style box. You are given the following three choices. Select one.

- **Basic:** The simplest method but not most efficient
- **Template:** Just fill in the blanks
- **Boolean:** Construct a search with Boolean connector

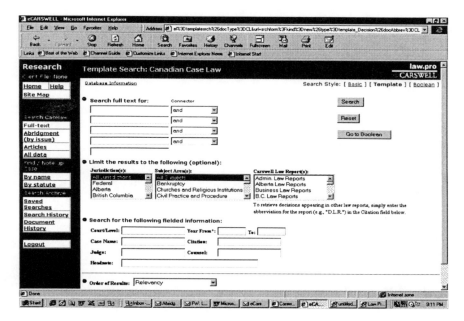

Legal Problem Solving

Step 4: If you are searching the **Abridgment (by issue)** for case digests, you have the following options:

- **Search digests via template:** Search by keywords
- **Search the key:** Classification system
- **Browse digests classification:** Table of contents

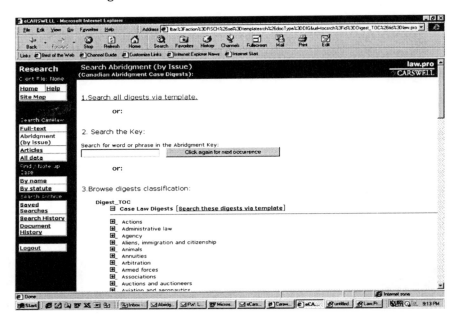

Step 5: If you choose to find or note-up a particular case, you will be shown a template with the following boxes to help you narrow down your search:

- Case name
- Citation
- Jurisdiction
- Subject
- Court Level
- Year
- Judge
- All Text

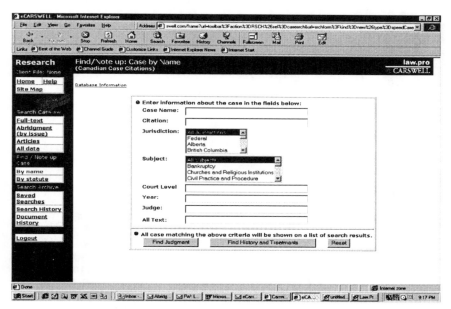

Then you are given two options at the bottom of the page:

- If you want the actual case: press **Find Judgment**; or
- If you want to note up the case: press **Find History and Treatments**.

Step 6: If you choose to note up a statute, you will be shown a template with the following boxes to help you narrow down your search:

- Jurisdiction
- Short Title
- Citation
- Section

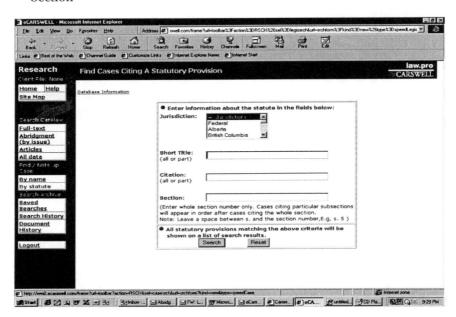

When you press the **Search** button at the bottom of the page, you will be shown a list of statutory provisions that match your search terms. By then clicking on the words **Cases Citing** beside any item on this list, you will see the cases that have considered that provision.

All illustrations in this appendix reprinted by permission of Carswell, a division of Thomson Canada Limited.

Appendix E: A Sample LEXIS Search

Step 1: Phone Butterworths to obtain access and a password and use your web browser to go to www.LEXIS.com. Always read the opening screen in detail. Note the *Search Advisor*.

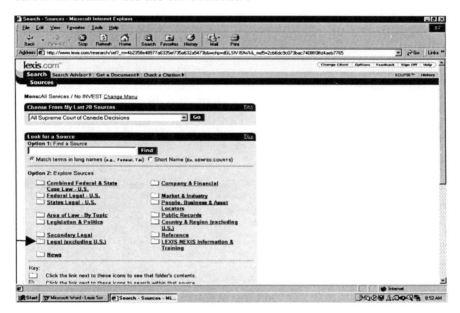

Step 2: From the main menu you have two initial options:

- **Find a Source:** Select this if you know the exact database you wish to search
- **Explore Sources:** Select this if you wish to select a database from a list of databases.

These two options are provided on almost every screen.

Under *Explore Sources* select **Legal (excluding U.S.)** to find Canadian sources.

Step 3: In the databases relating to Canada you will be given the same two choices. Under *Explore Sources* you will see:

- **Treaties & International Agreements**
- **Case Law**
- **Legislation & Regulations**
- **Journals**
- **Law lists & Directories**

Select the box that contains the information you are looking for. Note the list of terms at the bottom of the page. The lower-case **i** is your most valuable source of information about what is included in any database. You should always press this **i** before going into the database.

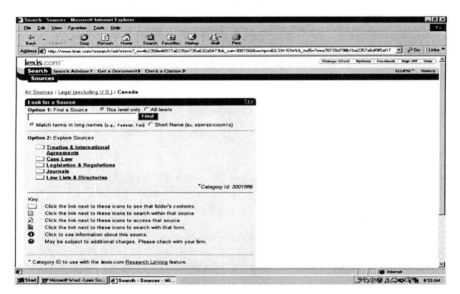

Step 4: If you select **Case Law** you will be shown the following:

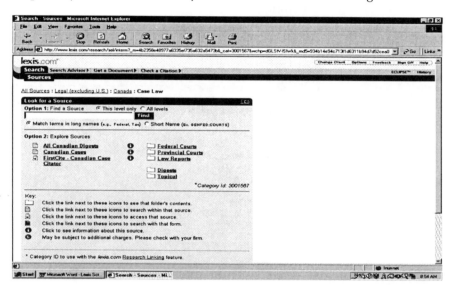

Again you are given the same two choices: *Find a Source* and *Explore Sources*. Under *Explore Sources* you will see:

- All Canadian Digests
- Canadian Cases
- First Cite - Canadian Case Citator
- Federal Courts
- Provincial Courts
- Law Reports
- Digests
- Topical

Press the small **i** beside any of the selections to find out what is in that database. Then select the relevant database.

Step 5: If you select **Legislation & Regulations** from the *Canada* page you will be shown the following:

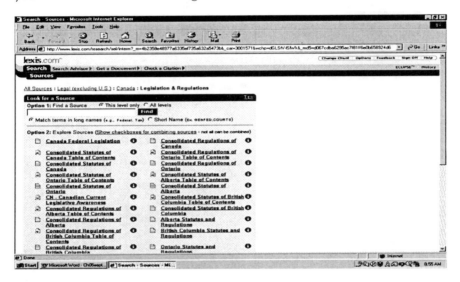

Again you are given the same two choices. Under *Explore Sources* you will find:

- Canadian Federal Legislation
- Consolidated Statutes of Canada
- Etc.

Step 6: If you select **Journals** from the *Canada* page you will be shown the following:

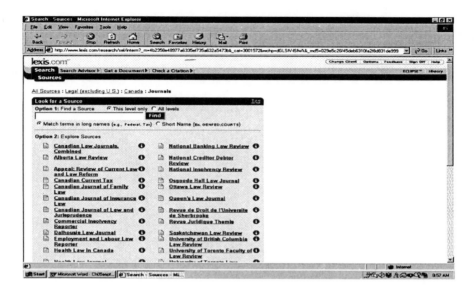

Again you are given the same two choices. Under *Explore Sources* you will find:
- Canadian Law Journals
- Alberta Law Review … etc.

How to Find Secondary Materials 6

As mentioned in Chapter 4, secondary materials are those books and other sources that assist researchers in doing two things: understanding the law and locating the law. They are essential to most research problems and are usually the first sources referred to upon entering a law library.

This chapter describes how to locate and use the most popular secondary sources.

Sources used to explain the law:

- Textbooks
- Periodicals and periodical indexes
- The *Canadian Encyclopedic Digest*
- Legal dictionaries

Sources used to locate the law:

- Case digests
- Books of words and phrases
- Tables of cases
- Citators

Learning Objectives

At the end of this chapter you will be able to:

- Locate and use textbooks and legal dictionaries
- Use periodical indexes to locate journal articles
- Find and use the *Canadian Encyclopedic Digest*
- Locate case digests and case indexes
- Explain what a citator is
- Cite secondary sources

The use of secondary sources will be demonstrated with the following fact pattern, which is the same fact pattern used in Chapters 2 and 3.

Fact Pattern

Paul Quint and Melody Jones

Paul Quint and Melody Jones, after ten years of marriage, are getting divorced. They have two children, Lindsay and Wayne, and have agreed that the children will stay with Melody. However, they cannot reach an agreement as to the division of property. They own a house and a boat on Salty Island. In addition, two years ago, Melody was given a $20,000 gift from her grandmother, which she put into a separate bank account in her own name. She wants to know whether the judge will consider the gift to be a family asset when making a decision about the division of property.

Sources Used to Explain the Law

Researchers should look at secondary sources in almost all research situations. Even if you know the name of the particular statute or case you are looking for, secondary sources will put this law into context and explain how the cases and statutes work together to form the law. They are created by editors and experts who know the law well, so it is a good idea to read what they say and refer to the cases that they mention.

Textbooks, Treatises, and Casebooks

Textbooks are books designed to teach a single subject and usually summarize the law on a specific legal topic. Treatises include textbooks and usually cover broader subject areas than textbooks. Textbooks and treatises are extremely useful to those new to a particular area of law. They provide summaries of the law and often include helpful tables of contents and subject indexes.

Every law library has a collection of law textbooks that can be located by using a computer catalogue. Researchers can search the catalogue by subject, title, author, or call number.

Although textbooks and treatises are not authoritative (*i.e.*, they are not primary sources of law), they have come to be regarded as having a considerable degree of authority because they are often written by academics and scholars. The major legal publishers in Canada are Butterworths, Carswell, and Canada Law Book.

Other useful sources are materials published by continuing legal educators, law societies, and Bar associations. Often materials are published as part of a course or workshop for practising lawyers and are written by experts. These materials can be found at law libraries or through the originating organization. Sometimes they can be purchased online through the organization's website.

Casebooks, unlike textbooks, do not summarize the law. They are collections of excerpts of cases and brief discussions about these cases. They are almost exclusively used in first-year law classes and are designed to help students learn by the case method. These books are used almost exclusively for educational purposes and are rarely referred to after the first year of law school.

Legal Literature and Periodical Indexes

Journals publish articles written by experts and academics. If you happen to locate a very recent article on your topic you will save hours of research. This section discusses paper and electronic journals and periodical indexes.

Paper and Electronic Journals

Journals are periodic soft-cover publications consisting of journal articles and other legal literature. They are in magazine format and include very current information. Many lawyers subscribe to periodicals relevant to their area of practice in order to stay up-to-date on the law. Recently periodicals have begun to appear in electronic form on websites.

Legal periodicals are particularly helpful when researching new or changing areas of the law. They include articles by academics that summarize and analyze the law. In addition to articles, many periodicals include other useful information, such as advertisements and job postings, case comments, book reviews, and current news.

The following are a few types of legal journals:

- General interest (*e.g.*, *Canadian Lawyer Magazine*)
- Special interest (*e.g.*, *Family Law Journal*)
- Bar association (*e.g.*, *Canadian Bar Review*)
- Scholarly (*e.g.*, *Modern Law Review*)

Common features of periodicals are helpful research tools such as subject headings, subject indexes, author and title indexes, tables of cases commented on, and book review indexes.

The vast majority of the full text of published journals are not yet in electronic form so you must go to the library to read them. A few journals are now available in full text through online service providers. For example, Quicklaw and LEXIS have journal databases. However, there is a budding industry of electronic journals where authors simply post their articles on websites. These articles tend to be edited less than the print versions but are extremely current.

Paper and Electronic Periodical Indexes

Periodical indexes are research aids designed to assist researchers in locating periodicals. Although most in the indexes are now on CD-ROM, the print versions are still useful for narrowing down your legal concepts and selecting the precise words to search.

Paper versions of periodical indexes typically list periodicals by subject, author, and title so that researchers can approach the periodical indexes in any of the following ways:

Option 1:   If you know the *title* of the journal, such as the Family Law Journal, but do not know the title or author of the article, it is often easier to go directly to that periodical and leaf through its index rather than using the periodical indexes.

Option 2:   If you do not know the title of the journal but know the *author or the title* of the article, look in the author or title index in one of the many paper-based or CD-ROM periodical indexes.

Option 3:   If you know only the *subject*, look in the subject indexes in one of the many periodical indexes.

The paper versions are particularly helpful when trying to find out how a legal subject is categorized or to narrow down a subject area. This is because you can scan back and forth quickly searching for key words that can ultimately be used for your electronic search. Each legal publisher describes subjects differently and there are usually a number of topics that are relevant to any research problem.

Paper periodical indexes are hardbound and thus are updated by supplements, so you must look in both. Occasionally, the supplements are consolidated into cumulative volumes, so it is always important to read the spine of the volume to determine whether the index is a consolidation or a supplement. It is usually necessary to search through several hardbound volumes and several soft-cover supplements to do a thorough search. Often the indexes provide instructions at the front of the volumes to assist researchers in using them. Most indexes include a list of all of the periodicals referred to in that index.

Many periodical indexes are published by geographical region. For example, the *Index to Canadian Legal Periodical Literature* includes only Canadian periodicals. There are five main legal periodical indexes. They are as follows:

Index to Canadian Legal Literature **(ICLL)**: Includes Canadian journals, books, book reviews, and other legal literature. It does not include all Canadian journal articles. It is available online through Quicklaw (db ICLL), and on CD-ROM.

Current Law Index **(CLI)**: Includes periodicals from most countries in the world. A hardbound cumulative volume is published quarterly and annually.

Index to Legal Periodicals (and Books) **(ILP)**: Indexes about 500 journals from the United States, Canada, the United Kingdom, Ireland, Australia, and New Zealand. It is hardbound and updated by supplements. A cumulative volume is published quarterly and annually. It is available online through Westlaw (ILP and CILP), LEXIS, and on CD ROM.

Index to Canadian Legal Periodical Literature **(ICLPL)**: includes legal periodicals and some non-law periodicals that include law-related articles. It includes about 100 Canadian periodicals. It is not available in electronic form.

Illustration 6.1
Index to Canadian Legal Periodical Literature

A-48 Index to Canadian Legal Periodical Literature

MARRIAGE ***(Continued)***

Consequences of a January/December marriage: a cautionary tale. A.H. Oosterhoff. (1999) 18 Estates J 261-284

Des empêchements matrimoniaux en droit canonique et en droit civil français. B. Callebat. (1999) 33 Studia Can 399-440

Les incidences pastorales de la dissolution du mariage non sacrementel en faveur de la foi. J.P. Labelle. (1999) 33 Studia Can 27-70

L'ordre public dans les relations de famille. J. Pineau. (1999) 40 Cahiers 323-344

Cases

Banton v. Banton, (1998) 164 D.L.R. (4th) 176.
A.H. Oosterhoff. (1999) 18 Estates J 261-284

Debora v. Debora, (1999) 43 R.F.L. (4th) 179.
J.G. McLeod. (1999) 43 Rep Fam L (4th) 179-181

MARRIAGE: PROPERTY

Business interests and family law. S.M. Grant. (1999) 17 Can Fam L Q 67-85

Consequences of a January/December marriage: a cautionary tale. A.H. Oosterhoff. (1999) 18 Estates J 261-284

Creditors and partition of the marital home. J.R. Williamson. (1999) 15 Solicitor's J 2:8-14

Family law and bankruptcy. T.A. Gutkin. (1999) 16 Nat Ins Rev 26-40

The need to reform the division of property provisions in the Family law act. A.S. Raphael. (1999) 21 Advocates' Q 380-396

L'ordre public et les rapports patrimoniaux dans les relations de couple. C. Dubreuil et B. Lefebvre. (1999) 40 Cahiers 345-365

Sagl v. Sagl: Valuation of an interest in a discretionary trust under Ontario's Family law act. L.H. Wolfson (1998-1999) 16 Can Fam L Q 521-531

Cases

Appleyard v. Appleyard, (1999) 41 R.F.L. (4th) 199.
J.G. McLeod. (1999) 41 Rep Fam L (4th) 199-200

Banton v. Banton, (1998) 164 D.L.R. (4th) 176.
A.H. Oosterhoff. (1999) 18 Estates J 261-284

Caisse populaire de Saint-Boniface ltee. v. Hong-Kong Bank of Canada, (1999) 19 R.P.R. (3d) 165.
J.W. Lem. (1999) 19 R.P.R. (3d) 166-171

Gallant v. Gallant, (1999) 42 R.F.L. (4th) 353.
J.G. McLeod. (1999) 42 Rep Fam L (4th) 355-357

Harris v. Harris, (1999) 47 R.F.L. (4th) 106.
J.G. McLeod. (1999) 47 Rep Fam L (4th) 107-108

M. v. H. (1999) 46 R.F.L. (4th) 32.
M. Buist. (1999) 46 Rep Fam L (4th) 331-338

MacNeill v. Pope, (1999) 43 R.F.L. (4th) 209.
J.G. McLeod. (1999) 43 Rep Fam L (4th) 209-211

Martin v. Martin, (1999) 42 R.F.L. (4th) 251.
J.G. McLeod. (1999) 42 Rep Fam L (4th) 253-257

Mazzarello v. Mazzarello, (1999) 44 R.F.L. (4th) 142.
J.G. McLeod. (1999) 44 Rep Fam L (4th) 142-144

Pastway v. Pastway, (1999) 49 R.F.L. (4th) 375.
J.G. McLeod. (1999) 49 Rep Fam L (4th) 376-379

Sagl v. Sagl, (1997) 31 R.F.L. (4th) 405.
L.H. Wolfson. (1998-1999) 16 Can Fam L Q 521-531

SWAN, v. Canada (Attorney General) (1999) 47 R.F.L. (4th) 282.
J.G. McLeod. (1999) 47 Rep Fam L (4th) 282-286

Wamsley v. Wamsley, (1999) 41 R.F.L. (4th) 454.
J.G. McLeod. (1999) 41 Rep Fam L (4th) 455-458

MARRIAGE (CIVIL LAW): PROPERTY

La transmissibilité du droit au partage du patrimoine familial sous l'eclairage de la jurisprudence recente. J. Beaulne. (1999) 101 R du N 141-154

Cases

Fine (Succession de) c. Bordo, [1998] R.J.Q. 1823.
J. Beaulne. (1999) 101 R du N 141-154

Illustration 6.1: This is an excerpt from the *Index to Canadian Legal Periodical Literature*. As you can see, the sections that relate to the Paul and Melody situation are the main heading "Marriage" and the subheading "Marriage: Property."

Most indexes are published a few times throughout the year (*e.g.*, quarterly), and a cumulative volume is usually published annually.

Perhaps the most useful source for electronic journals is the University of Toronto law library alphabetical list of electronic journals at http://www.law-lib.utoronto.ca/resources/locate/journals.htm. It lists all available periodicals and where they can be viewed or purchased.

When searching electronic journals it is best to narrow your search down as much as possible before beginning. You can do this in three ways:

- Select a specific database that only contains certain journals (*e.g.*, Canadian journals);
- Select a specific field search so that your search will be limited to such fields as author or subject; or
- Construct a word search that uses connectors such as and/or, not, or adjacent words.

Encyclopedias

There is only one Canadian legal encyclopedia. It is called the *Canadian Encyclopedic Digest* (CED) and is published by Carswell. Legal encyclopedias are similar to other encyclopedias in that they summarize large amounts of information. They are heavily footnoted with references to both statutes and cases.

These summaries are not the law. They include only an editor's opinion about what the law is, what the cases stand for, or what statutes mean. All cases and statutes referred to should be checked to ensure that the editors of the encyclopedia have interpreted their meaning correctly.

Encyclopedias consist of multi-volume loose-leaf sets with legal subjects organized alphabetically by topic. Because the law is categorized into specific legal topics, researchers must have some understanding of the way in which the subjects are categorized before beginning research. This is accomplished by reviewing the indexes and tables of contents in the encyclopedias. Specific steps are recommended below.

The CED is a good place to start research if you know very little about the legal topic you are researching. It is available in most law libraries in print or on CD-ROM from Carswell.

There is a western version (CED, Western 3rd ed.), which contains the law of the western provinces and an Ontario version (CED, Ontario 3rd ed.), which contains the law of Ontario. The two sets consist of about 40 loose-leaf volumes each. Each volume contains a number of legal subjects (called titles). Each title contains a brief overview of the law and refers to specific statutes and cases. The CED uses an indexing system that categorizes all of Canadian law into approximately 160 different subject areas.

The loose-leaf version of the CED consists of the following three parts:

* *Key*
* *Main Set* (multi-volume)
* *Supplements* (yellow pages)

The way to use the CED is by looking at each of these parts as described here in three steps.

Step 1: **Go to the *Key* volume. Look in either the Contents Key or the Index for areas of law that might be relevant to your problem. These sources will refer you to specific volumes in the *Main Set*.**

The *Key* is the first volume in the set. It includes a Research Guide that explains how to use the *Canadian Encyclopedic Digest*. It also includes the following four indexes:

* **Contents Key**: Lists all the titles of each of the subject areas (about 160)
* **Statutes Key**: Lists statutes alphabetically
* **Rules Key**: Lists rules alphabetically
* **Index**: Lists the subject titles alphabetically with subheadings

Each of the indexes directs the researcher to the location in the *Main Set* where the topic is discussed. A researcher who is unfamiliar with a legal topic will typically go first to the *Contents Key* and peruse it for one or two titles that might be relevant and then peruse the *Index* to find more specific areas of law that might be relevant.

In the CED there is a main heading called Family Law (General) and several subheadings such as family assets, bank accounts, and property division. Note that all of these subjects are found in title 63.1 in Volume 14A. A few of these sections could potentially apply to the Paul and Melody situation. Therefore all should be read.

Step 2: **Go to the *Main Set* of volumes and look in the volumes that include your topics. Peruse the table of contents in that volume, locate the relevant topic and read the relevant paragraphs. Record citations of relevant cases and statutes.**

The *Main Set* of volumes of the CED contains all the summaries of the law organized alphabetically by subject area. For example, the first volume includes a summary of the law on adoption and the last volume contains a summary of the law on wills. The volumes are loose-leaf and supplements are included at the front of most of the titles on yellow pages. These supplements are cumulative.

By reading the text, the researcher can gain an overview of the topic and also record the citation of statutes and cases on point. These statutes and cases provide a springboard for further research.

Illustration 6.2
Contents Key: List of Titles

CONTENTS KEY

LIST OF TITLES

The following is a list of the subject titles in C.E.D., showing the volumes in which they appear and their respective title numbers.

Subject Title		Volume
1.	Absentees	1
2.	Actions	1
3.	Administrative Law	1

THE KEY TO C.E.D.

Subject Title		Volume
36.	Coroners and Medical Examiners	8
37.	Corporations	8
62.	Extradition	14
63.	Family Law (Divorce)	14
63.1.	Family Law (General)	14A
63.2.	Federal and Provincial Taxation	14A

Canadian Encyclopedic Digest (Western) Third Edition, Key, Release June 2000. Reprinted by permission of Carswell, a division of Thomson Canada Limited.

Illustration 6.3
The Key to CED Index

INDEX

This Index covers all titles published up to and including **Release 2000-4**.

References are to volumes, titles and paragraphs within those titles, except for references to the title "Employment Law", which include a part number. For example, 1-5§44 refers to Volume 1, Title 5, paragraph 44, and 11D-54.1-VI§1050 refers to Volume 11D, Title 54.1, Part VI, paragraph 1050. "(Supp.)" in the reference indicates material found in a supplement to the title.

INDEX

FAMILY LAW (GENERAL) – *cont.*

R.R.S.P. 14A-63.1§322.1 (Supp.)
refusal of, reconciliation possible 14A-63.1§306
reviewable transfers of property 14A-63.1§§320, 330
settlements 14A-63§108 (Supp.)
tax consequences 14A-63.1§355
transfers to third parties 14A-63.1§331
valuation 14A-63.1§§317, 324-26, 348, 358
void marriages 14A-63.1§302
property division (British Columbia). *See also* **family assets (British Columbia).**
actions for 14A-63.1§§363, 365, 366, 404
applicability of legislation 14A-63.1§§359-61, 371
bankruptcy, effect of 14A-63.1§365.1 (Supp.)
business assets 14A-63.1§§370, 398-403, 434
commencement of action 14A-63.1§369.1 (Supp.)
common law marriages 14A-63.1§361
compensation orders 14A-63.1§442
court's powers 14A-63.1§§439, 439.1 (Supp.), 440-46, 448-50, 450.1 (Supp.), 451
declaration of irreconcilability 14A-63.1§§364, 364.2 (Supp.), 365-67

matrimonial home 14A-63.1§§422, 423, 432, 436
"other assets" 14A-63.1§§370, 370.1 (Supp.), 405-17, 417.1 (Supp.), 437
practice and procedure 14A-63.1§§369.1 (Supp.), 369.2
preservation orders 14A-63.1§451
"property" 14A-63.1§370.1 (Supp.)
reapportionment, factors in 14A-63.1§§375, 424-34, 436, 437, 438.2 (Supp.), 439
reapportionment, general 14A-63.1§§418, 419
registrar's recommendations 14A-63.1§449
separation agreements 14A-63.1§§364, 368, 369
set-off, maintenance arrears 14A-63.1§§280, 281
short marriage 14A-63.1§423.1 (Supp.)
triggering events 14A-63.1§§364, 364.1 (Supp.), 365-69
uncertainty of economic inequality 14A-63.1§369.2 (Supp.)
valuation 14A-63.1§§391, 396, 420, 421, 425, 447
property division (Manitoba)
actions 14A-63.1§§484, 491, 492, 493 (Supp.), 495, 500, 504-506
accounting and equalization 14A-63.1§§458, 471-74, 479-81, 499, 500
annuities 14A-63.1§§467, 477
applicability of legislation

Canadian Encyclopedic Digest (Western) Third Edition, Key. Reprinted by permission of Carswell, a division of Thomson Canada Limited.

Illustrations 6.2 and 6.3: These are excerpts from the Contents Key and the Index of the western version that relate to the Paul and Melody situation.

Illustration 6.4
CED Family Law: Contents

Title 63.1

FAMILY LAW (GENERAL)

prepared by

D.D. PETERSON, B.A., LL.B.
of the Alberta Bar

and updated by

NANCY A. FLATTERS, B.A., LL.B.
of the Alberta Bar

Canadian Encyclopedic Digest (Western) Third Edition. Reprinted by permission of Carswell, a division of Thomson Canada Limited.

Illustration 6.5
CED Family Law: Text

PART VIII – DIVISION OF MATRIMONIAL PROPERTY   §429

D. INHERITANCES AND GIFTS

§428 Where property has been acquired by inheritance or gift, it may be excluded from division as the property does not form part of the product of the marriage.[93]

> 93. See s. 51(*d*); *Bateman v. Bateman* (1979), 10 R.F.L. (2d) 63 (B.C.S.C.) (R.R.S.P. purchased with gift from mother); *Bandiera v. Bandiera* (1979), 13 B.C.L.R. 327 (S.C.) (inter vivos gift); *Caskey v. Caskey* (1979), 14 B.C.L.R. 193 (S.C.) (gift in form of loan at low interest rate taken into account); *Richardson v. Richardson* (1982), 32 R.F.L. (2d) 82; reversed on other grounds 43 R.F.L. (2d) 312 (B.C.C.A.) (husband's participation in litigation involving wife's inheritance not a "venture" within meaning of s. 45(3)(e) since no element of risk present; inheritance not family asset); *Barnard v. Barnard* (1987), 7 R.F.L. (3d) 163 (B.C.C.A.) (husband's use of inheritance as part of purchase price of property justifying unequal division); *Jasich v. Jasich* (1984), 40 R.F.L. (2d) 441 (B.C.S.C.) (inheritance kept intact and separate from family assets not constituting family asset); *Rushton v. Rushton* (1984), 38 R.F.L. (2d) 308 (B.C.S.C.) (term deposit held by wife and originating from sale of wife's mother's cottage not family asset); *Gullickson v. Gullickson* (1990), 26 R.F.L. (3d) 220 (bonds purchased by wife's mother and held by mother with wife having no access not family asset); *Maclean v. Maclean* (1990), 28 R.F.L. (3d) 103 (B.C.S.C.) (husband's trust divided 60% to husband and 40% to wife); *Gifford v. Gifford*, [1991] W.D.F.L. 914 (B.C.S.C.) (wife's inheritance a family asset as parties intending it to be basis of secure future; inheritance divisible with exception of inheritance in specie or yet to be paid).

Canadian Enclyclopedic Digest (Western) Third Edition. Reprinted by permission of Carswell, a division of Thomson Canada Limited.

Illustrations 6.4 and 6.5: These are excerpts from the *Main Set* of the CED.

Step 3: Look at the yellow pages Supplements in the relevant volume to see if the law has changed since the white pages were printed.

The CED is updated by supplements on yellow pages. Researchers should refer to these pages to see whether the law has changed since the white pages were printed. Every page in the CED is dated to indicate the cut-off date of the information. It is important to note this date to ensure that the information is current and search other sources for more current information.

CED in Electronic Form

The CED is also available on CD-ROM and online through *e*Carswell in Law.pro. There are essentially two ways to search a CD-ROM: by scanning the table of contents, or by using the template and filling in the blanks. It is best to scan the contents first to get a general sense about what is included on a CD-ROM and then you can refine your search on the template once you have a better sense about your topic and where it might be located.

When searching online you simply follow the instructions provided. More instructions on how to search electronic sources are in Chapter 5.

Other Secondary Materials

A description of secondary legal materials would not be complete without mention of the following.

Legal Dictionaries

Legal dictionaries define legal terms and common words with special legal meanings. Like standard dictionaries, they list words alphabetically. The most frequently used dictionary is *Black's Law Dictionary*, an American publication. The two main Canadian dictionaries are the *Canadian Law Dictionary* by Yogis (Barron's Educational Services) and *The Dictionary of Canadian Law* by Dukelow and Nuse (Carswell). Dictionaries are typically located in the reference sections of libraries.

Books of Words and Phrases

In some situations legal research is conducted on the basis of particular words or phrases. To assist researchers in this search there are secondary materials called "books of words and phrases." These sources list and define words and phrases that have been interpreted by courts. They also provide citations to cases and statutes that contain certain words or phrases. Here are two Canadian words and phrases sources:

> *Words and Phrases Judicially defined in Canadian courts* (*Canadian Abridgment*). This source consists of two bound volumes that are updated by supplements. It includes over 50,000 judicial consider-ations of words and phrases and provides citations for the cases referenced.

> *Words and Phrases, Legal Maxims*: This source consists of three loose-leaf volumes and defines words and phrases interpreted by Canadian courts. It was originally published by DeBoo.

Government Documents

Several government bodies produce studies or publications on different areas of the law. For example, federal and provincial law reform commissions investigate problems in the law and recommend changes. These commission reports are very useful summaries and critiques of the law. Often parliamentary committees or royal commissions produce reports on investigations or controversial areas of law. In law libraries these are often treated like textbooks and categorized by subject and call number. Often they are listed in periodical indexes and, more recently, they can be located on government websites.

Case Digests

Case digests are summaries of reported and unreported cases. They are written by editors and compiled in periodic publications and newsletters. They are prepared primarily for use by lawyers so that they can quickly read about current cases in their area of practice. A lawyer who wants the full text can order it from the publisher or the courts. The digests are arranged according to subject matter. Unlike the CED, digests are simply abstracts and rarely used by beginning researchers.

The main Canadian case digest collection is the *Canadian Abridgment: Case Digest*. It is organized in a fashion similar to the CED; cases are filed according to a similar classification scheme. Each topic is assigned a multi-level number. Digests can also be found online. The case digests are explained in more detail in Chapter 9.

Citators

Citators are annotations of the law. They typically state the law and all of its updates and judicial considerations. There are both statute and case citators. Statute citators consist of lists of statutes, revisions, and cases that refer to statutes. Case citators consist of lists of decided cases and lists of cases in which other cases have been judicially considered. The two most comprehensive paper-based citators are published as part of the *Canadian Abridgement*: *Canadian Case Citations* and *Canadian Statute Citations*. Citators are explained in more detail in Chapters 7 and 9.

Forms and Precedents

There are a few publications of forms and precedents. These are used primarily by lawyers in practice. Examples include: *O'Brien's Encyclopedia of Forms* (Canada Law Book) and *Canadian Forms and Precedents* (Butterworths). They include forms related to commercial law, corporate law, banking, real estate, and wills.

Citation of Secondary Materials

The authoritative book on Canadian legal citation is the *Canadian Guide to Uniform Legal Citation* ("the McGill Guide": Carswell). The main rule of citation of any source is to remain consistent. Each part of a citation has a purpose with the ultimate goal of enabling the reader of the citation to locate the source. The following is an example of a proper citation:

Author	Title	Edition	Publication Info.	Page
↓	↘	↘	↓	↓

P.W. Hogg, *Constitutional Law of Canada*, 2d ed. (Toronto: Carswell, 1985) at 73.

The following are some tips about textbook citation:

Author:	Full initials before the author's last name, followed by a comma
Title of textbook:	Italicize or underline, followed by comma
Volume:	If there is one
Edition:	Use abbreviations
Place of publication:	Name of city followed by a colon
Publisher:	Full name of publisher (unless well known)
Year of publication:	Of that particular edition
Page reference:	Only if referring to a specific passage

The following are the parts of a journal article citation and some tips:

L.E. Weinrib, "Learning to Live with the Override" (1990), 35 McGill L.J. 541 at 562.

Author:	Full initials before the author's last name, followed by a comma
Title of article:	Put in quotation marks
Year of publication:	Place in brackets
Volume number:	If there is one
Name of journal:	Use proper abbreviations
First page of article:	Always included in citation
Page reference:	Only if referring to a specific passage

Self Test

The answers to these questions are found at the end of the book in the "Answers to Self Tests" section.

1. How do you locate a textbook?
2. How do you locate journal articles by subject?
3. What is the *Canadian Encyclopedic Digest*?
4. What is a book of words and phrases?
5. What is a case digest?
6. What is a citator?

Sample Exercises — Finding Secondary Materials

Objectives

At the end of this exercise you should be able to:

- Locate and use relevant textbooks and treatises
- Locate and use relevant journal articles and periodical indexes
- Locate and use the *Canadian Encyclopedic Digest*
- Properly cite a journal periodical and a textbook

Instructions

- Do background reading on secondary materials.
- Keep a record of all the steps and the time taken to complete the exercise.

Canadian Encyclopedic Digest

Read the following fact pattern and answer the following questions.

Fact Pattern

Mr. Bark

Your client, Mr. Bark, has just been visited by the police. He apparently has been charged with both causing unnecessary pain and suffering to and unlawfully killing his dog, Wolff. Last week Wolff attacked the four-year-old girl next door. Mr. Bark fought off Wolff with a hockey stick and in the process killed him. He can't understand why he is now being charged with an offence, when he actually saved the little girl's life. What are his rights?

1. Brainstorm and list five words that you might look for in the library. Before looking at the law, list the facts you think are relevant.

   Words:

   Relevant facts:

2. Go to the *Canadian Encyclopedic Digest* (West 3rd) and look in the *Key* volume in the Contents Key and Index. List those titles and volumes that appear to be relevant to the fact pattern. Or look in the CD-ROM version in the Table of Contents.

   Subject titles/volumes:

3. Go to the specific *Canadian Encyclopedic Digest* volume that contains the most relevant subject title (from Question 2). Look in the Index to that volume and find the most relevant sections. List

the most relevant heading, subheading(s), and paragraph(s) that appear to be relevant to the fact pattern.

Number:

Heading:

Subheading(s):

Paragraph Numbers:

4. Read the other relevant titles *briefly*. List any new paragraphs you find that may be relevant to the fact pattern. Look in the yellow page supplements (if any) and list those paragraphs you selected above which have been updated. *Do not solve the problem.*

New paragraphs:

Paragraphs that have been updated:

Textbooks

1. Use the card or computer catalogue in the library to locate a treatise/textbook on the subject of *Criminal Law*, by D. Stuart. Provide the proper citation and record the call number.

Citation:

Call number:

2. Find the treatise/textbook in the above question and locate the topic and pages where cruelty to animals is mentioned.

Pages:

Periodicals

Go to the legal periodical indexes (paper or electronic). Give the proper citation for one periodical that addresses the following:

1. By subject (use the *Index to Legal Periodicals*):

A 1990 article on the Pacific Region and the proposed "driftnet free zone."

Citation:

2. By author (use the *Index to Canadian Legal Periodical Literature*):

A 1980 article by N. Bala on unmarried couples.

Citation:

3. By table of cases (use *Current Law Index*):

    A 1994 article or case comment on *R. v. Osolin*.

    Citation:

Dictionaries

Give a complete clear and succinct legal explanation in your own words for the following term. Name the source you used.

> *Res judicata*

> Source:

Answers to Exercises

Canadian Encyclopedic Digest

1. Animal; dog; self defence; neighbour; children.

    Relevant Facts: A man killed his dog with a hockey stick during an attack on a four-year-old girl. He has been charged with causing unnecessary pain and suffering to the dog and unlawfully killing it.

2.

Title Numbers	Subject Titles	Volumes
6	Animals	2
40 and 40.1	Criminal Law	10 and 10A

4. Volume 2, title 6, section XII: Offences relating to Animals, part 1: causing unnecessary suffering at par. 558. And section IX: Dogs, part 5: Liability for injuries inflicted by dogs at par. 330.
5. No new paragraphs.

Textbooks and Treatises

1. D. Stuart, *Canadian Criminal Law: A Treatise*, 3d ed. (Toronto: Carswell, 1987).

    Call Number: KM520.S8849(R) (The call number may be different in different libraries.)

2.   Offences, cruelty to animals: pages 81 and 202.

Defence of person, defense of other: page 446.

Periodicals

1.   M.R. Islam, "The Proposed 'Driftnet-Free Zone' in the South Pacific and the Law of the Sea Convention" (1991), 40 Int'l Comp. Law Q. 184.
2.   N. Bala, "Consequences of Separation of Unmarried Couples: Canadian Developments" (1980) 6 Queen's L.J. 72.
3.   "Medical Records of Rape Victims" (1994) 36 Crim L.Q. 257 (Note: the author is not listed in the index so you must go to the specific journal to get the author's name).

Dictionaries

Res judicata: An issue that has been settled by judicial decision.

Source: *Black's Law Dictionary*, 7th ed. (St Paul, Minn.: West Publishing Co., 1990).

Appendix A: Checklist: How to Find Secondary Materials

Locating and reading secondary materials to gain an overview of the law should be your first research step. Record references to specific cases, statutes, and other secondary sources referred to in the secondary materials.

Textbooks

❑ *In the library*: Look in a computer library catalogue to locate textbooks or go to library shelves and browse. Read generally at first. After you have focused your research, go back and record the relevant cases and statutes that are referenced. Some researchers photocopy relevant pages from textbooks for future reference.

❑ *Electronically*: Some library catalogues are available over the Internet. However, very few textbooks are available in electronic form. One other way to find textbooks is through online bookstores.

Legal Journals and Periodical Indexes

❑ *In the library*: Look in a couple of the paper legal periodical indexes to confirm or narrow your choice of subject area for research. At the same time you may find some relevant journal articles on your subject. Most law libraries have collections of journals that you can read and photocopy.

Electronically

Very few journals have full text available online.

❑ *CD-ROM*: Several periodical indexes are available on CD-ROM. Scan the indexes for words that represent the issue you are researching. If the CD-ROM provides a query template use that as well to construct a more defined search.

❏ *Online*: Quicklaw and LEXIS have periodical indexes and periodical databases. Scan the directory of databases of each provider.

Canadian Encyclopedic Digest

Western or Ontario Version

❏ *In the library*: Locate and review the *Key* (the first volume in the set) and locate relevant subject areas or titles in the Contents Key or the Index. Go to the volumes in the *Main Set* and read generally at first. After you have focused your research, go back and record cases and statutes that are referenced.

❏ *Electronically*: the CD-ROM version of the CED is usually available free to use in law libraries. You can search the CD-ROM by scanning the contents or by using the template provided.

How to Find and Update Statutes 7

Statute research involves locating and updating statutes and locating cases that have interpreted or applied statutes. For example, a researcher confronted with a situation involving the dismissal of an employee would look for labour and employment statutes, determine whether they have been repealed or revised, and then search for cases that have considered or interpreted those statutes. Often cases that apply statutes add a new interpretation to a statute, so a researcher should always look for the most recent cases even if a statute is new.

The following should be kept in mind when conducting statute research:

- Statutes work in combination with cases;
- There may be more than one applicable statute;
- There may be overlap between provincial and federal statutes;
- Statutes are revised regularly, so research must always be current; and
- Cases interpret statutes and can affect the meaning of statutes.

This chapter describes two basic ways to find statutes and provides a step-by-step technique. It explains how statutes are published, provides instruction on how to find cases that have considered statutes, and demonstrates how cite a statute.

Learning Objectives

At the end of this chapter you will be able to:

- Describe how statutes are published or reported
- Locate a statute by title in the library and electronically
- Locate a statute by subject in the library and electronically
- Note up a statute
- Locate cases that have considered statutes
- Write a citation for a statute

How Statutes Are Published

In order to research statutes properly you must understand the stages through which a statute passes and the way in which statutes are published.

As explained in Chapter 4, governments are constantly introducing or repealing statutes and thereby creating new law. Proposed legislation goes through a lengthy legislative process before becoming law. To determine whether a bill has become law, a researcher must trace the progress of a bill through each of its publications. Statutes are published by the federal government and by each provincial government. These governments also publish research aids such as indexes of statutes, although many of the tools researchers use to locate statutes are published by commercial publishers.

Provincial parliaments consist of single legislatures, whereas the Canadian Parliament consists of the Senate and the House of Commons. A provincial bill must be read three times in the legislature. A federal bill must receive the consent of both houses before legislation can be effective.

The five basic stages of the creation of statutes are as follows:

Bill/First Reading	➔ Second Reading	➔ Third Reading
➔ Royal Assent	➔ Proclamation (or Delayed Effective Date)	

There is one set of federal statutes published by the federal government and one set of statutes for each of the provinces and territories, published by their respective governments.

Within each of set of statutes (provincial and federal) there are the following four main components:

Format	Stage
Bills/First Reading	Not yet approved
Gazettes/First Printing	First publication of statutes (loose- or softbound)
Annual or Sessional Volumes	Formal bound set, usually published annually
Revised Statutes	Consolidation of statutes

Each of these is described in detail here. It is important to note that, at least for the time being, there is only one official version of statutes. These are the government-printed versions. Electronic versions or commercially published versions are unofficial versions.

Bills/First Reading

A statute is first introduced in a provincial legislature or the federal Parliament as a bill. At first reading, bills are assigned a number and then sent to a committee to be debated. This reading is merely a formality. A bill may be either a public bill, which deals with public policy, or a private bill, which affects individuals or institutions.

The Parliament of Canada consists of two houses — the House of Commons with 301 seats, and the Senate with 104 seats. Federal laws must be passed by each house. A statute is introduced in the House of Commons as a commons bill or in the Senate as a senate bill. The bills are assigned alpha-numeric numbers indicating where they were introduced (C = Commons; S = Senate) and when it was introduced in a particular session. A bill at first reading contains explanatory notes that can be helpful to researchers when determining the intent of a statute. The statute is read three times in the House of Commons and three times in the Senate. The statute then receives royal assent by the Queen's federal representative, the Governor General. Some statutes also require a proclamation by the federal cabinet (*e.g.*, if it has a delayed effective date).

Each of the provincial parliaments consists of one house. The legislation making process is similar for all provinces. A statute is introduced as a bill and must receive three readings and royal assent by the Queen's provincial representative, the Lieutenant Governor, before becoming law. Some statutes also require proclamation by provincial cabinet.

Bills are made only when Parliament is in session, so laws are categorized by session — usually one or two years in length. Any bills that do not become law in a session die and must be reintroduced in the next session. Each sitting of Parliament is numbered after each election. For example, the 36th Parliament since Confederation in 1867 began in June 1997 after that federal election.

The first reading of the bill is particularly important to researchers because it contains explanatory notes that help determine the intent of the statute. The third reading of a bill is also published, but is only important because it exists as the statute until the statute is formally published a few months later.

Royal Assent

Royal assent is the symbolic acceptance by the sovereign and simply involves signing the statute by the Governor General (for federal statutes) or Lieutenant Governor (for provincial statutes). Royal assent occurs after the bill is approved by both houses (federal) or the legislature (provincial). However, not all statutes become law upon royal assent.

Proclamation or Delayed Effective Date

The effective date of some statutes may be delayed. This results in the statute coming into effect upon the introduction of a regulation or proclamation, or on a specified date. Finding the effective date of the statute is discussed in the next chapter on regulations.

Research Tools

Most law libraries have print copies of federal and provincial bills and research aids that explain what stage the bill is at. Bills may also be obtained directly from the federal and provincial governments. There are several publications that list the progress of a bill. The most current can be found online. For example, the several government sites have progress of bills information, and Quicklaw and LEXIS have statute databases. But if you are looking for a very current bill, it is best to telephone the libraries at the federal or provincial legislatures.

The following are examples of some of the paper-based research aids that can assist researchers in locating bills and determining their status:

Federal Bills

- *Ottawa Letter*: A newsletter that contains information entitled "Progress of Legislation," which describes the progress of federal bills through Parliament. This is a useful source for determining the status of a bill in the House of Commons or the Senate, but it is not always accurate.

- *Order Paper and Notices*: Parliament's agenda, outlining what will happen to a bill that day. This is rarely used for research.

Provincial Bills

Each provincial legislature publishes similar lists that can be used by researchers to determine the status of a bill. Each of these publications contains similar information from province to province. The following are some of the tiles used:

- *Orders of the Day*: A daily agenda of a provincial legislative assembly. It contains information on bills and the stage they are at.

- *Legislative Digest* or *Legislative Record*: Both resources list bills and what stage they are at. This is the most up-to-date tool and reasonably easy to use.

- *Votes and Proceedings*: A program of what happened on a particular day during a legislative sitting.

A bill is debated at its second reading. At the third reading, the bill is reviewed in final form. This is the version that usually becomes law.

Gazettes/First Printing of Statutes

After bills receive royal assent, they are assigned new numbers, collected together, and printed. The numbers assigned to federal statutes are usually alpha-numeric. The first letter is the same as the first letter in the title of the statute (*e.g.*, L-1 is the *Labour Code*).

Federal statutes are printed in the *Canada Gazette*, Part III and provincial statutes are published in what is typically called the *Third Reading Bills*. These softbound publications fill the gap between the printing of the original bill and the publication of the hardbound volume of statutes. Because they are softbound, libraries receive them within a few months of royal assent.

Illustration 7.1
Canada Gazette, Part III

Vol. 23, No. 2		Vol. 23, n° 2
Canada Gazette		**Gazette du Canada**
Part III		Partie III

OTTAWA, WEDNESDAY, AUGUST 9, 2000

Statutes of Canada, 2000

Chapters 8 to 12

Acts assented to from 14 April, 2000
to 29 June, 2000

OTTAWA, LE MERCREDI 9 AOÛT 2000

Lois du Canada (2000)

Chapitres 8 à 12

Lois sanctionnées du 14 avril 2000
au 29 juin 2000

NOTICE TO READERS

The *Canada Gazette* Part III is published under authority of the *Statutory Instruments Act*. The purpose of Part III is to publish public Acts as soon as is reasonably practicable after they have received Royal Assent in order to expedite their distribution.

Part III of the *Canada Gazette* contains the public Acts of Canada and certain other ancillary publications, including a list of Proclamations of Canada and Orders in Council relating to the coming into force of Acts, from the date of the previous number to the date shown above.

AVIS AU LECTEUR

La Partie III de la *Gazette du Canada*, dont la publication est régie par la *Loi sur les textes réglementaires*, a pour objet d'assurer, dans les meilleurs délais suivant la sanction royale, la diffusion des lois d'intérêt public.

Elle présente en outre certains textes complémentaires, comme la liste des décrets d'entrée en vigueur et des proclamations du Canada ultérieurs au numéro précédent.

Reproduced with permission from Public Works and Government Services Canada. Not an official copy.

Illustration 7.1: This illustration gives the "look" of an opening page of the *Canada Gazette*, Part III.

The following describes the contents of the publications that accompany the hardbound federal statutes:

- *Canada Gazette, Part I*: Contains formal notices required by statute to be published.
- *Canada Gazette, Part II*: Contains new regulations.
- *Canada Gazette, Part III*: Contains new statutes and a table of proclamations.
- *Table of Public Statutes*: A cumulative list of all federal public statutes in force.

Provincial sets of statutes are fairly similar to the federal set, although they go by slightly different titles. Because it is difficult to recall all of the detailed steps involved in statute research, it is better to understand these fundamental parts. If you understand the *framework* of statutes, you will be able to do research in any jurisdiction.

Annual or Sessional Volumes

At the end of each year or legislative session, all of the statutes from that year or session are collected and published in hardbound volumes called the "annual" or "sessional" volumes. These volumes are received by libraries about a year after the end of the year or session.

Annual or sessional volumes also typically include helpful research tools such as tables of contents, tables of statutes, and tables of proclamations. Each volume is identified by the year or session on its spine. Some sessions may span more than one year or there may be more than one session in a single year.

Revised Statutes

The federal government and most provincial governments periodically consolidate their statutes into a "revised" set of statutes in force. This involves reprinting all statutes and incorporating all amendments up to that time. The revisions effectively repeal and replace all prior legislation. They are essentially consolidations of all public statutes in effect at the time of publication.

The federal government did this in 1886, 1906, 1927, 1952, 1970, and 1985. The most recent federal consolidation is the *Revised Statutes of Canada, 1985*, which consists of 14 blue volumes.

The volumes that contain statutes from before the consolidation are rarely used and remain in the library mainly for historical purposes (*e.g.*, to see a statute in its original form). Researchers should rarely have to consult the pre-consolidated version of a statute.

Illustration 7.2

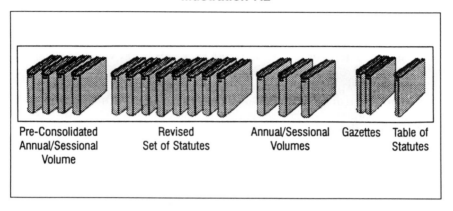

| Pre-Consolidated Annual/Sessional Volume | Revised Set of Statutes | Annual/Sessional Volumes | Gazettes | Table of Statutes |

For federal research, it is important to note that it took four years to produce the 1985 revision. Statutes that were amended or introduced between 1984 and 1988 were placed in supplements to the revised set. Therefore, the *Revised Statutes of Canada, 1985* consists of eight main volumes plus five supplements: one for each of the years from 1985 to 1988 and an Appendix volume. The main volumes and four supplements include all statutes enacted up to December 12, 1988. A researcher should always keep this problem in mind since this situation is true for most provinces; many statutes are passed while the revised set is being compiled.

When you go to the library, you will find not only the official version of the statues, but unofficial versions as well. These are usually published by commercial publishers and are edited in a way that makes them useful to researchers.

Office Consolidations of Statutes

A few of the more popular statutes are published individually, with all current amendments incorporated into them. They often include the regulations and are in soft-cover. Examples include the company acts from various provinces and the *Criminal Code*.

Loose-Leaf Editions of Statutes

There are several sets of loose-leaf editions of statutes. These are extremely useful tools because they are updated regularly by inserts so that you can avoid having to go through several volumes of statutes to determine which sections have been revised. As well, they are often annotated with lists of any cases that have considered a statute. These are called "annotation" or "statute citator."

Electronic Versions of Statutes

Computers have revolutionized statute research in three key ways:

- Statute databases can be searched by a simple key word command;
- The electronic form can be kept fairly current because no time is needed to print, publish and distribute the statutes; and
- The electronic version can be consolidated — meaning that it incorporates changes right into the statute so you do not have to search through several print volumes of statutes to locate amendments to those statutes.

However, the electronic versions are still not viewed by all courts as official, so paper-based research is still necessary. Keep in mind that many of the statute databases are kept filed in databanks much like on the shelves of a library. For example, one database may contain the consolidated set of statutes, one may contain bills and one may contain recent gazettes. If this is so, then you must look in each of these databanks for information relating to your statute. The best databases contain all of the changes since the last government consolidation incorporated right into the text.

There are three types of electronic versions of statutes: CD-ROM, commercial online versions, and government Internet versions.

CD-ROM: There are many CD-ROM versions of statutes. Most of the provincial governments placed their statutes on CD-ROM in the early 1990s. The CD-ROMs are like the loose-leaf versions of statutes in that they are updated regularly in a consolidated form so you only need to do library research from the disk date forward. When the statutes are updated, a new CD-ROM is issued and the old one can be thrown away. These disks are usually free to use in most law libraries. These can also be purchased and used at your own computer.

Commercial online service providers: There are two main providers of online statute research services: Quicklaw and LEXIS. They have many databases of statutes and regulations including all federal statutes and most provincial statutes. The main difference between the two is not so much in content as it is in the interface and search tools. Try both and remember to always look at the content of the database you are looking at to see how current it is. For example, LEXIS provides a small "i" beside each database selection so you can hyperlink to check the currency of the database before you do a search.

Government Internet sites: The federal government and most provinces maintain websites that can be accessed over the Internet. A list of these websites is appended to this chapter. Just as with other electronic sources, it is critical that you find out what exactly is in the database and how current the information is. Note whether the statutes are consolidated, and if not, what other databases update these databases. For example, you may have to look in three databases: the revised statutes, gazettes, and bills. You will need to search in the library to see what changes, if any, have been made since the latest update.

The Five Steps to Locating and Updating Statutes

There are essentially two ways to find statutes: by title or by subject. If you know the name of a particular statute, you can search by title in various indexes or tables of statutes. If you know only the subject area, subject indexes or other research tools must be used.

Statutes are generally much easier to find than cases because the federal and provincial governments publish indexes with the statutes.

There are five steps to finding, updating and noting up statutes. They are as follows:

Step 1: Find a statute by subject.
Step 2: Find a statute by name or citation.
Step 3: Ask whether the statute in force. Does it have a delayed effective date?
Step 4: Update the statute. Has the statute been amended?
Step 5: Note-up the statute. Find cases that considered it.

A summary of these steps is appended to this chapter. Each section below discusses how to use both the library and the computer for each step.

Step 1: Find a Statute by Subject

There are two ways to find a statute by subject: by using secondary materials or by going directly to the statutes. The most effective method is to use secondary sources first, but you should do both.

The two most helpful secondary materials are the *Canadian Encyclopedic Digest* and textbooks. Both of these secondary materials are essentially restatements of the law and are described in detail in Chapter 6. They provide an overview of the law and direct the researcher to specific cases and statutes.

A few governments publish subject indexes as part of their set of statutes. These indexes list statutes by subject and provide citations. These subject indexes are usually bound volumes and are typically included with the latest set of revised statutes. They list statutes by subject and provide citations (*i.e.*, year and chapter numbers). Unfortunately, subject indexes are slowly disappearing with the introduction of electronic sources. Many are out of date, since they are often only prepared as part of a consolidation. For example, the last subject indexes published for federal statutes was in 1985, called the *Revised Statutes of Canada, 1985* English Index. Provincial indexes go by various titles.

Although computers enable you to drill through tons of information, you can spend substantial time on your computer searching for a statute by subject unless you set fairly clear parameters. You could also overlook a statute if, for example, you find three relevant statutes and stop your search at that point. For example, you might find a statute that deals with matrimonial property on death and miss a statute that deals with matrimonial property on divorce. The other problem with electronic searches is that they search by word. This means that unless you know the specific word that defines the concept you are looking for, you will not find the relevant statute.

The best way to conduct a subject search on your computer is by refining your search by using the library and then searching for the statute by title on the computer.

As mentioned above, there are CD-ROM collections of statutes, there are government sites that allow public access to statutes, and there are online service providers that collect statutes in databases.

Step 2: Find a Statute by Name or Citation

It is fairly easy to locate a statute if you have the name of the statute or its citation. Although the easiest way is by searching on your computer, this is not always the most effective route.

The quickest way to locate a paper version of a statute is by looking in a loose-leaf statute citator. This is the first place lawyers look. Although citators are not the official version of statutes, they will give you the proper title of the statute, any revisions to that statute, and, in some publications, cases that have considered the statute. Citators are excellent research tools but you should confirm the information in the official set of statutes.

If you know the title of the statute, you should first locate the consolidated federal or provincial table of statutes. Most provincial governments and the federal governments publish comprehensive tables of statutes. The tables are cumulative, alphabetical lists of all statutes in force and are constantly updated. Other important information is usually included in the tables, such as the date the statute came into effect and the way it was brought into effect (*e.g.*, by regulation). It also lists amendments to the statute. These tables are a researcher's most important tool for finding statutes.

Simply locate the title of your statute in the index and note the year and chapter number of your statute. This tells you where to locate it in the main set of statutes.

The federal table is called the *Table of Public Statutes* and is published in hard-cover for each session of Parliament. It is also published as a separate volume up to three times annually. Until recently, it was published as part of the Gazette, Part III.

Provincial tables of statutes have various titles and various frequencies of publication. Some provinces, such as British Columbia, no longer publish these tables but publish a list of legislative changes instead. In these situations you must look in the most recent table of statutes published in the revised consolidated set and then look in each of the sessional volumes since that revision.

Instructions on how to read tables of statutes are at the end of this chapter. You will want to find the statute title in the alphabetical listing. The table will describe the location of the statute by the year, volume, and chapter number of the statute. This is called the citation. The table also lists amendments.

Illustration 7.3
Statutes of Canada: Table of Public Statutes

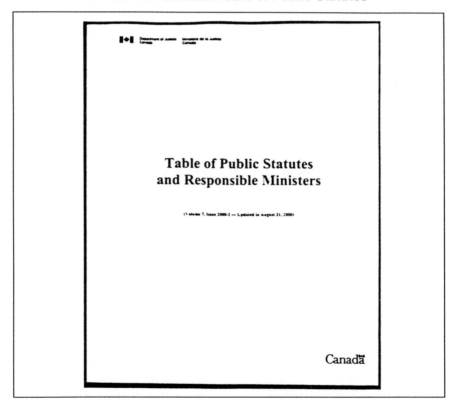

Illustration 7.3 — cont'd

Citizenship Act — R.S., 1985, c. C-29
(Citoyenneté, Loi sur la)

Minister of Citizenship and Immigration (SI/94-86)

s. 2, R.S., c. 28 (4th Supp.), s. 36(2) (Sch., item 2); 1992, c. 21, s. 6; 2000, c. 12, s. 74
s. 3, 1995, c. 5, s. 25(1)(e)
s. 5, R.S., c. 44 (3rd Supp.), s. 1; 1992, c. 21, s. 7; 2000, c. 12, s. 75
s. 9, 1992, c. 21, s. 8
s. 14, 1995, c. 15, s. 23
s. 19, 1992, c. 1, s. 144 (Sch. VII, item 22)(F); 1997, c. 22, s. 1
s. 19.1, added, 1997, c. 22, s. 2
s. 19.2, added, 1997, c. 22, s. 2
s. 19.3, added, 1997, c. 22, s. 2
s. 20, 1997, c. 22, s. 3
s. 22, R.S., c. 30 (3rd Supp.), s. 11; 1992, c. 47, s. 67, c. 49, s. 124; 1999, c. 31, s. 42; 2000, c. 24, s. 33
s. 35, R.S., c. 28 (1st Supp.), s. 49
s. 37, 1993, c. 28, s. 78 (Sch. III, item 18)
Conditional amendments, 2000, c. 12, ss. 76, 77
General, 1995, c. 5, s. 25(2)
Transitional, 1997, c. 22, s. 10
CIF, R.S., c. 28 (1st Supp.), s. 49 proclaimed in force 30.06.85 *see* SI/85-128
CIF, R.S., c. 30 (3rd Supp.), s. 11 proclaimed in force 30.10.87 *see* SI/87-251
CIF, R.S., c. 44 (3rd Supp.), s. 1 proclaimed in force 15.02.88 *see* SI/88-32
CIF, R.S., c. 28 (4th Supp.), s. 36(2) proclaimed in force 01.01.89 *see* SI/88-231
CIF, 1992, c. 1, s. 144 (Sch. VII, item 22)(F) in force on assent 28.02.92
CIF, 1992, c. 21, ss. 6 to 8 in force 30.06.92 *see* SI/92-126
CIF, 1992, c. 47, s. 67 in force 01.08.96 *see* SI/96-56
CIF, 1992, c. 49, s. 124 in force 01.02.93 *see* SI/93-16
CIF, 1993, c. 28, s. 78 (Sch. III, item 18) in force 01.04.99 *see* s. 79
CIF, 1995, c. 5, s. 25 in force 13.05.95 *see* SI/95-65

Source: Department of Justice Canada. Reproduced with the permission of the Minister of Public Works and Government Services Canada, 2001.

Illustration 7.3: This is a copy of the cover pages and excerpts from the federal tables of statutes.

A citation is simply an abbreviated reference used to help locate statutes. If the abbreviation starts with an "R" then you know that the statute you are looking for is part of a revised (consolidated) set of statutes. If it starts with an "S" then you know the statute was published after the revised set and can be found in the sessional or annual sets. The remaining few first letters represent the jurisdiction:

Examples	
Abbreviation	**Full Title**
R.S.C.	*Revised Statutes of Canada*
S.C.	*Statutes of Canada*
R.S.B.C.	*Revised Statutes of British Columbia*
S.B.C.	*Statutes of British Columbia*

How to Write a Citation for a Statute

A citation provides information about where to locate a source. Therefore, the fundamental rule in all citation is to include enough information in the citation to enable a reader to locate the material referred to. There is a reason why citations take the form they do, and researchers should be aware of the logic underlying citation, as well as the precise rules of citation itself.

There are three parts to the citation of a statute:

1. Title
2. Location
3. Section Number

Example:

> *Powers of Attorney Act*, R.S.O. 1990, c. P.20, as am. by S.O. 1992, c. 32, s. 24; 1993, c. 27, Sched.

Title

The title of the statute is obviously a critical part of a statute citation. Several statutes have very similar titles, so precision is important. It is acceptable to refer to a short title if there is one. This short title is often stated in the first section of a statute.

The title must be capitalized and any quotations or references to years in the title must appear in the citation exactly as they do in the title. For example, many statutes have a date in the title that distinguishes them from other statutes with the same name. The title must be italicized or underlined.

Location

Statutes are labelled by the year they were brought into effect (or revised) and a specific chapter number. Each statute is published in the gazettes and then in an annual or sessional volume. The following abbreviations describe the volumes:

- Statutes = S. (*i.e.*, annual or sessional volumes)
- Revised Statutes = R.S. (*i.e.*, consolidated volumes)
- R.S.B.C. = *Revised Statutes of British Columbia*
- R.S.C. = *Revised Statutes of Canada*
- c. = chapter

Section Number

If you refer to a specific section in a statute, you must refer to that section in the citation. The following abbreviations are used to describe section numbers:

- s. = one section
- ss. = several sections
- subs. = one subsection
- subss. = several subsections

Amendments

If the statute has been amended, you must specify which statute amended it. Note that the title of the amending statute is omitted in the citation. The following abbreviations are used to describe amendments:

- as amended = am. by.; as am.; *or* as am. by
- repealed = rep. by; as rep.; *or* as rep. by

Punctuation

Some basic rules of punctuation in statute citation are as follows:

- Use periods after abbreviations.
- Use commas after the title and the year.
- Use commas before notations (*i.e.*, as am.).

How to Search Electronically

As mentioned in Chapter 4, there are some fundamental ways to search through electronic data. The three most important things to understand are:

- The content of the source you are looking at;
- The automated search mechanism used to search through the data; and
- How to formulate a proper word search.

When using a CD-ROM, try to scan the contents first and then construct a search through a template. When using an online service, use the templates provided and read the instructions carefully. When using the Internet it is recommend that you use either the search engines you are familiar with or use your own browser search engine.

To locate a statute electronically by name or citation you need only do a word search for a unique word in the title of the statute. Although it can be difficult to search by the date or chapter number (since you must understand how the number should be placed), it is worthwhile trying if there are no unique words in your statute.

For example, if you search a database containing all federal statutes and regulations, you will have to wade through hundreds of regulations and several statutes before locating your statute. If you are new to research you will not be able to tell which statute or regulation is relevant to your situation. For example a search of the words "labour code" lists several federal statutes and many regulations with the words "labour" and "code" in them.

Be careful when using electronic sources, because each database contains different information. For example, the following are Quicklaw databases (db):

Examples	
Database	**Content**
db RSCT	Statutes of Canada updated by Quicklaw
db RSC	Canada statutes (Department of Justice)
db SCNF	Statutes of Canada not in force
db CB	Canada bills

Statutes are not always updated regularly and you will need to search from that date on to see what changes, if any, have been made.

Step 3: Is the Statute in Force?

While you are looking at the statute, it is a good idea to determine whether the statute has a delayed effective date. This can be done by looking for a commencement clause, which is usually located at the end of the statute.

You can determine whether a statute is in force by finding out whether it has a delayed effective date. If so, it will have a commencement clause in the original version of the statute. This clause is usually at the end of the statute. Note that subsequent printings of a statute will not contain a commencement clause if the statute is in effect because by then it is irrelevant. In simple terms, this means that if you statute has no effective clause it is likely in effect. However, you may wish to confirm this.

If there is a commencement clause (*i.e.*, it is brought into effect at a later time by a regulation or order in council), you must determine the effective date of the statute. To do this, refer to Chapter 8.

Step 4: Update the Statute

It is very important to determine whether and how a statute has been amended. There is always the possibility that a statute has been repealed or replaced with a new statute. There are two ways to find out how a statute has been amended: the official way and the unofficial way.

The Unofficial Way

The unofficial way to locate amendments to a statute is by using a statute citator. These books, which are discussed below, are used primarily for locating cases that consider statutes, but they also list all statutes, their amendments, and any cases that have considered them. They are a wonderful staring point but all of the information must be confirmed because they are not considered official and may have errors.

The Official Way

To find out if a statute has been amended, go back to the table of statutes (if there is one) to see whether the relevant section has been amended. The tables list each statute and sections of the statute that has been amended, in numerical order. They also provide a citation for the amending statute and when the amendment came into effect.

Illustration 7.4
Table of Public Statutes

Citizenship Act — R.S., 1985, c. C-29
(Citoyenneté, Loi sur la)

Minister of Citizenship and Immigration (SI/94-86)

s. 2, R.S., c. 28 (4th Supp.), s. 36(2) (Sch., item 2); 1992,
   c. 21, s. 6; 2000, c. 12, s. 74
s. 3, 1995, c. 5, s. 25(1)(e)

Illustration 7.4 — cont'd

---

s. 5, R.S., c. 44 (3rd Supp.), s. 1; 1992, c. 21, s. 7; 2000, c. 12, s. 75

s. 9, 1992, c. 21, s. 8

s. 14, 1995, c. 15, s. 23

s. 19, 1992, c. 1, s. 144 (Sch. VII, item 22)(F); 1997, c. 22, s. 1

s. 19.1, added, 1997, c. 22, s. 2

s. 19.2, added, 1997, c. 22, s. 2

s. 19.3, added, 1997, c. 22, s. 2

s. 20. 1997. c. 22. s. 3

CIF, R.S., c. 28 (1st Supp.), s. 49 proclaimed in force 30.06.85 *see* SI/85-128

CIF, R.S., c. 30 (3rd Supp.), s. 11 proclaimed in force 30.10.87 *see* SI/87-251

CIF, R.S., c. 44 (3rd Supp.), s. 1 proclaimed in force 15.02.88 *see* SI/88-32

CIF, R.S., c. 28 (4th Supp.), s. 36(2) proclaimed in force 01.01.89 *see* SI/88-231

CIF, 1992, c. 1, s. 144 (Sch. VII, item 22)(F) in force on assent 28.02.92

CIF, 1992, c. 21, ss. 6 to 8 in force 30.06.92 *see* SI/92-126

CIF, 1992. c. 47. s. 67 in force 01.08.96 *see* SI/96-56

Source: Department of Justice Canada. Reproduced with the permission of the Minister of Public Works and Government Services Canada, 2001.

Illustration 7.4: This is an excerpt from the federal *Tables of Statutes*, highlighting the federal *Citizenship Act*. Appendix A contains instructions on how to read tables of statutes.

In the illustration, s. 2 of the *Citizenship Act* was amended in the *Revised Statutes of Canada, 1985*, Chapter 28 (4th supplement) by s. 36(2) (Schedule, Item 2), and again in 1992 in the *Statutes of Canada* Chapter 21 by s. 6. If you look at the CIF (coming into force) references, you can see that these two amendments came into effect on 01.01.89 and 30.06.92, respectively.

Each of the provincial legislatures keeps track of bills and statutes and records any ammendments. These records are maintained by the government office that oversees the proceeding of the legislature. They are available to the public but are usually kept at law library desks because they must be updated continually. Indeed, expert researchers will simply call the legislative library to find out the most recent revisions to particular statutes, since they can be changed daily.

For the most recent amendments to statutes (*i.e.*, those published after the date of publication of the most recent table of statutes), you can look in the various publications from the various legislatures.

Publications that assist in updating federal statutes include the *Canada Legislative Index*, which contains the following:

- *Title Index*: To locate a statute and any amending legislation;
- *House of Commons Bills and Senate Bills*: To determine the status of any amending legislation;
- *Proclamations*: To determine if amending legislation requires pro-clamation.

Typically the most current versions of statutes are either on government websites or online services. Information found on these sites is updated regularly. CD-ROMs tend to get out of date. Look very closely for the date that the information was updated. If it is a few days old, it is best to update even further by speaking to law librarian or calling the legislative library.

Locate the Amending Statute

Armed with the citation of the amending statute, a researcher can locate the amending statute. The amending statute may amend more than one statute. If so, you must locate the specific sections that amend your particular statute. For example, if you look up the first amendment to s. 2 of the *Citizenship Act* (in c. 28 (4th supplement) of the *Revised Statutes of Canada, 1985*), you will see that the title of the statute is *An Act to Amend the Immigration Act and to amend other Acts in consequence thereof*. Section 36 of that act amends the *Citizenship Act*.

You can ensure that the amendment is effective by looking up the regulation that brought the amendment into effect. For example, you can see from the *Table of Public Statutes* above that the first amendment to s. 2 of the *Citizenship Act* came into effect on 01.01.89 by regulation (statutory instrument) SI/88-231. Locating regulations and statutory instruments is discussed in Chapter 6.

Armed with the citation of the amending statute, you can go directly to the statute by looking for it by year of volume and chapter number. The amending statute may amend more than one statute. If so, locate the specific sections that amend your particular statute.

Step 5: Note-Up the Statute

The way in which a court interprets a statute is as important to statute research as locating the statute itself. Cases tell a researcher how a statute has been interpreted by the courts and whether it is consistent with the constitution and other statutes. Therefore, locating cases that have considered statutes is a vital part of statute research. This step is called noting-up a statute.

What Are Statute Citators?

Statute citators are the most useful tools for noting-up statutes. They are specific research aids designed specifically to locate cases that have considered statutes and to find amendments to statutes. Statute citators are essentially annotated statutes. They are books that list statutes, amendments to the statutes, and summaries or lists of cases that have considered the statutes.

Citators are particularly useful because they are usually in loose-leaf or on CD-ROM and are continually updated. However, they are secondary sources and should not be relied on as a final version of the law. Information in the citators should be confirmed in the official statute and specific cases.

When you go in the library you will typically find the following statute citators:

All Canada: *Canadian Statute Citations* (*Canadian Abridgment*, Carswell), also on CD-ROM and through *e*Carswell. This citator consists of a set of volumes listing federal and provincial statutes by title as well as those cases that have considered each statute. Statutes are listed alphabetically by jurisdiction.

Federal Statutes: *Canada Statute Service* (Canada Law Book), also on CD-ROM.

Provincial Statutes: There are also numerous provincial citators, since each province has its own set of statutes. The main legal publishers each have their own version. The following are examples of a few British Columbia statute citators:

- *British Columbia Statute Services* (Canada Law Book), also on CD-ROM
- *Statutes of British Columbia Judicially Considered* (Carswell), also on CD-ROM and through *e*Carswell
- *British Columbia Decisions: Statute Citator* (Western Legal Publications)

Because there are often several statute citators, an easy way to distinguish them is by publisher.

A few of the online service providers have citators that are contained in distinct databases. These are compiled by researchers in the same way that the paper version are. Some providers do not keep citators. In these situations you can search through case databases for words that are in your statute.

Illustration 7.5
Canada Statute Citator

CANADA
STATUTE
CITATOR

R.S.C. 1985

VOLUME 2

Canada Post Corporation Act to Energy Supplies Emergency Act

Legal Editor
Rebecca Y. Tobe, B.A., LL.B.

Production Editor
Lilly Della Posta, B.Sc.

CANADA LAW BOOK INC.
240 EDWARD STREET, AURORA, ONTARIO, L4G 3S9
JUNE 2000

Illustration 7.5 — cont'd

CITIZENSHIP ACT

R.S.C. 1985 Chap. C-29

Amended R.S.C. 1985, c. 28 (1st Supp.), s. 49
Amended R.S.C. 1985, c. 30 (3rd Supp.), s. 11
Amended R.S.C. 1985, c. 44 (3rd Supp.)
Amended R.S.C. 1985, c. 28 (4th Supp.), s. 36
Amended 1992, c. 21, ss. 6 to 8; brought into force June 30, 1992 by SI/92-126. *Can. Gaz., Part II,* July 15, 1992
Amended 1992, c. 47, s. 67; to come into force by order of the Governor in Council
Amended 1992, c. 49, s. 124; brought into force February 1, 1993
Amended 1993, c. 28, Sch. III, s. 18; in force April 1, 1999
Amended 1995, c. 5, s. 25(1)(e); brought into force May 13, 1995 by SI/95-65. *Can. Gaz., Part II,* May 31, 1995
Amended 1995, c. 15, s. 23; brought into force July 10, 1995 by SI/95-76. *Can. Gaz. Part II,* July 12, 1995
Amended 1997, c. 22, ss. 1 to 3; brought into force May 20, 1997 by SI/97-64. *Can. Gaz., Part II,* June 11, 1997
Amended 1999, c. 31, s. 42; in force June 17, 1999
Administered by the Department of Citizenship and Immigration

Generally

NOTE: SI/94-86 (P.C. 1994-1122, June 30, 1994), *Can. Gaz., Part II,* July 27, 1994, designates the Minister of Citizenship and Immigration as Minister of this Act.

NOTE: 1997, c. 22, s. 10 provides as follows:

10. If, before section 1 of this Act comes into force, a legal proceeding has been commenced with respect to an investigation under subsection 19(4) of the *Citizenship Act,* a final decision in that proceeding that the Review Committee must cease its investigation is deemed to be a decision of the Review Committee under subsection 19(4.1) of that Act, as enacted by subsection 1(2) of this Act.

Section 2

Subsec. (1) definition "disability" repealed 1992, c. 21, s. 6.

Subsec. (2)(c)(i) repealed and the following substituted R.S.C. 1985, c. 28 (4th Supp.), s. 36:

(i) unless all rights of review by or appeal to the Immigration Appeal Division of the Immigration and Refugee Board, the Federal Court of Appeal and the Supreme Court of Canada have been exhausted with respect to the order and the final result of those reviews or appeals is that the order has no force or effect, or

Section 3

Subsec. (2)(c) amended 1995, c. 5, s. 25(1)(e) by replacing the expression "Secretary of State for External Affairs" with the expression "Minister of Foreign Affairs".

Section 5

Subsec. (1.1) new R.S.C. 1985, c. 44 (3rd Supp.), s. 1:

(1.1) Any day during which an applicant for citizenship resided with the applicant's spouse who at the time was a Canadian citizen and was employed outside of Canada in or with the Canadian armed forces or the public service of Canada or of

Illustration 7.5: This is an excerpt from a statute citator. Note that it does not provide the "official" text of the statute.

Illustration 7.6
Canadian Abridgment

CANADIAN STATUTE CITATIONS

RÉFÉRENCES LÉGISLATIVES CANADIENNES

OCTOBER 1999 TO DECEMBER 1999

OCTOBRE 1999 À DÉCEMBRE 1999

The treatment of international treaties, federal, provincial and foreign statutes, and rules of practice.

Illustration 7.6 cont'd

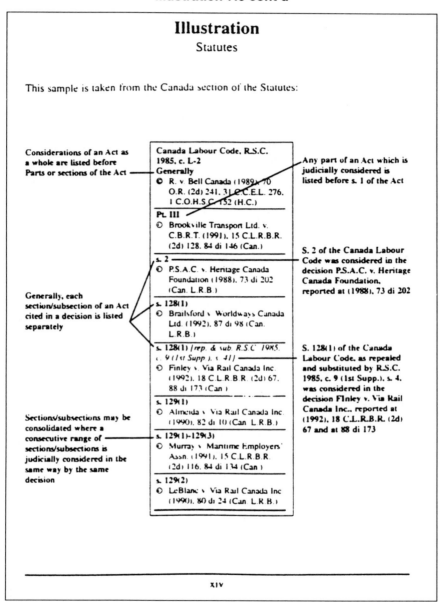

Illustration

Statutes

This sample is taken from the Canada section of the Statutes:

Considerations of an Act as a whole are listed before Parts or sections of the Act

Canada Labour Code, R.S.C. 1985, c. L-2
Generally
 ☉ R. v Bell Canada (1989), 70 O.R. (2d) 241. 31 C.C.E.L. 276. 1 C.O.H.S.C. 152 (H.C.)

Any part of an Act which is judicially considered is listed before s. 1 of the Act

Pt. III
 ☉ Brookville Transport Ltd. v. C.B.R.T. (1991), 15 C.L.R.B.R. (2d) 128. 84 di 146 (Can.)

s. 2
 ☉ P.S.A.C. v. Heritage Canada Foundation (1988), 73 di 202 (Can. L.R.B.)

S. 2 of the Canada Labour Code was considered in the decision P.S.A.C. v. Heritage Canada Foundation, reported at (1988), 73 di 202

Generally, each section/subsection of an Act cited in a decision is listed separately

s. 128(1)
 ☉ Brailsford v Worldways Canada Ltd. (1992), 87 di 98 (Can. L.R.B.)

s. 128(1) *[rep. & sub. R.S.C. 1985, c. 9 (1st Supp.), s. 4]*
 ☉ Finley v. Via Rail Canada Inc. (1992), 18 C.L.R.B.R. (2d) 67. 88 di 173 (Can.)

S. 128(1) of the Canada Labour Code, as repealed and substituted by R.S.C. 1985, c. 9 (1st Supp.), s. 4, was considered in the decision Finley v. Via Rail Canada Inc., reported at (1992), 18 C.L.R.B.R. (2d) 67 and at 88 di 173

s. 129(1)
 ☉ Almeida v Via Rail Canada Inc. (1990), 82 di 10 (Can. L.R.B.)

Sections/subsections may be consolidated where a consecutive range of sections/subsections is judicially considered in the same way by the same decision

s. 129(1)-129(3)
 ☉ Murray v Maritime Employers' Assn. (1991), 15 C.L.R.B.R. (2d) 116. 84 di 134 (Can.)

s. 129(2)
 ☉ LeBlanc v Via Rail Canada Inc. (1990), 80 di 24 (Can. L.R.B.)

XIV

Illustration 7.6: This is an excerpt from the *Canadian Abridgment*.

Self Test

The answers to these questions are found at the back of the book in the "Answers to Self Tests" section.

1. Where on the Internet could you locate a statute?
2. How are stautes arranged in a library?
3. What is a table of statutes?
4. Name a Canadian company that provides access to statutes on their database.
5. Where can you find the most recent amendments to a statute?
6. What is a statute citator?

Sample Exercises — Finding and Updating Statutes

Objectives

At the end of this exercise you should to be able to:

- Locate a statute and its amendments
- Determine the effective date of a statute
- Locate cases that have considered a statute
- Properly cite a statute

Instructions

- Do background reading on how to locate, update, and cite statutes.
- Keep a record of all of the steps and time taken to complete the exercise.

Statutes

Provincial Statutes

Read the following fact pattern and answer the following questions. Assume the research situation occurred in your province.

Fact Pattern

Mr. Chapps

Mr. Chapps has recently acquired the property of his dreams. After years of saving he finally was able to purchase an old farmhouse on a piece of property overlooking a lake. He moved into the farmhouse last month and has just begun to renovate.

Two days ago, he received a letter from the Minister of Municipal Affairs. The letter stated, "This letter will serve as notice of expropriation." It went on to explain that Mr. Chapp's property was going to be expropriated so that the city could build a sewage treatment plant on it. Mr. Chapp is very upset and wants to know what he can do to fight the expropriation.

---

1. Before entering the library, brainstorm for possible legal subject areas. List about five words relating to the above research situation that you might search for in the library.

   Words:

2. Using either a provincial subject index or a table of statutes find a statute relevant to your research situation. Give the proper citation to the statute.

   Citation:

3. Go to that statute and see if it has a commencement clause that delays its effective date. If so, record the section number.

   Section:

Amendments

4. Use the most recent table of statutes or table of legislative changes to determine whether the statute was amended. Locate one amendment and give the full citation of the amending statute. Locate that statute and record the name. If the statute amends more than one statute, include the specific section number that amends your statute.

   Citation:

Statutes Judicially Considered

5. Using the *Canadian Abridgment, Canadian Statute Citations*, locate your statute and record the name of a case that has considered the statute. Record the section number of the statute that has been considered by the case. If the statute has been judicially considered, state this.

    a.   Case name
    b.   Section number:
    c.   Judicial consideration:

Federal Statutes

1.   Give the proper citation for the following federal statute: S.C. 1990, c. 22.

    Citation:

Amendments

2.   Using the most recent federal *Table of Public Statutes*, determine whether the statute was amended. Note the amendment to s. 46 and record the citation. Locate the amending statute and give the full citation, including the name of the statute.

    Citation:

Statutes Judicially Considered

3.   Locate the *Canada Statute Citator* (Canada Law Book) and the *Canadian Abridgment, Canadian Statute Citations* (Carswell). Find your statute in both sources and record the name of a case that has considered the statute. Record the section number of the statute that has been considered by the case. If the statute has not been judicially considered, state this.

    a.   Case name:
    b.   Section number:
    c.   Name of citator:

Answers to Exercises

Note: Amendments ocurring after the publication of this text will not be shown in these answers.

Provincial Statutes

(British Columbia was used to answer this question.)

1.   Municipal affairs; property; expropriation; sewage treatment.
2.   *Expropriation Act*, R.S.B.C. 1996, c. 125.
3.   There is no commencement clause.

Amendments

4. The Table of Legislative Changes (changes in force) says that amendments were made to ss. 1 and 2., the citation to s. 1 is 1997-45-50. If you look up this statute in volume 1997, c. 45, s. 50 you find the *Builders Lien Act, 1997*, S.B.C. c. 45. Section 50 of that act amends the *Expropriation Act*.

Statutes Judicially Considered

5. a. *Reti v. Sickamous (District)* (1999), 66 L.C.R. c.35, 118 B.C.A.C. 297, 192 W.A.C. 297 (B.C.C.A.).

   b. Generally

Federal Statutes

1. *Plant Protection Act, 1990*, S.C. 1990, c. 22.

Amendments

2. *Miscellaneous Statute Law Amendment Act, 1993*, S.C. 1993, c. 34, s. 102. The *Table of Public Statutes* states: S.C. 1993, c. 34, s. 102, CIF 1993, c. 34, ss. 102 and 103 in force on assent 23-06-93. (Confirm this by going to statute.)

Statutes Judicially Considered

3. a. *Edwards v. Canada (Min. of Agriculture)* (1992), 53 F.T.R. 262 (Fed. T.D.).

   b. Generally

   c. *Canadian Abridgment, Canadian Statute Citations* (Jan. 1994 to Sept. 1999).

No case mentioned in the citator.

Appendix A: How to Read Tables of Statutes

The next few pages describe how to read the *Canada Table of Public Statutes* and the *British Columbia Table of Statutes*.

Reading the Canada Table of Public Statutes

The following is an example of how to read the federal *Table of Public Statutes*. If you look up the *Citizenship Act* in the *Table of Public Statutes*, you will find the following information:

Citizenship Act — R.S., 1985, c. C-29
(Citoyenneté, Loi sur la)

Minister of Citizenship and Immigration (SI/94-86)

s. 2, R.S., c. 28 (4th Supp.), s. 36(2) (Sch., item 2); 1992, c. 21, s. 6; 2000, c. 12, s. 74
s. 3, 1995, c. 5, s. 25(1)(e)
s. 5, R.S., c. 44 (3rd Supp.), s. 1; 1992, c. 21, s. 7; 2000, c. 12, s. 75
s. 9, 1992, c. 21, s. 8
s. 14, 1995, c. 15, s. 23
s. 19, 1992, c. 1, s. 144 (Sch. VII, item 22)(F); 1997, c. 22, s. 1
s. 19.1, added, 1997, c. 22, s. 2
s. 19.2, added, 1997, c. 22, s. 2
s. 19.3, added, 1997, c. 22, s. 2
s. 20, 1997, c. 22, s. 3
s. 22, R.S., c. 30 (3rd Supp.), s. 11; 1992, c. 47, s. 67, c. 49, s. 124; 1999, c. 31, s. 42; 2000, c. 24, s. 33
s. 35, R.S., c. 28 (1st Supp.), s. 49
s. 37, 1993, c. 28, s. 78 (Sch. III, item 18)
Conditional amendments, 2000, c. 12, ss. 76, 77
General, 1995, c. 5, s. 25(2)
Transitional, 1997, c. 22, s. 10
CIF, R.S., c. 28 (1st Supp.), s. 49 proclaimed in force 30.06.85 *see* SI/85-128
CIF, R.S., c. 30 (3rd Supp.), s. 11 proclaimed in force 30.10.87 *see* SI/87-251
CIF, R.S., c. 44 (3rd Supp.), s. 1 proclaimed in force 15.02.88 *see* SI/88-32
CIF, R.S., c. 28 (4th Supp.), s. 36(2) proclaimed in force 01.01.89 *see* SI/88-231

Published by the Department of Justice Canada. Reproduced with the permission of the Minister of Public Works and Government Services Canada, 2001.

This information reads as follows:

Top Line — The *Citizenship Act* (Canada) can be found in the *Revised Statutes of Canada, 1985* in c. C-29.

Line 1 — Section 2 was amended in the *Revised Statutes of Canada, 1985* in c. 28 (4th supp.) by s. 36(2) of the schedule, item 2. (If you look up c. 28, you will see that the title of the statute is *An Act to amend the Immigration Act and to amend other Acts in consequence thereof*) and s. 36(2), schedule, item 2 specifically amends the *Citizenship Act*). Section 2 was amended again in the Statutes of Canada, 1992 in c. 21 by s. 6, and in 2000, in c. 12, by s. 74.

Line 11 — Section 2 came into force (CIF) in c. 28 of the *Revised Statutes of Canada, 1985* (4th Supplement) on January 1, 1989 (see SI/88-231 for confirmation). Note that each revision has corresponding CIF information.

The proper citation for this statute is:

Citizenship Act, R.S.C. 1985, c. C-29.

Note: For provincial statutes, "O.C." means the statute came into effect by an order-in-council and "Proc." means the statute came into effect by a proclamation. Statutes brought into effect by either order-in-council or proclamation require that a regulation be introduced.

Appendix B: Checklist: How to Find and Update Statutes

Step 1: Locate a statute by name or citation.

In the Library

☐ If you know the title of the statute, look in the most recent consolidated federal or relevant provincial tables of statutes. These are typically called tables of public statutes. Statutes are listed alphabetically.

☐ Find your statute title and note the location of the statute by the year and chapter number. If the table lists amendments, take note since you will need this information at Step 5 below.

☐ Armed with the citation of the statute, you can go directly to the statute by looking for it by year, volume and chapter number.

☐ Read the statute and find the sections relevant to your problem.

Electronically

☐ CD-ROM: Some statute collections are on CD-ROM and are available for use in law libraries. You can search the table of contents to locate the title of your statute or do a word search in the templates provided.

☐ Online Service Providers: Quicklaw and LEXIS both have federal and provincial statute databases. Search the relevant statute, gazettes, and bills databases by using the templates.

☐ Public Access Websites: Many governments have statutes on their websites. A list of websites is appended to this chapter. View the alphabetical listing to locate your statute. Update by looking in gazettes and bills databases and by doing library research; see Step 5.

Step 2: Search for statutes by subject.

❏ If you do not know the title of the statute, read secondary sources such as the *Canadian Encyclopedic Digest* or textbooks first, before going to the statutes.

Secondary Materials in the Library

❏ Locate the *Canadian Encyclopedic Digest*, textbooks, and periodicals. Read these sources generally and record any statutes mentioned.

❏ Locate any federal or provincial statute subject indexes. Scan the topics for relevant statutes.

Electronic Secondary Materials

❏ CD-ROM: Some secondary materials such as the *Canadian Encyclopedic Digest*, textbooks, and periodicals are available on CD-ROM. Read these sources generally and record any statutes mentioned.

❏ Online Service Providers: Quicklaw and LEXIS have several databases of secondary materials, including journals and some textbooks. Search for unique words using the templates provided, and note statutes that are mentioned.

❏ Public Access Websites: Some journals are available on the Internet. Locate, read, and take note of any statutes mentioned.

Electronic statutes: Although full-text statutes can be found on CD-ROM and online, it is best not to search by subject in electronic statutes until you have completely refined your word search. Ideally, you will know the exact statute you are looking for. Otherwise, you will spend significant time searching several databases that contain thousands of pieces of information.

Step 3: Find the statute.

❏ Armed with the citation of the statute, you can go directly to the print version of the statute by looking for it by year, volume, and chapter number.

❏ You can also retrieve your statute from a full-text statute database, on CD-ROM, on the Internet, or online through a service provider.

❑ Read the statute and find the sections relevant to your problem.

Step 4: Is the statute in force? Does it have a delayed effective date?

❑ You can determine whether a statute is in force by finding out whether it has a delayed effective date. If so, it will have a commencement clause in the original version of the statute. This clause is usually at the end of the statute. Note that subsequent printings of the statute will not contain a commencement clause if the statute is in effect.

❑ If there is a commencement clause and it is brought into effect at a later time by a regulation, you must determine the effective date of the statute. To do this, refer to Chapter 8.

Step 5: Update the statute. Has the statute been amended?

In the Library

❑ To determine if a statute has been amended, go back to the tables of statutes (Step 1) and look in the alphabetical list for your statute.

❑ If there is no table of statutes, look in the table of legislative changes.

❑ The sections of each statute that have been amended are listed numerically.

❑ The tables provide information on when the amendment came into effect and how (*e.g.*, by regulation).

❑ Note the date of the table and look in the gazettes from that date forward for recent amendments.

❑ To further update the statute and its amendments, look in the most recent publications from the various legislatures, such as legislative indexes or votes and proceedings.

❑ Armed with the citation of the amending statute, you can go directly to that statute by looking for it by year, volume, and chapter number.

❏ The amending statute may amend more than one statute. If so, locate the specific sections that amend your particular statute.

❏ You can ensure the amendment is effective by looking up the regulation under which the amendment came into effect. Locating regulations is discussed in Chapter 8.

❏ Note that statutes can also be updated by referring to commercial loose-leaf statute citators which include not only amendments to statutes but also judicial considerations. If you use these citators, confirm the information in the official version.

Electronically

❏ Select and locate the electronic source you wish to use: CD-ROM or an online source.

❏ Try to find a statute index or table of public statutes. If there is one, start there.

❏ Scan the table for your statute and note any amendments.

❏ Go to the full-text statute database. Note whether the information is consolidated. This means that all of the revisions have been inserted into the text of the statute. If so, you will only need to locate revisions since that consolidation.

❏ If the electronic version is not consolidated then you must look in other databases that contain the revisions.

❏ Update from the statute database by looking in other databases that consist of sessional or annual sets, gazettes, and bills. You must then update in the library from that point on (see above).

Step 6: Note up the statute. Has it been considered in any cases?

In the Library

❏ The best place to look for cases that have considered statutes is in statute citators. Some examples of citators are: *Canada Statute Citator* (Canada Law Book) and *Canadian Statute Citator* (Carswell).

Electronically

❏ CD-ROM: there are a few citators on CD-ROM. They are published by commercial publishers and are available in many law libraries. Examples include: the *Canada Statute Service* and the *Ontario Statute Service*.

❏ Online Service Providers: Not all online providers have statute citators. If they do, you can use them in two ways: by going into the citator database and searching, or by hyperlinking from the statute database. If there is no statute citator, search case databases for references to your statute.

❏ Public Access Websites: See Appendix C.

Appendix C: Electronic Statutes on Government Websites

Jurisdiction	Government Site
Federal	Statutes: http://canada.justice.gc.ca/stable/EN/Laws/ Chap/ index.html
	Gazettes: http://canada.gc.ca/gazette
	Bills: http://www.parl.gc.ca
British Columbia	www.qp.gov.bc.ca/stat_reg
	www.legis.gov.bc.ca
Alberta	www.gov.ab.ca/qp
Saskatchewan	www.lawsociety.sk.ca
	www.saskjustice.gov.sk.ca
Manitoba	www.gov.mb.ca
Ontario	www.attorneygeneral.jus.gov.on.ca
Quebec	http://doc.gouv.qc.ca
Newfoundland/ Labrador	www.gov.nf.ca/hoa/sr
Prince Edward Island	www.gov.nb.ca/justice
Nova Scotia	www.gov.ns.ca/legi
Yukon	http://legis.acjnet.org (Yukon)
Northwest Territories	http://legis.acjnet.org (Northwest Territories)
Nunavut	http://legis.acjnet.org (Nunavut)

How to Find and Update Regulations

8

As explained in Chapter 4, regulations, rules, and municipal bylaws are delegated legislation. They are laws created by a delegated authority and are sometimes called subordinate legislation.

This chapter describes a step-by-step technique for finding regulations. It also explains how regulations are published and describes how to determine the effective date of a statute through use of regulations.

Learning Objectives

At the end of this chapter you will be able to:

- Locate a regulation
- Provide a proper citation for a regulation
- Describe what a municipal bylaw is
- Determine whether a statute is in effect by looking in the regulations

This chapter is divided into the following three parts with distinct steps in each part:

1. How regulations are made and published
2. How to locate a regulation:
   Step 1: Find the title of the regulation
   Step 2: Find the regulation
   Step 3: Update the regulation
3. How to ensure a statute is effective:
   Step 1: Did statute receive royal assent?
   Step 2: Is there a delayed effective date?
   Step 3: Locate and update the regulation

How Regulations Are Made and Published

Legislatures are continually making subordinate legislation or regulations. These regulations provide the "flesh on the bones" of statutes.

There are three types of subordinate legislation: regulations, rules, and proclamations.

Unlike statutes, in order for regulations to become law they need only be "passed" by the authority described in the statute, "filed or deposited," and published.

Passed: Regulations are passed by the executive arm of governments. For example, they are usually passed by the lieutenant governor in council (provincial cabinet) or the governor in council (federal cabinet) without the need for approval in the House of Commons.

Filed: Federal regulations are effective when filed with the clerk of the Privy Council. Provincial regulations are effective on the date deposited with a government office such as the registrar of regulations. These effective dates are specified in the regulation.

Published: Because regulations do not go through the House of Commons or the Senate, and do not go through readings like bills, they are only published once — in the official gazettes (provincial or federal).

Rules, regulations, and proclamations are published in sets called regulations. They can be found in law libraries right beside the statutes for each particular jurisdiction. When first published, regulations appear in the federal or provincial softbound gazettes. Federal regulations are published in the *Canada Gazette,* Part II. After a number of gazettes have accumulated, they are usually hardbound.

Periodically, governments consolidate their regulations. The federal government and some provinces have consolidated their regulations into "revised" sets, much like the revised versions of statutes. An example of a consolidation is the 1978 federal government consolidation of all federal regulations: the *Consolidated Regulations of Canada, 1978* (C.R.C. 1978). The C.R.C. 1978 incorporates all regulations and amendments to the regulations up to the date of publication. Examples of provincial consolidations include the 1990 Ontario consolidation (R.R.O. 1990).

Thus, on the library shelves there are usually four parts to each set of regulations:

- A consolidated set of regulations. The federal set is called the *Consolidated Regulations of Canada, 1978* (18 volumes).
- Annual or sessional regulations. The federal set consists of the Gazette, Part II, hardbound for each year.
- Current regulations. The federal version is the Gazette, Part II, which includes the most recent regulations.
- An index. The federal Gazette, Part II includes the most recent *Consolidated Index of Statutory Instruments.*

Some provinces have loose-leaf sets of consolidated regulations. These are very useful because amendments to the regulations are inserted directly into the set and you avoid looking in several volumes for amendments to the regulations. Some of the more popular regulations are published by commercial publishers and annotated. These annotated sets usually include the relevant statute and revisions to both, and refer to cases that considered the statute or the regulations. The rules of the courts are also published as separate publications since they are referred to regularly by litigators.

Electronic Publications

There are three types of electronic publications of regulations: CD-ROM, online service providers, and public access Internet sites. Many governments have placed their regulations on CD-ROM and some commercial publishers publish the more popular regulations on CD-ROM. Quicklaw and LEXIS have regulations and rules databases. Some are more comprehensive and up to date than others, but this changes daily so it is important to look at what each provider has available. Most provincial governments maintain websites that contain legislation, including regulations. These websites are upgraded frequently so it is best to look here first. A list of government websites is appended to Chapter 7. The two federal sites for regulations are:

- Cumulative consolidation: http://www.canada.justice.gc.ca/loireg/index_en.html
- Consolidated Index: http://www.canada.justice.gc.ca/

How to Read a Regulation

It is important to be able to read a regulation so you can find out quickly how it impacts the law and when it came into effect. A regulation typically consists of the following five parts:

- Regulation number (*e.g.*, SOR/93-246 (federal), or B.C. Reg 91/80 (provincial));
- Date of filing or deposit (*e.g.*, 11 May 1993, or March 21, 1980);
- Title (and sometimes the short title);
- Enabling statute (*e.g.*, *Citizenship Act*, s. 27, or the *Name Act*, s. 13); and
- How it was brought in (PC: Privy Council; OC: Order in Council).

The parts of regulations can be seen in the following excerpts from a federal and a provincial regulation:

Illustration 8.1
Citizenship Regulations

Registration

SOR/93-246 11 May, 1993

CITIZENSHIP ACT

Citizenship Regulations, 1993

P.C. 1993-943 11 May, 1993

His Excellency the Governor General in Council, on the recommendation of the Minister of Multiculturalism and Citizenship, pursuant to section 27 of the Citizenship Act, is pleased hereby to revoke the Citizenship Regulations, C.R.C., c. 400, and to make the annexed Regulations respecting Citizenship, in substitution therefor.

REGULATIONS RESPECTING CITIZENSHIP

Short Title

1. These Regulations may be cited as the *Citizenship Regulations,* 1993

Source: Canada Gazette, Part II, Justice Canada. Reproduced with the permission of the Minister of Supply and Services Canada. Not an official version.

Illustration 8.2
British Columbia Name Act Regulation

B.C. Reg. 91/80 Filed March 21, 1980

O.C. 617/80

Name Act

NAME ACT REGULATION

[effective June 1, 1980]

1. Under the *Name Act* the fee

　(a)　on filing an application for a Change of Name shall be $137 for the applicant and $27 for each person who is listed in the application as a person whose name will be changed by reason of a change of name of the applicant, which fees include the issuance of one certificate of Change of Name for the applicant and each listed person and the cost of publication of the certificates in the Gazette following approval of the application.

Illustration 8.2 — cont'd

> (b) for a search of one registration of Change of Name shall be $27 for each 3 year period or part of a 3 year period covered by the search, and
>
> (c) for each certificate of Change of Name shall be
>
> > (*i*) $27 including the fee for a search covering one 3 year period, or
> >
> > (*ii*) $60 including, where same day search service is offered and requested, the fee for a search that same day covering one 3 year period.
>
> [am. B.C. Regs. 326/84; 73/87; 121/88; 111/90; 133/91; 87/92; 79/94; 132/95; 554/95; 110/97].
>
> [Provisions of the *Name Act* relevant to the enactment of this regulation: section 13]

By permission of the Province of British Columbia — Queen's Printer. Not an official copy.

Empowering Statute

All regulations are made under the authority of a statute. Therefore you must know the statute under which the regulation is made. Since law-making power is delegated through statutes, each regulation must have an empowering statute, which authorizes an executive arm of the government to create regulations. This is evidenced by an "enabling section," which describes who has the power to make regulations and the matters about which regulations can be made. The following is an example of such an enabling section.

Illustration 8.3
Enabling Section, Citizenship Act

> Regulations 27. The Governor in Council may make regulations
>
> > (*a*) prescribing the manner in which and the place at which applications and registrations are to be made and notices are to be given under this Act and the evidence that is to be provided with respect thereto;
> >
> > (*b*) fixing fees for
> >
> > > (i) the making of any application under this Act,
> > >
> > > (ii) the issuing of any certificate under this Act,
> > >
> > > (iii) the registration of any person as a citizen under this Act,

Illustration 8.3 — cont'd

> (iv) the provision of any certified or uncertified copy of a document from the records kept in the course of the administration of this Act or prior legislation,
>
> (v) the administration of any oath, solemn affirmation or declaration filed, made, issued, delivered or administered pursuant to this Act or the regulations, or
>
> (vi) any search of the records referred to in sub-paragraph (iv);
>
> (c) providing for the remission of fees referred to in paragraph (b);
>
> (d) providing for various criteria that may be applied to determine whether a person
>
> > (i) has an adequate knowledge of one of the official languages of Canada,

Source: Citizenship Act, R.S.C. 1985, c. C-29, s. 27, Justice Canada. Reproduced with the permission of the Minister of Supply and Services Canada. Not an official version.

How to Find and Update Regulations

There are three steps to finding and updating regulations:

Step 1. Find the title of the regulation
Step 2. Find the regulation
Step 3. Update the regualtion

Step 1: Find the Title of the Regulation

In the library, regulations are filed according to their enabling statute. Therefore, researchers must determine the title of the statute before attempting to locate a regulation. Finding the title of the statute is made easy because most jurisdictions publish two tables: one that lists all *regulations* and their corresponding statutes (called a concordance) and one that lists all *statutes* and their corresponding regulations. These tables are usually consolidated and therefore include all regulations in force at the time of publication and all their amendments. They are called different things in each province but federally they are called Table I and Table II. Carswell also publishes the *Canadian Regulations Index*, which is a very useful research tool if you know the name of the relevant statute. It is in loose-leaf form and lists all regulations made pursuant to each federal statute.

Examples of Titles of Regulations Tables

Federal: *Consolidated Index of Statutory Instruments* (in *Canada Gazette*, Part II)

1. Table I (Table of Regulations, Statutory Instruments (other than Regulations) and Other Documents). All regulations and their corresponding statutes are listed.
2. Table II (Table of Regulations, Statutory Instruments (other than Regulations) and Other Documents Arranged by Statute). The regulations (SOR and SI) pertaining to each statute are listed underneath each statute.

British Columbia: *Consolidated Regulations of British Columbia*

1. Regulation/Act Concordance is found in the front of the *Consolidated Regulations of British Columbia* (CRBC Volume I). It lists all regulations and corresponding statutes.
2. Table of Contents or Index of Current B.C. Regulations. Both list all statutes of British Columbia and their corresponding regulations.

If you know only the title of the regulation, look in the first table. If you know the title of the statute, look in the second table. It is important to note the date on the table to ensure it is current. You must update from that date forward.

Example 1: Federal Regulations

If you know the name of the statute, look in Table II (Table of Regulations, Statutory Instruments (other than Regulations) and Other Documents Arranged by Statute).

Legal Problem Solving

Illustration 8.4
Table of Regulations – By Statute

II— TABLE OF REGULATIONS, STATUTORY INSTRUMENTS (OTHER THAN REGULATIONS) AND OTHER DOCUMENTS ARRANGED BY STATUTE

SEPTEMBER 30, 2000

This Table provides a reference to regulations, statutory instruments (other than regulations), and other documents that were in force at any time in the current calendar year. For instruments published in the *Canada Gazette* Part II which have ceased to be in force in any previous year, reference should be made to the Consolidated Index of Statutory Instruments of December 31st of the year in question.

The documents included in this Table are listed alphabetically under the statute pursuant to which they were made. The registration number of each document is included after the title. If amendments are made to a document, each section amended will be indicated as well as the registration number of the amending order with the amending section.

Documents not published but registered are indicated as such and can be examined at the office of the Registrar of Statutory Instruments, Blackburn Building, Room 418, 85 Sparks Street, Ottawa, Canada.

Documents that are by the Statutory Instruments Regulations, exempt from registration and publication in the *Canada Gazette* Part II are listed under the appropriate Statute along with the place where they can be inspected and obtained.

Amendments to Acts or the Coming into Force of Acts will be listed for the year in which they are made. For any further reference please consult the Table of Public Statutes and Responsible Ministers which lists all amendments to Acts.

Abbreviations:

CRC 55 — 1955 Consolidation

CRC — Consolidated Regulations of Canada, 1978

s. — section

ss. — sections

(E) — Only the English version has been modified

(F) — Only the French version has been modified

CITIZENSHIP ACT [RS 1985, c. C-29]
(CITOYENNETÉ (LOI))
Citizenship Regulations, 1993, SOR/93-246
(Citoyenneté. 1993—Règlement)
   s. 3, SOR/94-442, s. 1
   s. 11, SOR/94-442, s. 2
   s. 12, SOR/94-442, s. 2
   s. 13, repealed, SOR/94-442, s. 2
   s. 14, SOR/94-442, s. 2
   s. 15, SOR/94-442, s. 3
   s. 22, SOR/94-442, s. 4
   s. 32, added, SOR/95-122, s. 1
   s. 33, added, SOR/95-122, s. 1
   sch., SOR/95-122, s. 2; SOR/97-23, s. 1
Order Designating the Minister of Citizenship and Immigration as Minister for Purposes of the Act, SI/94-86
(Décret chargeant le ministre de la Citoyenneté et de l'Immigration de l'application de la Loi)
Foreign Ownership of Land Regulations, SOR/79-416
(Propriété de terres appartenant à des étrangers—Règlement)
   s. 12, SOR/80-156, s. 1
   s. 22, SOR/80-156, s. 2
   s. 23, SOR/79-514, s. 1
   s. 25, SOR/82-544, s. 1
   sch., SOR/79-514, s. 2; SOR/80-156, s. 3; SOR/82-544, s. 2

CIVIL INTERNATIONAL SPACE STATION AGREEMENT IMPLEMENTATION ACT [SC 1999, c. 35]
(ACCORD SUR LA STATION SPATIALE INTERNATIONALE CIVILE (LOI DE MISE EN OEUVRE))

s. 2, "Division 3N", added, SOR/94-362, s. 1
s. 2, "Fishing Zone 4", SOR/79-713, s. 1
s. 2, "flag state", SOR/94-362, s. 4(F); SOR/94-362, s. 6(F)
s. 2, "International code of Signals", added, SOR/94-362, s. 1
s. 2, "master", SOR/94-362, s. 4(F)
s. 2, "NAFO", added, SOR/99-313, s. 1
s. 2, "NAFO Measures", added, SOR/99-313, s. 1
s. 2, "observer", added, SOR/79-713, s. 1; SOR/86-939, s. 1 (E). SOR/99-313, s. 1
s. 2, "permit", SOR/79-713, s. 1; repealed, SOR/85-527, s. 1
s. 2, "pilot ladder", added, SOR/79-713, s. 1
s. 2, "processing", added, SOR/79-713, s. 1; SOR/85-527, s. 1
s. 2, "Regional Director-General", SOR/83-264, s. 1; SOR/85-527, s. 1
s. 2, "round weight", added, SOR/85-527, s. 1
s. 2, "Signal L", added, SOR/94-362, s. 1
s. 2, "Signal SQ 1", added, SOR/94-362, s. 1
s. 2, "Signal SQ 3", added, SOR/94-362, s. 1
s. 2, "Subarea", added, SOR/81-729, s. 1; SOR/85-527, s. 1
s. 3, SOR/79-713, s. 2; repealed, SOR/85-527, s. 2; added, SOR/99-313, s. 2
s. 4, SOR/79-713, s. 3; repealed, SOR/85-527, s. 2
s. 5, SOR/78-447, s. 1; SOR/78-795, s. 1; SOR/79-138, s. 1; SOR/79-713, s. 4; SOR/80-186, s. 1; SOR/85-527, s. 3; SOR/86-939, s. 2; SOR/94-362, s. 4(F); SOR/94-362, s. 6(F); SOR/94-444, s. 1; SOR/95-261, s. 1; SOR/95-356, s. 1; SOR/96-309, s. 1; SOR/98-410, s. 1; SOR/99-474, s. 1; SOR/2000-36, s. 1
s. 6, SOR/80-186, s. 2; SOR/85-527, s. 4; SOR/94-362, s. 4(F); SOR/94-362, s. 6(F)
s. 7, SOR/80-186, s. 3; SOR/85-527, s. 5; SOR/94-362, s. 4(F); SOR/94-362, s. 6(F); SOR/98-410, s. 2; SOR/99-474, s. 2

As you can see, the regulations (SOR and SI) pertaining to each statute are listed underneath each statute. If the regulation was made before 1985, it will have a reference to a C.R.C. 1978. This table will provide information on the regulations.

At this stage, you should record the number and year of all of the relevant regulations and their citation (*i.e.*, the location in the *Canada Gazette*, Part II). For example, the first regulation under the *Citizenship Act* is the *Citizenship Regulations, 1993*, SOR/93-246.

Other regulations listed often amend prior regulations. For example, regulation SOR/93-246 was amended by SOR/94-442, and again by SOR/95-122. You should look at all of the regulations to ensure you have the most current version.

If you know the name of the regulation look in Table I (Table of Regulations, Statutory Instruments (other than Regulations) and Other Documents. All regulations and their corresponding statutes are listed.

Illustration 8.5
Table of Regulations

I— TABLE OF REGULATIONS, STATUTORY INSTRUMENTS (OTHER THAN REGULATIONS) AND OTHER DOCUMENTS

SEPTEMBER 30, 2000

This Table provides a reference to regulations, statutory instruments (other than regulations) and other documents that have been made under statutory or other authority and that were in force at any time during the current calendar year.

The instruments are listed alphabetically according to their title showing the authority under which they were made and are listed in Table II.

For instruments no longer in force, that were published in the *Canada Gazette* Part II, reference should be made to the Consolidated Index of December 31st of the year in question.

A.G. Girardin Remission Order Financial Administration Act	**Accounting for Imported Goods and Payment of Duties Regs** Customs Act	**Aerodrome Security Regs** Aeronautics Act
ACOA Loan Insurance Regs Atlantic Canada Opportunities Agency Act	**Accrued Interest under Canada Account Loans to Madagascar, Poland, Tanzania and Zambia Remission Order** Financial Administration Act	**Affiliated Persons (Banks) Regs** Bank Act
AECB Cost Recovery Fees Regs Atomic Energy Control Act		**Affiliated Persons (Insurance Companies) Regs** Insurance Companies Act
AECB Cost Recovery Fees Remission Order Financial Administration Act	**Acting Customs Excise Enforcement Officers Exclusion Approval Order** Public Service Employment Act	**Affiliated Persons (Trust and Loan Companies) Regs** Trust and Loan Companies Act
AECL Tandem Accelerator Superconducting Cyclotron Complex Remission Order Customs Tariff	**Action Loan Regs** Atlantic Canada Opportunities Agency	**African Development Bank Privileges and Immunities Order**

Reproduced with permission from Public Works and Government Services Canada. Not an official copy.

Example 2: Provincial Regulations

If you know the name of the provincial statute look in the table that lists the statutes and all the corresponding regulations. In British Columbia this is called the Regulation/Act Concordance and is found in the front of the *Consolidated Regulations of British Columbia* (C.R.B.C.). It lists all regulations and corresponding statutes.

Ilustration 8.6
B.C. Regulation Act/Concordance

REGULATION / ACT CONCORDANCE

REGULATION	ACT
Miscellaneous Registrations Regulation	Miscellaneous Registrations, 1992
Mission & District Community Health Council Regulation	Health Authorities
Mortgage Brokers Act Regulations	Mortgage Brokers
Motion Picture Act Regulations	Motion Picture
Motor Carrier Regulations	Motor Carrier
Motor Carrier Regulation No. 2	Motor Carrier
Motor Dealer Act Regulation	Motor Dealer
Motor Dealer Exemption Regulation	Real Estate
Motor Dealer Leasing Regulation	Motor Dealer
Motor Fuel Tax Regulation	Motor Fuel Tax
Motor Fuel Tax Refund and Remission Regulation	Motor Fuel Tax; Financial Administration
Motor Vehicle Act and Commercial Transport Act Retention of Fees Regulation	Financial Administration
Motor Vehicle Act Regulations	Motor Vehicle
Motor Vehicle Fees Regulation	Motor Vehicle
Motor Vehicle Insurance Policy Limits Regulation	Insurance
Motor Vehicle Prohibition Regulation	Wildlife
Motor Vehicle Prohibition (Temporary) Regulation	Wildlife
Mount Pleasant Commission Retention Regulation	Financial Administration
Mount Waddington Health Council Regulation	Health Authorities
Municipal Act Fees Regulation Nos. 1 & 2	Municipal
Municipal Act Tax Regulation	Municipal
Municipal Administration Certification Regulation	Municipal
Municipal Bylaw Enforcement Ticket Regulation	Municipal
Municipal Finance Authority Act Regulation	Municipal Finance Author.
Museum Fee Regulation	Museum Act
Muskwa Kechika Access Management Area Regulation	Wildlife Act
Nakusp Unorganized Territory	Curfew
Name Act Regulation	Name
Nanaimo Health Council Regulation	Health Authorities
Nanaimo Regional District Regulation	Municipal
Natural Gas Price Act Regulation No. 2	Natural Gas Price
Natural Products Marketing (BC) Act Regulations	Natural Products Marketing (BC)
Nelson and Area Health Council Regulation	Health Authorities
New Westminster Health Council Regulation	Health Authorities
Nicola Valley Health Council Regulation	Health Authorities
Non-Reporting Company Exemption Regulation	Financial Institutions
North Coast Community Health Council Regulation	Health Authorities

If you know the title of the statute, look in the table that lists all of the regulations and the corresponding statutes. In British Columbia this is called the Index of Current B.C. Regulations. It lists all regulations in British Columbia and their corresponding statutes.

Illustration 8.7
Index of Current B.C. Regulations

These regulations are still technically in effect, but not all are in active use. Most, but not all, have been published in the B.C. Gazette, Part II. Regulations made under a repealed Act but which are still in use are listed under the replacement Act. Some regulations which were previously listed no longer meet the definition of "regulation" under the present *Regulations Act* (S.B.C. 1983, c. 10) and so have been deleted from this index. Symbols used are as follows:

* = not published
# = published in Part I Gazette

Citations such as "1985-55-42" signify the year, chapter and section of a statute.

. . .

NAME ACT c. 295, R.S.B.C. 1979				
Name Act Regulation				91/80
amended	326/84	73/87	121/88	111/90
	133/91	87/92	79/94	

NATURAL GAS PRICE ACT c. 74, S.B.C. 1989		
Natural Gas Price Act Regulation No. 2		241/90
amended	104/93	355/94

NATURAL PRODUCTS MARKETING (BC) ACT c. 296, R.S.B.C. 1979

British Columbia Broiler Hatching Egg Scheme	432/88
amended	479/88

Note where to find the number and year of the regulation (*e.g.*, B.C. Reg. 91/80) and amendments to the regulation (*e.g.*, B.C. Reg. 326/84).

Computers have revolutionized regulation research in three key ways. You can now do a simple word search to locate a regulation, and the electronic version is usually consolidated — meaning you do not have to search through several volumes of statutes to locate the amendments to those statutes. The electronic form of information is also current. However, the electronic versions are still not viewed by all courts as the official version, so paper-based research is still necessary.

The main advantage of electronic regulations is that you do not need to know the related statute. You can simply do a search for a word in the statute of a word in the regulation. However, beware that these databases are huge and it can be very difficult to isolate the particular regulations that you may be looking for. As mentioned above, it is critical that you find out how current the site is and how recently the regulation has been updated. You will need to search in the library from that date forward.

As mentioned in Chapter 4, there are some fundamental ways to search through electronic data. The three most important things to keep in mind are:

- Determine the content of the source you are looking at;
- Identify the automated search mechanism used to search through the data; and
- Learn how to properly formulate a word search.

When using a CD-ROM, try to scan the contents first and then construct a search through a template. When using an online service, use the templates they provide and read their instructions carefully. When using the Internet, it is recommend that you use either the search engines you are familiar with or use your own browser search engine.

Step 2: Find the Regulation

You can find the regulation from the information obtained in Step 1. Most regulations are filed by number and date and sometimes by page. Once you have the proper number of the regulation you are looking for, it is most efficient to search for that number, rather than search for the title, which can be very long.

The paper version of federal regulations are located in the Gazette, Part II in either the consolidated set, the *Consolidated Regulations of Canada, 1978*, or the published versions since the consolidation. This is an excerpt from British Columbia Regulation 91/80 (made pursuant to the *Name Act*). Note that it repeals a prior regulation.

Illustration 8.8
B.C. Regulation 91/80

B.C. Reg. 91/80

                       Filed March 21, 1980

CHANGE OF NAME ACT
[Section 14]

Order in Council 617, Approved and Ordered March 20, 1980

On the recommendation of the undersigned, the Lieutenant-Governor, by and with the advice and consent of the Executive Council, orders that, effective June 1, 1980, Order in Council 3437, approved November 7, 1967 (B.C. Reg. 253/67), be repealed and the following regulation be made.

CHANGE OF NAME ACT REGULATIONS

1. Under the *Change of Name Act* the fee

    (*a*)   on filing an application for a Change of Name shall be $25, which fee includes the issuance of one certificate of Change of Name and cost of publication of the certificate in the Gazette following approval of the application,

    (*b*)   for a search of one registration of Change of Name shall be $2 for each three-year period or part of a three-year period covered by the search, and

    (*c*)   for each certificate of Change of Name shall be $5, including the fee for a search covering one three-year period.

K. R. MAIR
Minister of Health

W. R. BENNETT
Presiding Member of the Executive Council

. . .

apl -- 3506

Illustration 8.8: This is an excerpt from British Columbia Regulation 91/80 (made pursuant to the *Name Act*). Note that it repeals a prior regulation.

Illustration 8.9
B.C. Regulation 79/94

B.C. Reg. 79/94, deposited March 18, 1994, pursuant to the **NAME ACT** [Section 13 (1)]. Order in Council 365/94, approved and ordered March 17, 1994.

On the recommendation of the undersigned, the Lieutenant Governor, by and with the advice and consent of the Executive Council, orders that effective April 1, 1994, th Name Act Regulation, B.C. Reg. 91/80, is amended

1. in section 1 (c) (i), by striking out $20 and substituting $25, and
2. in section 1 (c) (ii), by striking out $50 and substituting $55. — P. RAMSEY, *Minister of Health and Minister Responsible for Seniors;* M. HARCOURT, *Presiding Member of the Executive Council.*

Illustration 8.9: This is British Columbia Regulation 79/94. It amends Regulation 91/80. It is important to note the effective date of the regulation.

Step 3: Update the Regulation

To locate the most recent amendments to regulations, you must look in the most recent publications from the legislature: either directly from the legislature, electronically, or in a law library.

For library research of federal regulations, this means looking in the index of each of the soft-cover editions of the *Canada Gazette,* Part II, that have come out since dated after the most recent *Consolidated Index of Statutory Instruments.* To further update, you must look at the *Canada Legislative Digest,* speak to a law librarian, or call the legislative library.

For provincial amendments to regulations, look at the most current soft-cover editions of the gazettes (often there is an index included) and the most recent legislative digest from a librarian or the legislature.

When using electronic sources, be sure to update in the library from the date noted on the electronic version.

How to Write a Citation for a Regulation

The citation of regulations is fairly straightforward.

Federal Regulations

The title of a federal regulation is the short title, which is often stated in the regulation. Although it is not necessary to state the title of the regulation in the citation, it is good practice to do so. Those published in the *Consolidated Regulations of Canada, 1978* can be cited as follows: *Civil Service Insurance Regulations,* C.R.C., c. 401. Note you do not need to put the date in because the only C.R.C. that was published is dated 1978.

Those published after the consolidation (*i.e.,* in the Gazettes) include both the SOR or SI number and the page reference. They are cited as follows: *Foreign Ownership of Land Regulations,* SOR/79-416, 2113. This means SOR number 416, published in 1979, at page 2113.

Provincial Regulations

The proper way to cite provincial regulations is by the name of the province (abbreviated) and the regulation number, for example: B.C. Reg 91/80. This means this was the 91st regulation made in 1980 and it can be located in the 1980 volume of regulations. Note again that the title of the regulation is not necessary.

How to Determine Effective Dates of Statutes

As mentioned in Chapter 7, a researcher must ensure that each statute is effective. If a statute has a delayed or retroactive effective date, the researcher must look in the regulations to see when the statute will come into effect.

There are three steps to finding the effective date of a statute:

Step 1: Find out whether the statute received royal assent.
Step 2: Find out whether there is a delayed effective date.
Step 3: Locate and update the regulation.

Step 1: Did the Statute Receive Royal Assent?

The first step in determining whether a statute is effective is ensuring that it has received royal assent. A statute must receive royal assent before becoming law. The date of royal assent is printed on the first page of the statute when it is first published. This date is not printed on the version found in the *revised* statutes, since statutes included in the revision are already in effect.

Therefore, if your statute is in the revised set, you can assume it received royal assent. If it is not, you must go to the version in which it was first printed. You can locate the original statute by looking in the table of public statutes from the relevant jurisdiction. See Chapter 7 for more details.

Step 2: Is There a Delayed Effective Date?

Not all statutes come into effect upon royal assent. Many have delayed or retroactive effective dates. Often governments will delay the operation of a statute until certain events take place, or until certain systems are in place. The drafters of legislation may change the effective date of a statute by placing a "commencement clause" in the statute. This commencement clause states either the specific day it will come into effect or that it will come into force upon the act of another authority. The commencement clause is usually at the end of the statute.

The second step, therefore, is to refer to the statute itself to see if there is a commencement clause. This clause will tell you whether the statute came into force by a given date, proclamation, or regulation. For example, if the commencement clause specifies a specific effective date that will usually be its effective date. This information can be confirmed by looking in the cumulative tables of statutes, such as the Federal *Table of Statutes*.

If the statute has no commencement clause, then the effective date of the act is the date of royal assent. Note that those statutes that are consolidated into the revised sets will no longer have a commencement clause because they are in effect.

Step 3: Locate and Update the Regulation

If a commencement clause states that the statute will come into effect by proclamation or regulation, this means the regulation that gave effect to the statute must be located to prove it is effective. This can be done in any of the following three ways:

Method 1: Table of Statutes

This method is the most direct way to locate the effective date of a statute. Recall from Chapter 7 that federal and provincial tables of statutes include information about when statutes came into effect. You can return to the table of statutes and look for your statute. The information contained will direct you to the specific regulation.

Method 2: Index to Regulations

Indexes to regulations usually list those regulations that bring statutes into effect. For example, in the following British Columbia regulation index there is a specific section devoted to "Acts in Force."

Illustration 8.10
B.C. Gazette, Part II

xx	THE BRITISH COLUMBIA GAZETTE — PART II		
O.C. No.		Reg. No.	Page
	Acts in Force—		
1200/94	Accountants (Management) Act, S.B.C. 1994, c. 17 — Act in force Sept. 15, 1994	327/94	362
1037/94	Agricultural Land Commission Amendment Act, 1994, S.B.C. 1994, c. 25 — Act in force August 26, 1994	278/94	322
905/94	Agriculture, Fisheries and Food Statutes Amendment Act, 1993, S.B.C. 1993, c. 7 — sections 3 to 6 [*Natural Products Marketing (BC) Act*], in force July 7, 1994	223/94	273
1027/94	Architects Amendment Act, 1994, S.B.C. 1994, c. 2 — sections 1 and 3 to 26 in force July 28, 1994	269/94	316
1480/94	Architects Amendment Act, 1994, S.B.C. 1994, c. 2 — section 2 in force January 1, 1995	461/94	611
484/94	Attorney General Statutes Amendment Act (No. 2), 1992, S.B.C. 1992, c. 32 — section 17 [*Liquor Control and Licensing Act*] in force April 14, 1994	111/94	117

In the above example the *Accountants (Management) Act* was brought into force on September 15, 1994, by Regulation 327/94.

Method 3: Tables of Proclamation

Many governments publish tables of proclamation with statutes. These tables include information about when statutes were proclaimed and provide citations for the regulations that brought them into effect. One example of such a table is the *Canada Gazette*, Part III entitled *Proclamations of Canada and Orders in Council Relating to the Coming into Force of Acts*.

Illustration 8.11
Table of Proclamation

PROCLAMATIONS OF CANADA AND ORDERS IN COUNCIL RELATING TO THE COMING INTO FORCE OF ACTS — 27 APRIL, 2000 TO 19 JULY, 2000		
—	Date in force	Canada Gazette Part II

Canada Grain Act and the Agriculture and Agri-Food Administrative Monetary Penalties Act and to repeal the Grain Futures Act, An Act to amend the, S.C. 1998. c. 22.
 (a) subsections 1(2) and 6(3), sections 8, 11 and 12, subsection 24(1) and section 25, and
 (b) subsection 88(1) of the *Canada Grain Act*, as enacted by section 17, other than
   (i) in the English version, paragraph (a), and
   (ii) in the French version, the following: "soit pénétrer dans une installation ou dans les locaux d'un titulaire de licence d'exploitation d'une installation ou de negociant en grains ou en cultures spéciales, s'il a des motifs raisonnables de croire que des grains, des produits céréaliers ou des criblures s'y trouvent, qu'ils appartiennent au titulaire ou soient en sa possession, ainsi que des livres, registres ou autres documents relatifs à l'exploitation de l'installation ou du commerce."		

Reproduced with permission from Public Works and Government Services Canada. Not an official copy.

The problem with most tables of proclamation is that they are not cumulative. As seen in the example, the table of proclamation covers only one period: April 27 to July 19, 2000. Therefore, each table must be searched in each of the annual volumes. In other words, to be thorough you must look at each table in the volume of the year in which the statute was created, as well as all subsequent volumes.

You will note that you are referred to the volume and page number of the *Canada Gazette*, Part II, rather than to a regulation number.

Finally, you must find the actual regulation. Regulations are located by the year and number in the gazettes. If you have the regulation number, you can go directly to the volume of regulations or statutory instruments and locate the regulation by date and regulation number.

For the most recent information on statutes coming into force, look in the softcover volumes of the federal or provincial gazettes, or current information from the various legislatures.

A Word about Municipal Bylaws

The Constitution does not mention legislative powers of municipalities. Municipal law-making powers are delegated provincial powers. These powers are delegated through statute and give municipalities the powers to create bylaws. Typically, each municipality has a governing statute which describes the areas in which municipalities have powers to make bylaws.

The process by which bylaws are adopted is different than that of statutes or regulations. Usually the method of adoption is outlined in a statute or another bylaw.

Some bylaws require that certain procedures be followed prior to their introduction. These include such procedures as public hearings or public votes. Bylaws usually require three readings; however, all three readings are often conducted in one sitting of municipal council. The committee work is usually done prior to the bylaw being introduced and there is usually "reconsideration" of the bylaw at least one day after third reading.

Because municipal bylaws are rarely the subject of litigation, they are rarely found in case law. Because law students tend to focus primarily on case law, they are often unfamiliar with municipal law when they graduate.

Self Test

The answers to these questions are found at the end of the book in the "Answers to Self Tests" section.

1. What is a regulation?
2. Explain how regulations become law.
3. What is a consolidation of regulations?
4. How do you locate regulations?
5. When will a statute not become effective on royal assent?

Sample Exercises — Finding Regulations and the Effective Dates of Statutes

Objectives

At the end of this exercise you should be able to:

- Locate a federal regulation
- Locate a provincial regulation
- Use the tables of concordance
- Determine the effective date of a statute
- Cite a regulation

Instructions

- Do background reading on how to determine the effective date of a statute.

- Do background reading on how to locate and cite regulations.
- Keep a record of the time taken to complete the exercise.

Effective Date of a Provincial Statute

1. Locate the *Tourism B.C. Act*. Give the proper citation for the statute.

    Citation:

2. Go to the statute and:
    a. Locate the commencement section, if there is one. Record the commencement section number and the means by which the statute came into force (*e.g.*, proclamation).

    Commencement section number:

    Means:

    b. Find the date of royal assent (usually on the front page of the original statute).

    Date of royal assent:

    c. Find the enabling section (which allows regulations to be made) and note the section number.

    Enabling section number:

3. Use the most recent *Table of Legislative Changes* to locate the regulation, if any, which brought the statute into force. Record the proper citation to the regulation.

    Citation:

4. Give the effective date of the statute (the day the statute came into force).

    Effective date:

5. Locate the regulation and record the date of deposit or date of filing.

    Date of deposit or filing:

Effective Date of a Federal Statute

1. Locate the federal *Coasting Trade Act* and give the proper citation for the statute.

   Citation:

2. Go to the statute and:
   a. Locate the commencement section, if there is one. Record the commencement section number and the means by which the statute came into force (*e.g.*, proclamation).

   Commencement section number:

   Means:

   b. Find the date of royal assent (usually on the front page of the original statute).

   Date of royal assent:

   c. Find the enabling section (which allows regulations to be made) and record the section number.

   Enabling section number:

3. Use the most recent *Table of Public Statutes* to locate the regulation (SOR or SI), if any, which brought the statute into force. Record the proper citation to the regulation.

   Citation:

4. Record the effective date of the statute (the day the statute came into force).

   Effective date:

5. Find the regulation and record the P.C. number.

   P.C. number:

Provincial Regulations

Answer questions 1–4 for the following regulation:

Christmas Tree Regulation (B.C.)

1. Record the proper citation for the statute that authorizes this regulation.

   Citation:

2. Record the basic citation of the regulation.

    Citation:

3. Record the citation for any amendments to the regulation.

    Amendments:

4. Find the regulation and record the date of deposit or date of filing.

    Date of deposit or date of filing:

Federal Regulations

Answer questions 1–4 for the following regulation:

Honey Regulations (Canada)

1. Record the proper citation for the statute that authorizes this regulation.

    Citation:

2. Record the basic citation of the regulation.

    Citation:

3. Record the citation for the top amendment to s. 2 of that regulation.

    Citation:

4. Find the regulation and record the P.C. (Privy Council) number for that amendment.

    P.C. number:

Answers to Exercises

Effective Date of a Provincial Statute

1. *Tourism B.C. Act*, S.B.C. 1997. c. 13.

2. a. Commencement s. 1, by regulation. Deemed to come into force on April 1, 1997 and part by the Lieutenant Governor in Council.

    b. June 27,1997.

    c. None.

3. In the *Table of Legislative Changes* up to December 31, 1998 all sections are brought into force on April 1, 1997 through regulation 259/97 per 1997-13-25(2).

4. April 1, 1997.

5. July 25, 1997.

Effective Date of a Federal Statute

1. *Coasting Trade Act*, S.C. 1992, c. 31.

2. a. Commencement s. 31, by order of the Governor in Council.

   b. June 23, 1992.

   c. None.

3. SI/92-175 *see also* s. 31(2) re application.

4. Dec. 1, 1992.

5. P.C. number 1992-2106 (Sept. 17, 1992).

Provincial Regulations

1. *Forest Act*, R.S.B.C. 1996, c. 157.

2. B.C. Reg. 166/2000.

3. None.

4. Date of deposit for Reg. 166/2000 is May 19, 2000.

Federal Regulations

1. *Canada Agricultural Products Act*, R.S.C. 1985 (4th Supp.), c. 20.

2. C.R.C. Vol. II, c. 287.

3. Section 2 was amended by SOR/91-524, s. 1.

4. P.C. number 1991-1631, Sept. 5, 1991.

Appendix A: Checklist: How to Find and Update Regulations

In the library you will find volumes of new regulations and consolidated sets of older regulations. Federal regulations are called statutory instruments (SI) and statutory orders and regulations (SOR). Each regulation is made pursuant to a statute.

In the library, you can locate a regulation by searching by the name of the statute or by searching for the title of the regulation.

Step 1: Find the Name of the Regulation

❑ Go to the most recent *consolidated* index of regulations or statutory instruments.

- For federal regulations, this index is titled *Consolidated Index of Statutory Instruments*.

- For provincial regulations, the index has various titles. In British Columbia it is called the *Consolidated Regulations of British Columbia*.

- There are also some commercially published consolidations avail-able.

If You Know the Title of the Regulation

❑ If you know the title of the *regulation,* look in the index for a table called a *concordance.*

❑ Note the date on the cover, since you will need to update from this date forward.

- For federal regulations, the concordance is titled: Table I: Table of Regulations, Statutory Instruments (other than Regulations) and Other Documents.

- For provincial regulations, the concordance has various titles. In British Columbia it is called the Regulation/Act Concordance.

- Record the number and year of all the relevant regulations and their citation.

If You Know the Title of the Statute

❏ If you know the title of the *statute*, look in the consolidation for the index that list statutes and their corresponding regulations.

- For federal regulations this index is called Table II: Table of Regulations, Statutory Instruments (other than Regulations) and Other Documents Arranged by Statute.

- For provincial regulations, this index has various titles. In British Columbia it is called the Index of Current B.C. Regulations.

❏ Record the number and year of all the relevant regulations and their citation. Note the date of the index so you can update from that date forward.

Electronic Regulations

❏ It is best not to search by subject in electronic regulations until you have completely refined your word search.

❏ If you have access to an electronic index of regulations it is best to start there, just as you would in the library.

Step 2: Find the Regulation

Regulations are filed chronologically by number. The citation of the regulation tells you both the year and the number to look for in each of the annual volumes of the Gazettes (*e.g.*, *Canada Gazette*, Part II). When looking for federal regulations keep in mind that C.R.C. refers to the *Consolidated Regulations of Canada, 1978* and SOR and SI are filed by number, date, and page (*e.g.*, SOR/79-416, date 13/06/79, and page 2113). SORs are published separately from SIs.

Electronically

- CD-ROM: there are a few sets of regulations on CD-ROM. They are published by commercial publishers and are available in most law libraries. See tips on how to research CD-ROMs in Chapter 5.

- Commercial Online Providers: Quicklaw and LEXIS have statute and regulation databases. Look for an index first and only go to the full text if you have refined your word search.

- Public Access Internet Sites: Most provinces are placing their regulations on their websites. The two federal websites are:

  - Cumulative consolidation: http://canada.justice.gc.ca/loireg/index_en.html

  - Consolidated Index of Statutory Instruments: go to http://canada.justice.gc.ca and click **Consolidated Index of Statutory Instruments** (under the Search Folio Views InfoBases heading).

Step 3: Update the Regulation

❑ To locate the most recent amendments to regulations, look in the index or table of contents of *each* of the soft-cover issues of the gazettes dated after the most recent consolidated index (above). For federal regulations these are the biweekly issues of the *Canada Gazette*, Part II.

❑ To further update, look at publications from the various legislatures.

❑ When updating using electronic sources, note whether the database you are looking at is consolidated. If it is then all of the revisions to the regulations have been inserted into the text and you need only update from the current date forward.

Appendix B: Checklist: How to Ensure a Statute is in Force

Step 1: Did Statute Receive Royal Assent?

- ❏ Determine whether the statute is effective. A statute must receive royal assent before becoming law.

- ❏ The date of royal assent is printed on the first page of the statute when it is first published (not the version found in the revised statutes).

Step 2: Is There a Delayed Effective Date?

- ❏ If there is a commencement clause in a statute, the effective date may be delayed or made retroactive.

- ❏ Refer to the *first printing* of the statute and see if there is a commencement clause that delays the statute's effective date. The commencement clause is usually at the end of the statute. This clause will tell you whether the statute came into force by a given date, by proclamation, or by regulation.

- ❏ If the statute has no commencement clause, then the effective date of the statute is the date of royal assent.

- ❏ If the commencement clause states a specific effective date, that will be the date it is in force.

- ❏ This information can be confirmed by either looking in the *Table of Public Statutes* or by locating the actual regulation that brought the statute into effect.

Step 3: Locate and Update the Regulation

- ❏ If you have the regulation number, go directly to the volume of regulations and locate the regulation by number.

❏ For the most recent information on statutes coming into force, look in the soft-cover issues of the gazettes, or information from the various legislatures.

❏ If the statute has a commencement clause, you should locate the regulation that brought the statute into effect. The title of the regulation can be found in one of the following three ways:

In the Table of Statutes

❏ Look at the most recent *Table of Statutes*.

❏ Locate the statute title.

❏ There is usually information in the table about the date the statute came into force and the number of the regulation that brought it into force.

- "O.C." means it came into effect by an order-in-council (*i.e.*, by regulation).

- "Proc." means it came into effect by a proclamation (*i.e.*, by regulation).

❏ To confirm this information, the regulation should be located.

❏ If the regulation number is not specified in the table, use the next method to locate the regulation number.

❏ For each entry in the federal *Table of Public Statutes* there is corresponding coming into force (CIF) information about the date the statute came into force and the number of the regulation (SI or SOR) that brought it into force. To confirm this information the regulation should be located.

In the Regulation Indexes

❏ Search the individual indexes of regulations contained in the federal and provincial gazettes. These indexes tell you the date and location of the regulation.

In the Table of Proclamations

❑ Search the annual tables of proclamations, which are included in the statutes in that year's volume and all years since that date. These tables tell you the effective date and the location.

❑ Note the dates and the locations, since the tables of proclamations are not often cumulative.

How to Find and Update Cases   9

Case law research involves locating relevant cases, seeing whether these cases have been appealed (updating), and locating cases that have considered those cases (noting-up). Thousands of cases are published each year provincially, federally, and internationally. In order to locate these cases, researchers must become familiar with how cases are published, how they are arranged in law libraries and databases, and the tools available to assist in locating them.

This chapter describes what cases are, how to read cases, and how cases are published in reports. It then describes step-by-step how to locate cases, and explains how to cite cases.

Learning Objectives

At the end of this chapter you will be able to:

- Read a case and define its parts
- Describe how cases are published
- Name a few specific case reports
- Locate a case by case name or citation
- Locate a case by subject
- Update and note-up a case
- Use proper case citation

What Is a Case?

A case is a decision of a judge or a tribunal. It is the written outcome of a dispute that has been tried in a court or an administrative tribunal. Since Canadian judges are required to follow previously decided similar cases, these cases must be made available to the judges and the public. They form the vast majority of the common law in Canada.

How to Read a Case

The ability to read a case is critical to legal analysis but also equally important to the task of locating relevant cases. If you can read cases quickly and accurately you can efficiently detect those cases that are relevant and exclude those that are not.

Reading cases involves some skill. Most cases follow a particular format and, after reading several cases, the researcher should be able to quickly find relevant information without getting bogged down in irrelevant information.

At the most basic level, researchers should be familiar with the format of published cases. A description of this format is provided in Appendix A to this chapter. This format is also important for computer research since you can narrow down your search by asking the computer to search only certain locations in the text of reported cases (*e.g.*, the parties or the date).

How Cases Are Published

The system of common law and the doctrine of precedent require that judges follow past judgments to the extent that they are similar and binding. Therefore, in a common law system, it is very important that judgments be written and published. This process is called case reporting.

Although many cases are in electronic form, computers are not always the most effective or efficient method of finding cases. As well, not all electronic cases are recognized by the courts and not all cases are in electronic form.

The location of cases in computer databases is similar to their location in paper compilations in the library. For example, the case report Dominion Law Reports contains the same cases as the databank on Quicklaw called Dominion Law Reports.

What Are Case Reports?

Case reports are sets of books containing decided cases. Case reports are also called case reporters, law reports, or case reporting series.

Various commercial publishers and government bodies collect the decisions of courts and administrative bodies and assemble and publish them for resale. There are over 100 distinct case reports in Canada. It is important to know that not all cases are reported. Usually only those that change or clarify the law are reported.

Each case report consists of many volumes of bound books, which are arranged in chronological order on the library shelves. Each hardbound volume contains many cases. As you can imagine, there are thousands of volumes of case reports, containing millions of cases, on the shelves of law libraries. Each case has a headnote or summary of the issues at the top. These are written by editors and sometimes include case comments and references to other cases. These headnotes are rarely found in electronic versions of cases unless the cases were originally published in hard copy or the editors can charge for the value added by this service.

When locating cases, particular attention should be paid to the publishers of legal materials. Although it may seem strange to the new researcher, the way in which cases are published directs much of legal research. This is because each publisher decides which cases are published, how they are categorized, and how they are indexed. In order to locate cases, therefore, researchers should be aware of the different publishers' indexing systems.

Which Cases Are in Case Reports?

Cases are organized and published in a number of ways. There is no single complete set of all decided cases in Canada. Cases from different jurisdictions and on different subjects are published in different case reports. This is one of the main reasons why legal researchers need research aids to assist them in locating cases.

Although computer research can eliminate some of this problem, at present there is no single computer system that contains all decided cases. The same case can often be found in several case reports. Most case reports include a list of what cases they publish and it is always a good idea for new researchers to check and ensure that the cases they are looking for are in that particular report. The following are some examples.

Federal Case Reports

There are three case reports that publish cases from the two federal courts: the *Supreme Court Reports* (S.C.R.), the *National Reporter* (N.R.), and the *Federal Court Reports* (F.C.). The *Supreme Court Reports* contains only Supreme Court of Canada decisions. The *National Reporter* publishes all of the judgments of the Supreme Court of Canada, the Federal Court of Appeal, and some decisions from the trial division of the Federal Court of Canada. The *Federal Court Reports* is the official report of the Federal Court of Canada and contains all of the decisions of the Federal Court (which typically involve matters of taxation and immigration).

General Case Reports

The only case report that publishes cases from all the provinces as well as the two federal courts is the *Dominion Law Reports* (D.L.R.). It is the best known case report in Canada.

Provincial Case Reports

Most provinces have their own set of case reports that include court decisions from that particular province and cases that are important to the law of that province. Examples include the *British Columbia Law Reports* (B.C.L.R.) and the *Ontario Reports* (O.R.).

Regional Case Reports

Regional case reports include cases from regions of Canada. For example, the *Western Weekly Reports* (W.W.R.) includes cases only from the western provinces.

Subject Case Reports

Recently there has been an increase in case reports that include cases on only particular subjects. This is because lawyers tend to specialize and will often only purchase case reports containing cases that are relevant to their particular specialty. *Canadian Criminal Cases* (C.C.C.) and *Canada Cases on Employment Law* (C.C.E.L.) are examples of such subject specific reports.

Administrative Tribunal Case Reports

The decisions of administrative tribunals are published in separate reports from those of cases decided by judges. Reports that include court cases do not, as a rule, include decisions of administrative bodies because they are not *per se* part of the common law (*i.e.*, law made by judges). An example of an administrative tribunal case report is the *Canadian Labour Relations Board Reports* (C.L.R.B.R.). It includes labour tribunal decisions from across Canada.

Digests of Cases

There are some so-called case reports that include only digests or summaries of cases not yet published in full. Researchers typically use these reports to locate very recent cases.

Digests are useful not only because they are very current but also because they enable you to quickly decide whether the case is worth reading in full. Most practising lawyers subscribe to digest services in order to stay current on the law. The digests are organized by subject area, so a busy lawyer only needs to read those summaries that are relevant to his or her practice area.

For example, *All Canada Weekly Summaries* (A.C.W.S.) includes digests of cases that will ultimately be published in full in *Dominion Law Reports* (D.L.R.). Researchers must contact the publisher or court for the full text of these decisions. The most comprehensive set of Canadian digested cases is the *Canadian Abridgement, Case Digests*, which is published by Carswell. The digests are collected in a multiple-volume set and sorted by a subject classification scheme. In order to locate digests you need to figure out the classification for your particular topic.

All of the online service providers, including Quicklaw, *e*Carswell, and LEXIS, have digest databases. Most are hyperlinked to the full-text version of the case, which simplifies the research process.

The most recent cases can be located at the particular court registry where the cases were heard, at a law library reference desk, online through a commercial service provider or on public access Internet sites. These are discussed in more detail below.

Format of Case Reports

Most case reports are published as soon as they are issued by the courts. However, this process of publication may take some time. Case reports are often not received in hard copy by law libraries until about four to six months after the decisions are written. Therefore, it is always important to check for most recent cases online, or directly through the courts.

Usually, case reports have tables of cases and subject indexes in each volume to assist in locating cases quickly. Some also have other aids for research, such as annotations of cases and statute indexes. When looking at a new case report, a researcher should try to become acquainted with the available research aids and the format of the particular case report.

Many case reports have been divided into several series (*e.g.*, 1st, 2d, and 3d series). For example, *Dominion Law Reports* has four series. This means that the numbering of the volumes begins over again every so often. In each series, the volumes are numbered consecutively for many years. At some point, the publishers decide to begin the numbering again and call it a new series. For example, a 2d series will begin once the numbering in the first series becomes unmanageable. A 2d series is not a second edition or reprinting of the cases in the first series. The series number is important for locating cases.

How to Find Cases

There is no simple way to find relevant cases. It is an art as well as a skill.
The main rule to keep in mind is to be systematic. If you proceed in a
systematic way and record your steps as you go, it is unlikely that you will
get off track or duplicate steps. Ideally, you should have a strategy or
plan of attack before you enter the library. Developing a research plan is
discussed in Chapter 13.

Before beginning your search, you should ask yourself the following
questions. The answers will help you narrow down the sources you will
look at.

- Do you want the full text of a case?
- Do you just want the citation of the case?
- Do you want a summary or digest of the case?
- Do you want a reported or a not-yet-reported case?
- Do you want a list of all the cases related to your case?
- Do you want the history of your case (*e.g.*, appeals)?

There are essentially two ways to find cases: by case name (or citation)
or by subject. If you know the name of a particular case, it can be
searched for by its title in various tables, case reports, and databases. If
you know only the subject, other tools must be used. No matter what
method you employ, once you find a case you must update it and note it
up.

How to Find a Case by Name or Citation

In some situations you may have enough information to locate a case by
finding the volume on the shelf. Often, however, you have only a case
name, maybe with a date.

Finding a case by its name is reasonably straightforward, whether in
the library or on your computer.

To locate a case by name or citation you can use any of the following
sources:

- in the *Consolidated Table of Cases (Canadian Abridgment)* in the library;
- on CD-ROMs published by commercial publishers;
- online through Quicklaw, *e*Carswell, or LEXIS; or
- on the Internet on university, government, or court websites.

Although your first impulse may be to head to your computer,
sometimes a quick library search can be faster and less expensive,
particularly if you need an original copy of the published version of the
case.

Source 1: The Consolidated Table of Cases

The *Consolidated Table of Cases (Canadian Abridgment)*, published by Carswell, is a multi-volume table of thousands of reported cases. It includes the titles of almost all published cases in Canada and many British cases. It contains case histories (*e.g.*, appeals) and citations for each case.

Illustration 9.1
Consolidated Table of Cases

THE
CANADIAN ABRIDGMENT
SECOND EDITION

CONSOLIDATED TABLE OF CASES
───
TABLE GÉNÉRALE DE LA JURISPRUDENCE

SUPPLEMENT
MARCH/MARS
2000

VOLUME 1
A – C

Containing all cases digested in the 1999 Supplement to the Canadian Abridgment
Revised Second Edition and [2000] Canadian Current Law – Case Digests issues 1-3.

Reprinted by permission of Carswell, a divison of Thomson Canada Limited.

Illustration 9.2

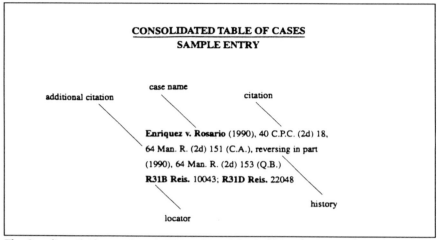

The Canadian Abridgment Second Edition "Consolidated Table of Cases — Supplement March 2000" Volume 1 A-C. Reprinted by permission of Carswell, a division of Thomson Canada Limited.

Illustration 9.1: This is an excerpt from the Consolidated Table of Cases (Canadian Abridgment).

In 1999, a new, cumulative, five-volume set of the *Consolidated Table of Cases* was published. This set of volumes consolidated all of the information on cases up to 1999. Therefore, when searching for cases, there is no need to search volumes published prior to this particular consolidation. A full search for a case citation would involve searching the 1999 volumes and the soft-cover supplements from that date forward. Use of the *Abridgment* is described in more detail below, but the main rule when searching in the *Abridgment* is to search in the hardbound volumes first, then the softbound volumes, then the loose-leaf volumes (*i.e.*, search from oldest to most recent). Once you have located a case citation in the *Abridgment,* it is always advisable to go to the actual case report and make sure the citation is correct. The *Canadian Abridgment* is a major research tool for Canadian law. The *Consolidated Table of Cases* is just one of a host of aids.

Other indexes are available for specific kinds of cases, such as Supreme Court of Canada cases. Two such commercial research aids are the *Supreme Court of Canada Report Service* and *Supreme Court of Canada Decisions*. Both are cumulative tables of cases from the Supreme Court of Canada. Many of these sources are available on CD-ROM and online.

Source 2: CD-ROM

There are many CD-ROMs published that contain collections of cases. Some contain cases identical to those in the print versions of the case reports, while others contain cases relevant to a particular area of law practice. The *Canadian Case Digests* from Carswell is available on CD-ROM.

The advantage of CD-ROMs is that the cases can be searched quickly and are often hyperlinked to other cases, such as appeals, or to statutes. The main disadvantage is that the information quickly becomes out of date. As well, you must be able to formulate a proper search in order to ensure accurate results.

As mentioned in Chapter 5, the main way to search a CD-ROM is to first scan the table of contents and then fill in the blanks in the templates provided. Your search will only be as strong as your ability to accurately choose words that are relevant to your research.

Source 3: Online through Quicklaw, eCarswell, or LEXIS

All of the big three online service providers, Quicklaw, *e*Carswell, and LEXIS, have hundreds of databases of cases: reported, unreported, and in digest form. They also provide research tools to help you construct searches. If you know what database(s) your case is likely to be in, you can do a word search in those databases for a name of one of the parties or search by citation.

All three providers have a simple way to search for a case by case name or citation. This is because lawyers often conduct these particular types of searches. In practical terms this means that you can do a very quick search not having to search through several different databases. The computer will use the citation to search only relevant databases. Refer to Chapter 5 on how to search electronically.

Source 4: Public Access Internet Sites

There are several websites that include collections of cases. However, because the Internet is a relatively recent phenomenon, the cases usually only go back a few years. The other difference between these cases and those provided online through paid service providers is that these cases have often been edited only lightly, if at all, and often do not have summaries or headnotes.

If you are fairly sure about the court that decided your case, you can search the court website, if there is one. At present the following collections of cases are on the Internet:

- Supreme Court of Canada cases from 1989
- Federal Court decisions: reported cases from 1993 and unreported cases from 1996
- B.C. Supreme Court and Court of Appeal decisions from 1996
- Alberta Court of Appeal decisions from January 1998
- Ontario Court of Appeal decisions from June 1998
- P.E.I. Supreme Court decisions from January 1997

A list of websites that have cases available is found in Appendix C to this chapter.

How to Find a Case by Subject

A case is more difficult to locate by subject than by title. As mentioned above, cases are published in a variety of ways in a variety of case reports and in a variety of databases.

Publishers, who recognized this problem, developed aids to assist researchers in finding cases by subject. One publisher, Carswell, has developed a subject classification scheme and has organized its published cases into these classifications. Therefore, researchers need only find the way in which the subject they are researching is categorized in order to find cases in that category.

This may sound easy, but in order to locate a case by subject you must first know the particular subject area and how it is categorized. As you can imagine, this is not an easy task for a person unfamiliar with a particular area of law. Many legal subjects fall into a host of areas of the law; different publishers often categorize the subjects differently and those categorizations may not be consistent with your thinking. To avoid searching under the wrong subject, most researchers read about the law generally to achieve a clearer sense of the way the law is categorized before delving into subject classification schemes and case reports.

The sources used to locate cases by subject are:

- the *Canadian Encyclopedic Digest* or textbooks in the library;
- the *Case Digests (Canadian Abridgment)* in the library;
- CD-ROM case law collections;
- online through Quicklaw, *e*Carswell, or LEXIS; and
- the Internet on university, government, or court websites.

Source 1: The Canadian Encyclopedic Digest and Textbooks

Both the *Canadian Encyclopedic Digest* (CED) and textbooks are summaries or overviews of the law. In Chapter 6, these sources were discussed as means to help researchers identify relevant facts and determine legal issues. Both sources are good starting points for any research situation. In addition to providing a general overview, both the CED and textbooks refer to specific cases and statutes in their discussion of the law.

Typically, researchers use these secondary materials to gain a general understanding of the law, and, at the same time, to gather citations of cases and statutes. These cases often provide a springboard for further case research. Use of these and other secondary materials is discussed in more detail in Chapter 6.

In order to locate a case by subject in the CED, you must find your subject in the classification scheme, which is contained in the first volume called the *Key*. The *Key* is in a thick, single, loose-leaf volume that contains the Contents Key and Index. Both list legal topics, and either is a good starting point for research. The CED is also available on CD-ROM. Very few textbooks are available electronically but more and more journals are becoming available on the Internet.

Source 2: Case Law Digests

The *Canadian Abridgment, Case Digests* is another tool which can be used to locate cases by subject. These *Case Digests*, which were discussed above, are summaries of cases. The entire set of digests includes almost every reported Canadian case and consists of about 130 volumes. These digested cases are arranged by subject pursuant to a classification system very similar to that used in the CED. This is because Carswell is the publisher of both. The CD-ROM version is called *The Abridgment, Canadian Case Digests*.

In order to locate a case by subject in the *Canadian Abridgment*, you must find your subject in the classification scheme, which is contained in the first volume, called the *Key & Research Guide*. The *Key* is a thick, single loose-leaf volume that contains the Classification System and a Subject Titles Table. Both list legal topics, and either is a good starting point for research.

Illustration 9.3
Subject Titles Table

EDITOR'S NOTE: The list of subject titles below is supplemented in the Key by an extensive system of cross-references. The cross-references appear in bold-face and may be of assistance in locating specific topics or related issues. In addition, each subject title includes a Scope Note describing its contents and the location of related issues in other subject titles.

Subject Title	Page
Absentees and Missing Persons	2-1
Actions	2-5
Administrative Law	2-9
Agency	2-17
Aliens, Immigration and Citizenship	2-25
Animals	2-31
Annuities	2-33
Arbitration	2-37
Armed Forces	2-41
Associations	2-47
Auctions and Auctioneers	2-51
Aviation and Aeronautics	2-55
Bailment and Warehousing	2-59
Banking and Banks	2-65
Bankruptcy	2-71
Barristers and Solicitors	2-85
Bills of Exchange	2-93
Boundaries and Surveys	2-103
Bulk Sales	2-107
Burial and Cemeteries	2-111
Carriers	2-115
Charities	2-123
Chattel Mortgages and Bills of Sale	2-127
Choses in Action	2-133

iii   Key & Research Guide 1994-3

The Canadian Abridgment Key and Research Guide, Revised Second Edition. Reprinted by permission of Carswell, a division of Thomson Canada Limited.

Illustration 9.3: This is an excerpt from the Canadian Abridgment Research Guide.

In addition, the *Canadian Abridgment Key & Research Guide* contains a General Index, which is an alphabetical list of legal concepts and key words arising out of the case law digests.

Illustration 9.4
Case Law Digests

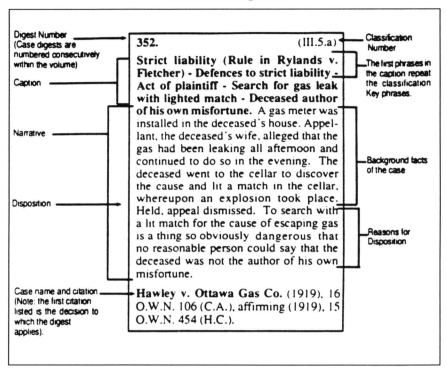

A Short Guide to the Abridgment and Related Products, May 1995. Reprinted by permission of Carswell, a division of Thomson Canada Limited.

Illustration 9.4: This is an excerpt from the Case Digests.

As you can see from Illustration 9.4, these digests are in order by "classification number" (see top right hand of digest: III.5.a). Carswell's classification scheme essentially divides all of Canadian law into a number of subject areas and then assigns each a number. The eight main headings are as follows:

- Commercial Law
- Criminal Law
- Family Law
- International Law
- Procedure and Courts
- Property
- Public Law
- Torts

You can see in Illustration 9.4 that the case of *Hawley v. Ottawa Gas Co.* was classified under III.5.a. If you look in the classification scheme you will see that III.5.a represents the following subjects:

Negligence
III: Strict Liability (rule of *Rylands v. Fletcher*)
5: Defences to strict liability
a: Act of plaintiff

Illustration 9.5
Classification System

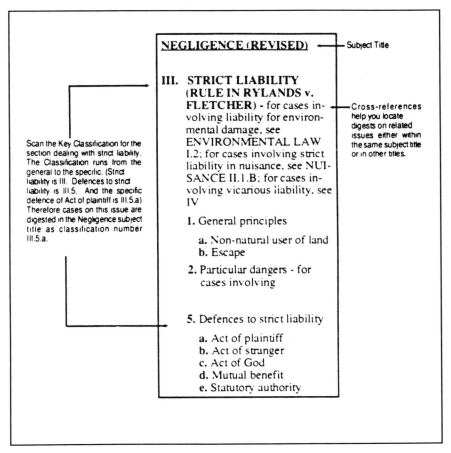

Remember when using the library set of the *Abridgment* you must look in *all* of the following parts:

❑ *Research Guide*: Look in the *Key* and Table of Contents.

❑ *Main Set*: Look under your title (*i.e.*, subject), note the classification number, and refer to the pages.

❑ *Supplements* (softcover): Refer to your classification number.

❑ *Canadian Current Law* – Case Digests and Canadian Case Citations:[1] Look for further updates.

Many Canadian researchers have become frustrated with the *Canadian Abridgment*, arguing that it is too difficult to use because of the number of supplements. This requires explanation. Because the *Canadian Abridgment* is a vital aid to case law research, it is important that researchers understand the underpinnings of the system.

All of the books in the *Canadian Abridgment* are out of date as soon as they are published. Therefore, the publisher must continually update these hardbound volumes with supplements. As soon as the supplements accumulate to a certain point, these supplements are bound. This process is continuous so that each source typically has one original volume or volumes (called the *Main Set*), as well as both hard- and softbound supplements. Periodically, the entire set is consolidated.

As a result of this ongoing process, the researcher is required to look in a number of volumes to find the information needed. As a rule of thumb, the three general steps in using the *Canadian Abridgment* are as follows:

1. Hardbound
2. Softbound
3. Loose-leaf

If you search in each of these volumes, you can ensure that your information is correct and up to date. Carswell has published a research flow chart that describes each of the steps necessary for the three types of research: statute law, case law, and literature. Researchers should have a copy of this flow chart and refer to it as they use the *Canadian Abridgment*.

Source 3: CD-ROM Collections of Cases

There are many CD-ROMs published that contain collections of cases. Some contain cases identical to those in the print versions of the case reports, while others contain cases relevant to a particular area of law practice.

When searching a CD-ROM by subject, the most important skill is formulating your search. Although you can scan a CD-ROM's table of

---

[1]   These are periodicals from Carswell.

contents, it is best to use the templates provided. However, recognize that the searches are usually based on Boolean logic and the particular combination of words you decide to search. Again, your search will only be as strong as your ability to choose words that are relevant to your research.

Source 4: Online through Quicklaw, eCarswell, or LEXIS

Each of the online law service providers, Quicklaw, *e*Carswell, and LEXIS, have hundreds of databases of cases: reported, unreported, and in digest form. When searching by subject you must use the research tools that they provide. Before you construct a search, however, you usually must know what database your case is likely to be in. More information on each of these providers and a sample search for each is in Chapter 5.

Source 5: Public Access Internet Sites

There are several websites that include collections of recent cases. Because these cases are not edited or compiled by publishers, they are not as easy to search as through online law service providers. Nor do they often contain headnotes, so your subject search may be very cumbersome. It is always best to refine your search as much as you can before going online or you may get sunk in all the information available. However, if you are fairly sure about the court that decided your case, you can search the court website if there is one.

How to Update and Note-Up Cases

After you have located the cases that are relevant to your situation, you will need to update them and note them up. This means ensuring that the cases are still "good law" and requires:

- Updating: Find the history of the cases. Have they been appealed or overturned?
- Noting-up: Find the judicial treatment of the cases. Have they been considered in other cases, and have these cases overruled it or followed it, etc.?

There are two paper-based research aids specifically designed to answer these two queries: "tables of cases", which list all decided cases and their history, and "case citators," which list all cases and their history and treatments (how they were considered in other cases). The two main Canadian sources are published by Carswell.

- To update, use the *Consolidated Table of Cases (Canadian Abridgment)*.
- To note-up, use the *Canadian Case Citations (Canadian Abridgment)*.

Tables of Cases

The *Consolidated Table of Cases* lists alphabetically almost every Canadian case, the history of the case, and citations. It is typically used to locate the citation of a case or to find out if a case has been appealed. It is now available on CD-ROM.

Some individual case reports also have indexes that provide information about the history and judicial treatment of cases. A researcher could consult case tables in those case reports where a case would likely be reported to locate this information. For example, if looking for a British Columbia tort case, a researcher might look in *British Columbia Law Reports* (B.C.L.R.) or *Canadian Cases on the Law of Torts* (C.C.L.T.).

Citators

The main tools used to update or note-up cases are called citators. These citators are lists of cases that are compiled by editors. Under each case there is information about whether the case has been appealed (history) and how the case has been considered in other cases (treatment). These tools greatly assist the ability of our courts to apply the rule of precedent.

The only cross-Canada citator is called *Canadian Case Citations (Canadian Abridgment)*. It consists of a set of ten hardbound volumes and supplements. It contains two types of information: prior and subsequent history (*e.g.*, the prior or subsequent treatment of that case in a lower or higher court), and treatment of the case by other cases.

Illustration 9.6
Canadian Case Citations

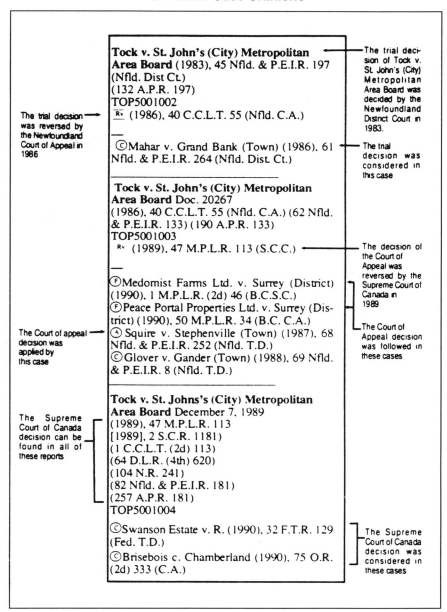

Tock v. St. John's (City) Metropolitan Area Board (1983), 45 Nfld. & P.E.I.R. 197 (Nfld. Dist Ct.)
(132 A.P.R. 197)
TOP5001002
Rv (1986), 40 C.C.L.T. 55 (Nfld. C.A.)

The trial decision of Tock v. St. John's (City) Metropolitan Area Board was decided by the Newfoundland District Court in 1983.

The trial decision was reversed by the Newfoundland Court of Appeal in 1986

©Mahar v. Grand Bank (Town) (1986), 61 Nfld. & P.E.I.R. 264 (Nfld. Dist Ct.)

The trial decision was considered in this case

Tock v. St. John's (City) Metropolitan Area Board Doc. 20267
(1986), 40 C.C.L.T. 55 (Nfld. C.A.) (62 Nfld. & P.E.I.R. 133) (190 A.P.R. 133)
TOP5001003
Rv (1989), 47 M.P.L.R. 113 (S.C.C.)

The decision of the Court of Appeal was reversed by the Supreme Court of Canada in 1989

The Court of appeal decision was applied by this case

ⒻMedomist Farms Ltd. v. Surrey (District) (1990), 1 M.P.L.R. (2d) 46 (B.C.S.C.)
ⒻPeace Portal Properties Ltd. v. Surrey (District) (1990), 50 M.P.L.R. 34 (B.C. C.A.)
ⒶSquire v. Stephenville (Town) (1987), 68 Nfld. & P.E.I.R. 252 (Nfld. T.D.)
©Glover v. Gander (Town) (1988), 69 Nfld. & P.E.I.R. 8 (Nfld. T.D.)

The Court of Appeal decision was followed in these cases

Tock v. St. Johns's (City) Metropolitan Area Board December 7, 1989
(1989), 47 M.P.L.R. 113
[1989], 2 S.C.R. 1181)
(1 C.C.L.T. (2d) 113)
(64 D.L.R. (4th) 620)
(104 N.R. 241)
(82 Nfld. & P.E.I.R. 181)
(257 A.P.R. 181)
TOP5001004

The Supreme Court of Canada decision can be found in all of these reports

©Swanson Estate v. R. (1990), 32 F.T.R. 129 (Fed. T.D.)
©Brisebois c. Chamberland (1990), 75 O.R. (2d) 333 (C.A.)

The Supreme Court of Canada decision was considered in these cases

A Short Guide to The Abridgment and Related Products, May 1995, Chapter 4 "To Find The History And Judicial Treatment Of A Case ('Updating' or 'Noting Up' A Case)." Reprinted by permission of Carswell, a divison of Thomson Canada Limited.

Illustration 9.7
Symbols Used in Canadian Case Citations

| Af | **Affirmed/judicial review refused** *Same decision affirmed on appeal or application for judicial review of same case refused* |

| Am | **Amended** *Same decision amended or altered by court* |

| Ar | **Additional reasons** *Additional reasons for same decisions are located at* |

| La | **Leave to appeal allowed** *Same decision to be considered by court of appeal* |

| Lr | **Leave to appeal refused** *Leave to appeal from same decision refused* |

| Rf | **Referred for further consideration/clarification** *Same decision referred back to lower level for further consideration/clarification* |

| Rg | **Reconsideration/rehearing granted** *Application for reconsideration or rehearing granted* |

| Rr | **Reconsideration/rehearing refused** *Application for reconsideration or rehearing refused* |

| Rv | **Reversed** *Same decision reversed on appeal or on reconsideration* |

| St | **Set aside/quashed** *Same decision set aside or quashed* |

| Vr | **Varied** *Same decision varied or modified on appeal or on reconsideration* |

( ) **Parallel citation** *Brackets are used to denote an additional citation for the same decision*

(F) **Followed** *Principle of law in cited decision binding*

(A) **Applied** *Principle of law in cited decision followed but not binding*

(D) **Distinguished** *Principle of law inapplicable because of difference in facts*

(N) **Not followed/overruled** *Cited decision expressly overruled or not applied*

(C) **Considered** *Some consideration given to cited decision*

A Short Guide to The Abridgment and Related Products, May 1995, Chapter 4. Reprinted by permission of Carswell, a divison of Thomson Canada Limited.

Illustration 9.6 and 9.7: The entries in Canadian Case Citations and the symbols used in them are set out in the these illustrations.

This citator is now available on CD-ROM and through *e*Carswell. There are a few differences between the print and the electronic version. Quicklaw and LEXIS both have an online case citators that compete with *e*Carswell. Quicklaw's is called QuickCite. It was originally created by

McGraw Hill Ryerson as CanCite. The LEXIS citator is called FirstCite and it was originally compiled by Canada Law Book.

Electronic citators can be used two ways.

Method 1: If you are in the case you need, you can select the citator function and you will be hyperlinked to all the history and judicial treatment of this case.

Method 2: If you go directly into the particular citator database you can do a word search for your case. Just as in the paper version it will list all those cases that mentioned your case.

There are other case citators that cover distinct areas of law that are equally useful. For example, the *Canadian Criminal Code Annotation Service* lists cases that have considered cases originally reported in *Dominion Law Reports*, as does the *Dominion Law Reports Annotation Service*.

How to Write a Case Citation

The citation of cases is fairly rigid. This is primarily because each component of the citation is necessary to enable a person to locate a case.

An example of a case citation is as follows:

Style of Cause	Date	Volume	Case Report	Series	Page	Court
↓	↓	↓	↓	↓	↓	↓
Jones v. Gas Co.	(1980),	2	D.L.R.	(2d)	555	(B.C.C.A.)

The following are some basic rules of case citation. For detailed rules of citation it is best to refer to a specific book on the topic.

Style of Cause

The style of cause is the title of the case or the names of the parties involved in the action. Some of the rules of citation of the style of cause are as follows:

- Always underline or italicize style of cause.
- Do not use full names of parties.
- Refer to the Crown as *R.*
- *Re* means "References" or "in the matter of a party named." These cases are usually applications to a court for an opinion or interpretation of someone's rights.
- Omit "the" before most styles of cause.
- *Ex Parte* means "on application of a party who is not present."
- In some family matters only initials are given (*e.g., M. v. L.*).

Date/Year

The year in the citation means either the date the case was published or the date of judgment.

If there are round brackets around the year, it means the date of judgment. If only round brackets are in the citation, you also need the volume number to locate the case. Square brackets are used to enclose the year of publication. In some cases it may be necessary to include both square and round brackets.

Volume

The volume is the number of the volume in which the case is published. Some reports resume numbering at volume 1 at the beginning of each year. Citations to these reports will have a year in square brackets followed by a volume number.

Case Report

The title of the case report is abbreviated. There are specific books in the library that provide the abbreviation of case reports.[2] Do not try to guess what the abbreviation is.

Series

The series number is an essential piece of information. Many case reports have several series spanning many years (*e.g.*, 1st, 2d, and 3d series). When citing a case report, you must cite the series in brackets after the title (*e.g.*, D.L.R. (2d)).

Page

The citation includes the page at which the report begins. If you are referring to a specific page within a case, include that page number at the end of the citation, preceded by "at" (*e.g.*, 434 at 437).

---

[2]   *E.g.*, J.A. Yogis *et al.*, *Legal Writing and Research Manual*, 5th ed. (Toronto: Butterworths, 2000); *Canadian Guide to Uniform Legal Citation*, 4th ed. ("the McGill Guide") (Scarborough: Carswell, 1998); and Carswell's *Canadian Abridgment, Consolidated Table of Cases*, at the beginning of Volume 1.

Court

The court is also part of the citation, and each court has its own particular citation (*e.g.*, B.C.C.A. stands for the British Columbia Court of Appeal). If the court is obvious from the title of the report, then the court does not need to be included in the citation (*e.g.*, S.C.R. includes only decisions of the Supreme Court of Canada).

Parallel or Alternate Citations

A parallel or alternate cite is another citation of the same case in a different case report. This is to assist those who may only have access to certain case reports.

The date does not need to be repeated in an alternate cite, but square bracketed years must be included when they are necessary to locate the case by volume. Alternate citations are separated by a comma.

Punctuation

General Rules about Punctuation in Citation	
Comma	Precedes date in square brackets Follows date of round brackets Between parallel citations
Period	After all abbreviations At end of citation
Brackets	Around date (round if date of judgment; square if date of volume) Around court Around series
Underline or italicize	Style of cause only
Semicolon	Between citations of different cases

History of a Case

The history of a case is the course of a case through all levels of appeal. Prior history means all that happened before. Subsequent history means all that happened after.

Use of *sub nom.*

The term *sub nom.* is the abbreviation for the Latin *sub nomen*, meaning "under the name of." It implies that the case also has an alternate title. In the citation, this other name appears in round brackets before the name of the case report in which it appears.

For example, *W. v. R.* (1984), [1985] 1 W.W.R. 122, (*sub nom. Re Walton and A.G. of Canada*) 13 D.L.R. (4th) 379 (Ont. C.A.).

Self Test

The following is a self test based on the information provided in this chapter. The answers to these questions are found at the back of the book in the "Answers to Self Tests" section.

1. Describe what a case report is.
2. Name a few case reports.
3. Name a research aid that assists in locating a case by name.
4. Name a research aid that assists in locating a case by subject.
5. What does "updating" a case mean?
6. Name a research aid that assists in updating a case.

Sample Exercises — Finding and Updating Cases

Objectives

At the end of this exercise you should be able to:

* Locate cases by title
* Locate cases by subject using the *Canadian Abridgment, Case Digests*
* Locate case reports
* Update and note-up cases
* Cite cases properly

Instructions

* Do background reading on how to locate, update, and cite cases.
* Keep a record of all the steps and the time taken to complete the exercise.

Find Cases By Title

Go to the *Canadian Abridgment, Consolidated Table of Cases* and give the proper citation for the following case. Provide an alternate citation as well.

Berwick v. Canada Trust Co. (S.C.C.)

Citation:

Alternate citation:

Find Cases by Subject Using the Case Digests (*Canadian Abridgment*)

Read the following research situation and answer the following questions.

Research Situation

Ms. Keener

Your client, Ms. Keener, a recent graduate from law school, has been going through the articling interview process over the last few weeks. She has received no offers and, although she admits that there is a recession, she has recently become suspicious of the interviewing process. In particular, at her last two interviews, she was asked whether she had ever been to a psychiatrist or suffered from any mental disorder. Being an honest person, Ms. Keener told both interviewers that she had indeed been to a shrink and has a family history of mental disorders. She has asked you to find her some case law that defines discrimination in order to determine whether her human rights have been violated.

Questions

1. Before entering the library, brainstorm for possible legal subject areas. List five or more words relating to the above research situation that you might search for in the library.

    Words:

2. Go to the *Canadian Abridgment, Key & Research Guide* and look at the section entitled Key Classification System. Find subjects relevant to the research situation. List one or two relevant subject titles, and also their subtitles and reference numbers (*e.g.*, Negligence; III. Strict Liability; 5. Defences; a. Act of Plaintiff).

    Titles; Subtitles; Reference Numbers:

3. Using these key classification numbers go to the multi-volume set of
    Canadian Abridgment, Case Digests and find the volume that
    contains your subject. Within that volume, find a case that appears
    to discuss your research situation. Give the citation for that case.
    Recall that you must look in the hard- and softbound volumes

    Citation:

Find Case Reports Using the *Canadian Abridgment, Canadian Case Citations*

Go to relevant case report and then the *Canadian Abridgment, Canadian
Case Citations* and give citations for the following cases.

1. [1973] 4 W.W.R. 417.

    Citation:

2. (1976), 12 O.R. (2d) 253.

    Citation:

    Alternate Citation:

3. (1982), 139 D.L.R. (3d) 407.

    Citation:

    Alternate Citation:

Find the History of a Case

Go to the *Canadian Abridgment, Canadian Case Citations* and list the courts
that heard the following case. Provide one citation for each level of court
that heard the case, starting with the highest level of court.

> *Industrial Acceptance Corp v. Canada Permanent Trust Co.* (Supreme
> Court of Canada)

Courts:

Citation one (S.C.C.):
Citation two (S.C.C.):
Citation three (S.C.C.):
Citation four (N.B.C.A.):
Citation five (N.B.K.B.):

Find Cases Judicially Considered

Go to the *Canadian Abridgment, Canadian Case Citations* and give the citation for the case by the Alberta Queens Bench that discussed *Slavutych v. Baker*, [1976] 1 S.C.R. 254.

Citation:

Answers to Exercises

Find Cases By Title

> *Berwick v. Canada Trust Co.* [1948] S.C.R. 151.
>
> Alternate citation: [1948] 3 D.L.R. 81 (S.C.C.).

Find Cases By Subject Using the Case Digests (Canadian Abridgment)

1. Human Rights; Discrimination; Employment; Labour; Articling.

2. Human Rights; III. What Constitutes Discrimination; 7. Handicap; b. Mental Handicap; ii. Mental Disorder (or III.7.b.ii.).

3. *Niagara North Condominium Corp. No. 46 v. Chassie* (1999), 23 R.P.R. (3d) 25, 173 D.L.R. (4th) 524 (Ont. Gen. Div.).

Find Case Reports Using the Canadian Abridgment, Canadian Case Citations

1. *Bank of Montreal v. Sperling Hotel Co.*, [1973] 4 W.W.R. 417 (Man. Q.B.).

   Alternate Citation: (1973), 36 D.L.R. (3d) 130 (Man. Q.B.).

2. *Mahood v. Hamilton-Wentworth (Region) Commissioners of Police* (1976), 12 O.R. (2d) 253 (Ont. H.C.).

   Alternate Citation: (1976), 68 D.L.R. (3d) 437 (Ont. H.C.).

3. *Sherwood v. Sherwood* (1982), 139 D.L.R. (3d) 407 (N.S.T.D.).

   Alternate Citation: (1982), 29 R.F.L. (2d) 374; *or* (1982), 52 N.S.R. (2d) 631; *or* (1982), 106 A.P.R. 631.

Find the History of a Case

Courts: Supreme Court of Canada (3 times), New Brunswick Court of
           Appeal, and New Brunswick King's Bench.

Citation one :   [1932] S.C.R. 661 (reversed)
Citation two :   [1931] S.C.R. 652 (set aside)
Citation three: [1931] S.C.R. 503 (refused leave)
Citation four: [1931] 4 D.L.R. 348 (N.B.C.A.) (affirmed)
Citation five: [1931] 2 D.L.R. 663 (N.B.K.B.)

This is a good exercise because it is such a complicated example. These
are five decisions by five courts about the same situation. The case was
first heard in the N.B.K.B. and then the N.B.C.A. It was considered by
three different sittings because leave was sought, refused, then overturned, and eventually heard.

Find Cases Judicially Considered

Dudley v. Jane Doe (1997), 53 Alta. L.R. (3d) 272 (Alta. Q.B.).

Appendix A: Format of a Printed Decision

1. The *style of cause* names the parties in the case. The name of the plaintiff (or on an appeal the name of the appellant) appears first.

2. The *name of the court* that decided the case.

3. The *name of the judge or judges*.

4. The *date of the judgment* is the date that the judgment was handed down, not the date it was heard or published.

5. The *keywords* classify the issues in the case. They are selected by publishers to fit a subject classification scheme.

6. The *headnote* is a brief summary of the case. It is written by the editors of the case report.

7. The list of *authorities* is those sources referred to by the court (e.g., cases, statutes, and literature).

8. The *history of the case* advises where the case originated.

9. The *names of counsel are the lawyers* representing the parties in the case.

10. The *name of the judge* who delivered or wrote the decision.

BUDAI v. ONTARIO LOTTERY CORP.

Ontario High Court of Justice, Divisional Court, O'Leary J., January 20, 1983.

Torts — Negligent misstatement — Plaintiff wrongly informed that he had won lottery prize — Plaintiff spending money to celebrate — Whether defendant liable for prize or for money spent.

The plaintiff was, because of a computer error, wrongly informed by the defendant that he had won \$835.40 in a lottery. He spent \$480 U.S. in an evening's celebration, but was informed the next day of the error. An action for the \$835.40 succeeded at trial. On appeal to the Divisional Court, held, allowing the appeal in part, the plaintiff had not, by the rules of the lottery, won the prize. However, the defendant was liable for negligently misinforming him, the extent of the liability being the money lost by the plaintiff in reliance on the misstatement, in this case \$480 U.S.

Statutes referred to

Ontario Lottery Corporation Act, R.S.O. 1980, c. 344

Rules and regulations referred to

O. Reg. 251/75, s. 9 (now R.R.O. 1980, Reg. 719, s. 8)

APPEAL from a judgment in favour of the plaintiff in an action for a lottery prize.

K. C. Cancellera, for appellant, defendant, Ontario Lottery Corporation
Robert Roth, for *amicus curiae*.
No one appearing for respondent, plaintiff, Jim Budai.

O'Leary J.:—This appeal involves the question of the right of the purchaser of a lottery ticket, who has been incorrectly and negligently told by the lottery operator that he is a winner, to collect from that operator some or all of the amount he was incorrectly told he had won where, prior to learning of the error he has squandered part of his expected winnings.

The appeal is brought by the defendant, Ontario Lottery Corporation, from the judgment dated February 29, 1980, of His Honour Deputy Judge D. Ceri Hugill, wherein he awarded the plaintiff the sum of \$835.40. The plaintiff, at a cost to him of \$7, in effect purchased seven tickets on a lottery operated by the defendant...

Appendix B: Checklist: How to Find and Update a Case

How to Find a Case by Name or Citation

❑ Use any of the following sources:

- The *Consolidated Table of Cases (Canadian Abridgment)* in the library
- CD-ROM sets of case law
- Online through Quicklaw, *e*Carswell, or LEXIS
- Internet on university, government, or court websites

❑ Select the source.

❑ Search for your specific citation.

- Look through the alphabetical listing, or
- Use the electronic templates or search boxes provided.

How to Find a Case by Subject

❑ The most direct way to identify relevant cases is through secondary materials.

❑ While reading these sources, note those cases that are cited and other cases that are referred to in those cases. The following are some main sources:

- The *Canadian Encyclopedic Digest*, textbooks, and periodicals (discussed in Chapter 6). Locate and read any of these sources to get an overview of your subject area.
- The *Canadian Abridgment, Case Digests*.

❑ Look at the *Key & Research Guide* and figure out how your subject is categorized in the key classification scheme.

❑ Find the volumes of case digests on that subject.

❑ Read the digests and record the citations of relevant cases, and locate those cases.

Electronic Cases

❏ Once you have a general sense of your subject, you can do a word search in any of the electronic case law databases.

❏ It is best to search in digests before going to full-text databases.

❏ Although full-text cases can be found on CD-ROM and on the Internet, it is best not to search by subject in electronic cases until you have completely refined your word search. Ideally you will know the exact cases you are looking for. Otherwise you will spend significant time searching several databases that contain thousands of cases. See instructions on electronic searches in Chapter 5.

How to Update and Note-Up a Case

❏ You must ensure that your cases have not been overturned by a higher court (*i.e.*, history) or considered adversely in another case (*i.e.*, judicial consideration).

❏ The best place to look for the basic history of a case is in the *Canadian Abridgment, Consolidated Table of Cases* in the library.

❏ The best place to look for cases that have considered other cases is in case citators.

❏ The main Canadian law citator is the *Canadian Abridgment, Canadian Case Citations*. There are a few case citators on CD-ROM.

❏ All online service providers have their own case citator. You can use them in two ways: by going into the citator database and searching, or by hyperlinking to the citator from the case that you are currently in.

❏ For further updating, check with the courts (on the Internet if available) to find out whether more recent cases have been decided.

Appendix C: Courthouse Electronic Cases

Jurisdiction	URL
Supreme Court of Canada	http://www.lexum.umontreal.ca/csc-scc/en/index.html
Federal Court	http://www.cmf.gc.ca
British Columbia	http://www.courts.gov.bc.ca
Alberta	http://www.albertacourts.ab.ca/
Saskatchewan	http://www.lawsociety.sk.ca
Manitoba	http://www.jus.gov.mb.ca
Ontario	http://www.ontariocourts.on.ca
Quebec	http://www.soquij.qc.ca/jugements/
Newfoundland	Not available as of January 2001.
Prince Edward Island	http://www.gov.pe.ca/courts/
Nova Scotia	Not available as of January 2001.
New Brunswick	Not available as of January 2001.
Yukon	Not available as of January 2001.
Northwest Territories	http://www.andornot.com/nwt/
Nunavut	Not available as of January 2001.

Introduction to Legal Analysis 10

After gathering the relevant law, researchers must review it and make sense of it. This skill is referred to as legal analysis and involves reading the law, interpreting it, and applying it to the facts.

"Thinking like a lawyer" is a skill improves that with practise. Each of the skills of reading, interpreting, and applying the law are continually learned throughout law school, professional legal training, and in practice. However, since new legal researchers often have not yet developed these skills before they are required to conduct research, this chapter serves as a basic introduction to the skill of legal analysis.

Legal analysis requires researchers to construct a picture of the law and apply this picture to a set of facts. This chapter explains how to analyze cases and statutes and how cases build upon each other and combine with statutes to form the law. It teaches legal analysis in a direct and simple manner and is not intended to replace the long-term development of legal analysis skills.

Learning Objectives

At the end of this chapter you will be able to:

- Describe the doctrines of precedent and *stare decisis*
- Name the three basic levels of court in Canada
- Name the three steps in case analysis
- Define what is meant by synthesizing the law
- Explain what "distinguishing between cases" is
- Name a rule of statutory interpretation

Case Analysis

The ultimate goal of research is to find cases and statutes that are relevant to a particular situation, analyze them, and apply them to that situation.

Analysis of cases involves determining the relevance of cases, reading these cases, and synthesizing them into a statement of law. It involves asking the following questions about the cases you find:

- Does the decision apply to the situation? (determining relevance of cases)
- What does the decision say? (reading cases)
- What does the decision mean? (synthesizing cases)

Determining Relevance of Cases

The first step in case analysis is determining whether the cases you have found apply to your situation or will be considered relevant by a court.

Relevant cases are those that have similar facts and issues and are persuasive or binding on the court that is likely to hear the case if it goes to trial.

Therefore, determining the relevance of cases involves determining which cases are similar, binding, or persuasive. An understanding of the system of common law and the Canadian court system is necessary to be able to determine relevance.

The Common Law

The system of common law developed through the use of precedents or decided cases. Precedents were, and continue to be, used as examples or authorities to assist judges in deciding cases.

From the system of precedent evolved the doctrine of *stare decisis*, which literally means "to stand by the decision." *Stare decisis* requires courts to follow prior decisions of courts from the same jurisdiction to the extent that those cases have similar facts and issues.

The doctrines of precedent and *stare decisis* promote consistency in law, ensure certainty, and provide tools to predict the likely outcome of a case. A coherent body of law results if these doctrines are applied consistently.

The Court System

The court system in Canada is structured in tiers of increasing authority. The courts form a hierarchy, whereby appeals from lower courts are heard by the higher courts and lower courts are bound by the decisions of higher courts. In Canada, there are three levels of courts: trial level, appellate level, and court of last resort. Each province has a trial and an appeal court. The court of last resort is the Supreme Court of Canada.

Trial courts are courts of original jurisdiction. This means they are the first courts to hear cases and make determinations about both fact and law. Often trial courts are divided by type of claim, amount of claim, or territorial jurisdiction. For example, the provincial court in British

Columbia consists of the following divisions: Family Court, Criminal Court, and Small Claims Court.

Appellate courts hear appeals from trial courts. They do not, as a rule, review factual determinations of trial courts, but review errors of law. There is no trial *per se* in the appellate court since no evidence is heard. The court instead reviews written briefs on the law (*i.e.*, factums) and hears arguments only.

The court of last resort in Canada is the Supreme Court of Canada. Prior to 1949 the court of last resort was the British Privy Council. Nowadays, the Supreme Court of Canada hears cases that are appealed from the various appeal courts. It also hears cases that are specifically referred to it for a determination about the meaning or application of a law. These are called "references."

There is also a federal court system that deals exclusively with federal matters, such as immigration and tax law. The system includes a trial and an appeal level: the Federal Court Trial Division and the Federal Court of Appeal. Appeals from this court go to the Supreme Court of Canada.

Illustration 10.1
Canadian Court Structure

Supreme Court of Canada
↗   ↖
Provincial Courts of Appeal   Federal Court of Appeal
↑   ↑
Provincial Trial Level Courts   Federal Court Trial Division

Illustration 10.1: This is a diagram of the Canadian court structure.

In Canada, all courts are bound by decisions of the Supreme Court of Canada and all courts are bound by higher courts in their own jurisdiction. For example, trial courts are bound by appeal court decisions. Appeal courts from one jurisdiction are not bound by appeal courts from another jurisdiction. For example, the British Columbia Court of Appeal does not bind the Alberta Court of Appeal.

Similar, Binding, or Persuasive

Those cases most similar to your legal problem are the best indicators of the likely outcome of your case. In other words, a case's predictive value is greatest when its facts and issues are most similar to yours. The converse is also true.

If a court is compelled to follow a case, that case is considered to be *binding*. There are a number of factors that will determine whether a case is binding on a court: the level of court, the jurisdiction of the court, the history of the case, the judicial consideration of the case, and how current the case is. In other words, when determining whether a case is binding, the following questions should be asked about each case:

Court Level: What is the court level? Is the decision from a higher level court?

Jurisdiction: What is the jurisdiction? Is the decision from the same jurisdiction?

History: What is the history of the decision? Has the decision been appealed or overturned by another court?

Judicial Consideration: Has the decision been considered by another court (*e.g.*, distinguished, applied, or followed)?

Currency: Has the decision been superseded by legislation?

The answers to these questions will not only determine whether a case is binding but will also contribute to the amount of weight the decision will be given by a court. Precedents that are binding are referred to as "mandatory," whereas those that are not binding are referred to as "persuasive." Although not binding, persuasive cases often assist judges in deciding cases. For example, a case from the United States will not be binding on a Canadian court but may be persuasive if the facts and issues are similar.

After selecting relevant cases, the researcher must read them and synthesize them into a coherent whole.

Reading Cases

Reading cases involves some skill. Most cases follow a particular format and, after reading several cases, the researcher should be able to quickly find relevant information without getting bogged down in irrelevant information.

At the most basic level, researchers should be familiar with the format of published cases. A description of this format is provided in Appendix A to Chapter 9. This format is also important for computer research, since computer searches are often conducted by a specific location in the text of reported cases (*e.g.*, by title or date).

Each case is the result of a judge's attempt to move through the research process. Therefore, as you read cases you will learn how to elicit from each case the products of the legal research process: facts, issues, law, analysis, and conclusion. By reading and dissecting cases, researchers enhance their research skills.

Synthesizing Cases

After all the relevant cases have been gathered and read they must be synthesized into a coherent description of the law. Synthesis requires comparing cases, recognizing their similarities and differences, and attempting to weave them together into a single picture of the law. It involves the exploration of the relationships between cases.

Judges do exactly this in their decisions as they apply the rule of precedent. Since similar cases must be decided in a similar manner, a crucial step for judges is to recognize the differences and similarities between the facts and issues of decided cases and the facts and issues of the case before the court.

Synthesis involves briefing cases, comparing them, and then constructing a description of the law.

Briefing Cases

A skill that can greatly assist researchers in synthesizing cases is briefing cases. Most law students become fairly proficient at the skill of summarizing cases into briefs, since much of law school learning is through cases.

Briefing cases involves summarizing cases into short, organized, and easily understandable formats. The basic format of a case brief is as follows:

The Basic Format of a Case Brief

1.	**Style of Cause:**	Name and citation of the case
2.	**Procedural History:**	Previous judicial treatment of case
3.	**Facts:**	Summary of relevant facts in the case
4.	**Issues:**	Specific legal questions that the court must answer
5.	**Decision:**	Disposition by the court of the case
6.	**Reasons:**	Reasons provided by the court for the answers to the legal issues
7.	*Ratio Decidendi:*	Rule of law for which the case stands
8.	**Commentary:**	Dissenting opinions, personal views on the case, and connections to other cases

Attached as Appendix A to this chapter is a sample case brief.

The obvious benefit of a briefed case is that it is in a form that can be quickly reviewed. Case briefs provide snapshots of the law as applied to a particular situation. These snapshots can then be pulled together to form a complete picture of the law.

Comparing Cases

The goal of legal research is to find cases that are so similar that they will predict the results of the current situation.

In order to find similar cases, the facts and issues of each case must be compared to other cases and to the current facts and issues. This is called analogizing and distinguishing. Analogizing is extracting the similarities between the cases. Distinguishing is noting the differences. Analogizing and distinguishing are very important intellectual skills in case analysis.

Whether a case is viewed as similar or different often depends on the level of generality and creativity applied. For example, a case that held that a landlord must supply a tenant with a heater could be considered similar to a situation in which a tenant complained that she had no running water. On the other hand, the case could be seen as fundamentally different because heating is a necessity of life but running water is not.

Often it is useful to gather together all of the case briefs into a one-page schedule.

Illustration 10.2:
Case Comparison Schedule

	Case 1	Case 2	Your Facts
Binding or Persuasive			
Facts			
Issues			
Decision			
Reasons and *Ratio*			
Commentary			

Illustration 10.2: This is a diagram of how a case comparison schedule might look.

When comparing cases, sometimes it is best to compare the decision of the court first and work back through the reasoning of the judge. For example, if the facts and the issues are very similar but the decisions are not, working back through the analysis might enable you to locate the distinguishing features or perhaps the inconsistent approaches taken by different judges. Do not assume, however, that because the decisions are the same that the same analysis was applied.

Constructing a Description of the Law

After comparing the relevant cases, the law should be synthesized into one general statement.

Synthesis involves pulling all the individual relevant cases together to form a complete picture of the law. Synthesis involves finding a collective meaning from the relevant cases. Synthesis does not simply involve describing case after case, but, rather, describing the law as a unified whole. Synthesis weaves the law together like a spider web. The result of synthesis is the development of a new "rule" from all of the cases that have been decided as they apply to your particular fact situation. Synthesis takes practice and is a skill that develops over time.

The difficulty of synthesis is finding common ground among the cases when there are wide-ranging similarities and differences. The following is a simple example of a synthesis.

Example of a Synthesis

Slip and Fall

Facts: A woman slipped and fell on a banana peel on the sidewalk in front of her neighbour's house. The banana had been on the sidewalk for days and had rotted in the sun, making it particularly slippery. She has sued the neighbour for negligence.

Case 1: A man fell on an icy sidewalk of a big department store. The sidewalk had daily been cleared of ice but there had recently been a massive snowfall. The department store was not liable because, although it was foreseeable that such an accident could occur, the store did all it could do to prevent the accident.

Case 2: A boy slipped and fell on an icy sidewalk. The ice was caused by faulty eavestroughs, which dripped water onto the sidewalk. The owner was liable because he could have foreseen the accident and did nothing to prevent it from occurring.

Case 3: An owner posted a sign on her property stating "enter at own risk" because she had flooded her property for irrigation purposes. A man slipped in the mud. The owner was not held liable because she had posted a warning.

Possible Synthesis: An owner or occupier of property will be held liable for injuries that occur on his or her property if the injury was reasonably foreseeable and the owner did nothing to prevent the injury from occurring.

Application to the Facts: The neighbour will likely be liable to the woman who slipped on the banana peel. Because the banana peel had been there for days, it was likely reasonably foreseeable that such an accident might occur. In addition, the owner did nothing to prevent the accident from occurring.

Statute Analysis

The system of common law has been altered significantly by the introduction of statutes. Indeed, some academics have argued that the law in Canada is no longer a true system of common law because of the weighty effect of statutes on almost every area of the law.

Statutes are codifications of the law. They are legal rules set out in legislative form to alter or clarify case law or create new areas of law. They cannot be separated from case law.

The law develops through both the creation of statutes and the interpretation of statutes by the courts in deciding cases. The rule of precedent suggests that the courts must apply statutes similarly to each set of facts.

Similarly to case analysis, statute analysis involves finding relevant statutes, reading these statutes, and interpreting them. It involves asking the following questions about the statutes you find:

- Does the statute apply to the situation? (relevance)
- What does the statute say? (reading statutes)
- What does the statute mean? (interpreting statutes)

Relevance

The first step in statute analysis is to determine whether the statute applies to a particular situation. This entails reading a statute and determining if the legislation was designed to cover the current situation.

Like case analysis, statute analysis involves distinguishing and analogizing the facts. The "facts" in a statute, however, are the words used in the statute. These words describe whether and how the statute applies. These "facts" must exist in order for a statute to apply to a situation. For example, all criminal law offences require that there be an act (*actus rea*) and intent (*mens rea*). Thus, a legal problem must involve both an act and intent to be considered a criminal offence.

Statutes are rules that apply to specific people or activities. If the current situation involves those specific people or activities referred to in the statute, then the statute probably applies. Often statutes have definitions at the beginning of the statute that describe the persons and activities covered in the statute. For example, s. 2 of the British Columbia *Insurance Act*[1] states as follows:

> This Act, except as provided, applies to every insurer that carries on any business of insurance in British Columbia and to every contract of insurance made or deemed made in British Columbia.

---

[1] R.S.B.C. 1996, c. 226, s. 2.

If it is not readily apparent whether the statute applies, you may need to resort to the rules of statutory interpretation described below.

Reading Statutes

If a statute is applicable, you must read those parts of the statute that are relevant.

Most statutes follow a particular format. Recognizing this format will enable researchers to better read and interpret statutes. The six components of a statute are essentially as follows:

1. Long title
2. Chapter number
3. Date of royal assent
4. Short title
5. Definitions
6. Parts, sections and subsections

Statutes are discussed in detail in Chapter 7.

Interpreting Statutes

Statutory interpretation involves some skill. There are three different, and often competing, approaches taken by the courts in interpreting statutes. They are as follows:

Literal or Grammatical Method

The literal or grammatical method of statute interpretation stresses the literal or plain meaning of a statute. This method assumes that complete understanding of the statute can be found within the ordinary meaning of the words of the statute. Therefore, interpretation is restricted to the actual text of the statute.

Aids used to interpret the statute, outside of the text, such as the intent of the legislators and previous versions of the statute, are not considered relevant. Taken to the extreme, this method requires interpretation of the ordinary meaning of the words within the statute even if it leads to an absurdity or inconsistency within the statute. Although the literal method is not appropriate where the wording of a statute is ambiguous, it is still the primary and preferred approach to interpreting statutes.

Contextual Method

The contextual method of statutory interpretation employs the "Golden Rule." This rule allows the court to depart from the literal meaning of a statute if it would lead to absurdity. Contextual interpretation is based on the assumption that statute law is meant to be rational and coherent. All legislation should be internally coherent and each must be coherent with any higher enactments; *e.g.*, a regulation must be coherent with its authorizing statute. Thus, the plain wording of a statute should be interpreted in a manner that will avoid any absurdity or inconsistency.

Purposive Method

Purposive interpretation of a statute gives primary importance to the intent of the legislators, rather than the words used, in enacting the legislation. This approach is called the "Mischief Rule." The original aim of this rule was to determine what mischief the legislators sought to overcome in enacting the legislation and to see that their goal was met. Today purposive interpretation of a statute is not limited to remedying mischief but rather to determining the purpose behind the legislation. With this method, in contrast to a literal interpretation, external aids such as legislative committee reports may be crucial to determining the purpose of the legislation.

Synthesis of the Three Approaches

According to E.A. Dreidger in the *Construction of Statutes*, there is only one approach to statutory interpretation:

> the words of an Act are to be read in their entire context and in their grammatical and ordinary sense harmoniously with the scheme of the Act, the object of the Act, and the intention of Parliament.

Just as important to statutory interpretation are court decisions that have construed statutes. These cases provide the opinions of both lawyers and judges on how the statute applies and what the statute means. The cases can be from other jurisdictions if those jurisdictions have similar statutes.

Thus, when looking at a statute, you should look at the specific words, the entire statute (*i.e.*, context), the history or creation process, the rules of construction of statutes, and cases that have considered the statute.

Because there will always be several interpretations of a statute, the skill required in statutory analysis, like case analysis, is to use analogy to extend or limit the application of the statute. For example, a statute that restricts vehicles from parks may or may not extend to skateboards or roller skates, depending on the interpretation.

This discussion is by no means exhaustive and other tools of interpretation can be found in treatises dealing specifically with statutory interpretation.

A synthesis of the law pertaining to the Paul and Melody situation, which was discussed in prior chapters, looks like this:

Synthesis of Law

Paul and Melody

Statutory law in British Columbia provides that upon marriage breakdown, "family assets" must be shared equally between the marriage partners. Family assets include gifts and inheritances obtained while in the marriage. However, a court may alter this division if the division would be unfair, having regard to a number of factors including "the extent to which property was acquired by one spouse through inheritance or gift." Cases that have interpreted this statute primarily look at whether the gift was intended to become part of the family assets. For example, in those circumstances where a gift of money was kept in a separate bank account and was received fairly close to the time of the marriage breakdown, the gift was not considered to be part of the family assets.

Applying the Law to the Facts

Once the cases and statutes have been read, analyzed, and synthesized, and the researcher has a good understanding of the law, the law may be applied to the current facts. This involves looking at the current facts and attempting to predict what would happen if the situation were brought to trial.

At this point, researchers should place themselves in the position of a judge. This entails looking at the law and stating how and why the law applies to the current facts. However, since researchers are not judges, they should not reach a final decision, but should only provide a best assessment of the outcome. In describing the outcome, words such as "probably" or "likely" should be used to show that the conclusion is only a prediction and not an absolute.

A sample application of the law to the Paul and Melody situation discussed in prior chapters looks like this:

Application of the Law

Paul and Melody

It is likely that Melody will be able to keep the $20,000 gift from her grandmother and not share it with Paul when they separate.

> Although the gift would likely initially be included in the "family assets," which must be shared equally between the marriage partners on marriage breakdown, it is likely that a court would alter this division on the basis that the division of the $20,000 would be unfair. Case law indicates that it would be considered unfair because the money was not intended to become part of the family assets. This is evidenced by the fact that the money was kept in a separate bank account and was received fairly close to the time of the marriage breakdown.[2]

A Word on Policy

When analyzing the law, policy should also be considered. Policy refers to the purpose or intent of the law or the reason behind the law. Policy usually relates to the underlying rights, interests, and obligations the law attempts to protect.

Policy can be used in two ways. It can be used to support the *status quo* or to introduce a change in the law. Often, if a case appears to be unfair, there is an underlying policy reason for the decision. This policy reason may be referred to when comparing cases and reconciling the differences.

As mentioned, courts are concerned with consistency in law and, therefore, will refer to policy in ensuring that the results reflect the intention of the law. But policy is not the law and should be used sparingly in legal analysis.

Self Test

The answers to these questions are found at the end of the book in the "Answers to Self Tests" section.

1. What is the doctrine of precedent?
2. What is meant by *stare decisis*?
3. What are the three basic levels of court in Canada?
4. What are the three steps in case analysis?
5. Define what is meant by "synthesizing the law."
6. What is the "Golden Rule" of statutory interpretation?

---

[2] This is an example only and should not be taken as an accurate description of the law.

Sample Exercise and Answers

Attempt a legal analysis for the following fictional problem by reading the law (statutes and cases), determining its relevance, synthesizing it, and applying it to the following facts.

Problem

Janet Smith

Janet Smith is a single woman who lives alone in Edmonton in a second-floor apartment with a balcony. She was recently the victim of an attempted sexual assault. A series of similar sexual assaults on single women living alone in second- and third-floor apartments with balconies had occurred recently, all within a few blocks of Smith's home. Although the police were aware of the assaults, the investigating constables chose not to warn women at risk, partly for fear of causing hysteria.

It was discovered that the chief of police had reassigned several officers from Ms. Smith's neighbourhood to the downtown area to protect personal property in response to rumors of rioting. As well, the board of police commissioners had decided to allocate funds to public relations rather than to a seminar for police officers entitled "The Female Victim and the Myth of Hysteria."

Question

You have been asked to answer the following question: Did the police constables breach a private law duty of care by failing to take steps to warn Smith about her particular risk from this attacker?

The Law

The following is a brief fictional description of the law relating to the duty of care of police officers. It consists of the *Police Act* and the following four cases.

The *Police Act* applies to all police officers in Alberta. It sets out the duties of a municipal police force and liability for police action. The relevant section of the Act is as follows:

> 21(1) No action for damages lies against a police officer ... for anything said or done or omitted to be said or done in the performance or intended performance of duty or in the exercise of power or for any alleged neglect or default in the performance or intended performance of duty or exercise of power. (fictional)

Four cases that discuss the duty of care of public officials are as follows:

Anders v. Calgary Council (Alta. C.A., 1915) (fictional)

A local building authority was sued when structural damage occurred in a residential building block. Although the building's plans had been approved by the authority, it was discovered that the block had not been constructed in conformity with the plans. Anders, the lessee, alleged that the building authority had a duty to ensure that the building was constructed in accordance with the plans, and that it had been negligent in not inspecting it. The Court of Appeal found that the authority owed a *prima facie* duty of care to the lessees of the building based on the relationship between them; that is, that there was "a sufficient *relationship of proximity* or neighbourhood such that, in the reasonable contemplation of the former, carelessness may have been likely to cause damage to the latter."

R. v. Dorse Boat Co. (H.L., 1930) (fictional)

Several prisoners escaped from custody and stole a yacht, and while escaping collided with the yacht of the plaintiffs. It was alleged that the officers in charge of the prisoners' custody had been negligent in their supervision. The majority of the courts found that the fact that the damage had been caused by third parties did not exempt the officers from a duty of care towards the plaintiffs because of the *foreseeability* of the damage caused as a result of their negligence in supervising the prisoners. A concurring majority decision found that the duty of care arose from the *special relationship* between the officers and the prisoners due to the former's *control* over the latter.

Hall v. Chief Constable of West Sheffield (H.L., 1969) (fictional)

An action was brought against the police by the estate of the last victim of the "Yorkshire Ripper," on the grounds that it was foreseeable that this criminal would commit further offenses against young women in Britain in the future. The court found that the police did not owe a general duty of care to individual members of the public absent a special *relationship of proximity* between the victim and the police, and that the identification of the victim as a young woman was not sufficient to locate her in a special class of persons to whom a private duty was owed. The court further held that the police should not be liable in such a situation.

Air Alaska Disaster Claimants v. Air Alaska (Ont. Dist. Ct., 1988) (fictional)

An action was brought against the police for not preventing, through proper security measures, an aircraft disaster caused by a bomb. The court held that, although a private law duty to the public generally could not be imposed on the police (as decided in *Hall*), this did not exclude the possibility of a duty of care to a more *limited* class of individuals such as the passengers of the aircraft. The court went on to suggest an expansion of the special relationship criteria to include such factors as the *control* that the defendants had over the situation (*i.e.*, the passengers and baggage allowed on board the aircraft), and the fact that they *knew or ought to have known* of the danger to Air Alaska flights.

Step 1: Determining Relevance of Statutes and Cases

The *Police Act* is relevant because it applies to all police officers in Alberta. The particular section of the statute has not been amended or repealed.

The relative relevance of the cases can be determined from the jurisdiction, dates, and court level of each of the cases. The only binding case is the Alberta Court of Appeal Decision, *Anders*. However, it is factually different (and fairly old), so may be fairly easily distinguished. Although two cases are from England, they are persuasive because they discuss duty of care. Therefore, although they are not binding, the court will likely apply them to Janet Smith's situation. *Air Alaska* is the most recent Canadian case and carries some weight in terms of precedent because it is a Canadian case — although an Alberta court is not bound by decisions from Ontario. The case that is most similar in fact to Smith's situation is *Hall*.

Step 2: Synthesizing the Law

Statute law and case law can be restated in a simplified form as follows:

The *Police Act* imposes on police a public duty to protect the public. In this role, the police are immune from liability. However, the common law has established that public officials can be found to have a private law duty of care to members of the public. This occurs in situations in which: there is a prior knowledge of the danger; harm is foreseeable; a special relationship of proximity exists between the police and that particular group or segment of the public; and the police have control over the situation.

In establishing the existence of a private law duty of care for police officers, the law appears to require four main elements: the foreseeability of harm; prior knowledge of the danger; the existence of a special relationship between the police and the member of the public; and control of the situation.

Step 3: Applying the Law to the Facts

An application of the law to Janet Smith's situation looks like this:

It is likely that the police constables owed a duty of care to Janet Smith. The police constables should have foreseen the possibility of another assault on a single woman in Smith's neighbourhood because they knew of the conditions surrounding the previous assaults and of the danger to women in the neighbourhood. The foreseeability of harm caused to a segment of the public is likely enough to establish a "special relationship" between the constables and the women in that neighbourhood, including Smith.

In addition, it is likely that there was a special relationship between the police and Ms. Smith based on Smith's membership in a small and identifiable group of potential victims. Smith and other women like her would likely be recognized by a court as being a sufficiently narrow class of potential victims and, as such, they may fit into the rule outlined in *Air Alaska*. Janet Smith's case can, therefore, be distinguished from *Hall*, for, unlike the "Yorkshire Ripper," for whom all young or fairly young women in Britain were targets, the assailant in this case targeted only single, white women living alone in second- or third-floor apartments with balconies, in Smith's neighbourhood.

There is no "control" factor in Janet Smith's case. No public authority exercised direct control over Smith's attacker. However, it seems unlikely that the lack of control over the assailant will affect the duty owed by the constables, given the extent to which the other elements apply.

Appendix A: Sample Case Brief

Style of Cause

Christie v. Davey, [1893] 1 Chancery Division 316.[1]

Procedural History

No previous judicial action.

Facts

Christie worked as a music teacher and had pupils in her home 17 hours per week. Her daughter, son, and a boarder frequently sang and practised their instruments. Davey had lived in the adjoining semi-detached house for the past three years. He worked out of his home as an engraver and had a musical evening once a week. Davey came to object to the noise from Christie's home and wrote a letter of complaint to Christie. Christie did not respond and the next day Davey began to make shrieking, banging, whistling, and pounding noises whenever Christie commenced musical activity.

Christie filed an action for an injunction to prevent Davey from making noises to annoy or injure Christie. Davey filed a counterclaim to prevent Christie from constant music to injure Davey.

Issue

May the occupier of property engage in an ordinarily legitimate activity on the property if the sole purpose for engaging in the activity is to deliberately annoy the neighbour?

Decision

The court allowed the claim by Christie and an injunction was issued restraining Davey from making noises in his house to annoy Christie, except for noise which resulted from of his engraving trade or his weekly musical evenings, which existed before the dispute.

The court disallowed the counterclaim by Davey finding that Christie's music lessons were not unusual or malicious.

---

[1]   1 Ch. 316, 62 L.J. Ch. 439, 3 R. 210.

Reasons

The court held that Christie was making reasonable use of her home, evidenced by no complaints by Davey in the past three years. Davey was making unusual noises to annoy and disrupt in a deliberate and malicious manner. Davey was not permitted to complain about a legitimate use of Christie's home.

Ratio Decidendi

An occupier of property may not engage in an activity on the property in a manner ordinarily legitimate if the sole purpose of the activity is to deliberately annoy the neighbour.

Comments

No dissenting opinions. The history of the situation and reasons for the noise (*i.e.*, pleasure or intentional annoyance) are important factors. No cases with which to compare.

Legal Writing

11

The final stage in the research process involves writing the results. Writing is a skill that develops over time. With practise, all writers can become more accurate, brief, and clear.

This chapter discusses the basics of good legal writing and introduces a three-stage process of legal writing. It then describes the format of legal writing and discusses two devices by which the law is communicated: the legal memorandum and the opinion letter.

Learning Objectives

At the end of this chapter you will be able to:

- Name a few rules of good writing
- List the three stages in the legal writing process
- Describe the five parts of a memorandum of law
- Explain the order in which to revise writing
- Describe the form of a typical opinion letter

Good Legal Writing

Good legal writing is accurate, brief, and clear. Good writers use plain English and target their writing to their readers. Although a lot has been written about the use of plain language in the law, the essential ideas are well articulated by Richard Wydick in his book *Plain English for Lawyers*.[1] Wydicks' six basic rules are as follows:

1. Omit surplus words.
2. Use familiar, concrete words.
3. Use short sentences.
4. Use base ve bs and the active voice.
5. Arrange words with care.
6. Avoid language quirks.

---

[1] Durham, N.C.: Carolina Academic Press, 1985.

Legal writing involves not only good basic writing skills, but, more specifically, the ability to write about the law. This may sound self-evident, but many lawyers who are good writers and knowledgeable about the law are still often unable to convey the law in a clear and concise manner.

Because legal writing is the articulation or written expression of legal thought, it requires all of the skills of good writing plus an ability to put the law in a form that is understandable. As researchers learn more about the law, their ability to communicate it improves: clearer thinking leads to clearer writing. However, before researchers can put pen to paper, they should have a general understanding of the process of legal writing and the way in which the law is usually articulated (*i.e.*, the form of legal writing).

The Process of Legal Writing

The process of legal writing, like other writing, has three basic stages:

1.   Planning
2.   Writing
3.   Revising

Stage 1: Planning

Planning involves the following four steps:

Step 1: Identify the reader;
Step 2: Determine the purpose of the writing;
Step 3: Gather, analyze, and organize the information; and
Step 4: Prepare an outline.

The following situation provides an example of the four-step planning process:

Scenario

A biology professor is deciding which first-year biology textbook to purchase and use in her first-year university biology class. You are a Ph.D. candidate in biology and the professor has asked you to review the available books and recommend one. She wants a book that is easy to read, inexpensive, and includes all of the topics that should be taught in a first-year biology course.

Step 1: Identify the Reader. The reader of your response is a biology professor who is very busy. It is likely that she expects thoroughness as well as conciseness. She will be familiar with the language of biologists and may even be familiar with some of the more popular biology textbooks.

Step 2: Determine the Purpose. The purpose of the project is to select a textbook to be used in a first-year biology class. The textbook should be easy to read, inexpensive, and cover all first-year biology topics. You must provide enough information to enable the professor to make an informed decision.

Step 3: Gather, Analyze, and Organize the Information. It is likely that you will go to a book store and contact publishers to gather information about first-year biology books available. Once you have gathered this information, you will be able to formulate a list of all of the books and organize and summarize the information. This information could then be organized into a schedule indicating the differences between the various options.

Step 4: Prepare an Outline. Once you have summarized all the information, you must decide how you will present it. Drafting an outline will enable you to put your ideas in order.

The following are samples of two potential outlines for the above example.

Sample Outline A:

1. Introduction
2. Body
   a. Book 1: Ease of reading, cost, and topics covered
   b. Book 2: Ease of reading, cost, and topics covered
   c. Book 3: Ease of reading, cost, and topics covered
3. Conclusion

Sample Outline B

1. Introduction
2. Body
   a. Ease of reading: Books 1, 2, and 3
   b. Cost: Books 1, 2, and 3
   c. Topics Covered: Books 1, 2, and 3
3. Conclusion

Beginning researchers often do not spend enough time on planning. New researchers should avoid the temptation to begin writing before the planning process is complete. Each of the four steps of planning are described here in more detail as they relate to legal writing.

Step 1: Identify the Reader

Writers should always keep in mind who their readers are. Identifying the audience enables a writer to focus on an audience's particular wants and needs and adjust the content, organization, and style accordingly. It also gives specific purpose and direction to writing. Some questions that might be asked in order to identify readers are:

- Who are the potential readers?
- How much do the readers already know about the subject?
- What do the readers want or expect in the writing?
- How busy are the readers?
- What are the readers' ages, gender, language, education, etc.?

Step 2: Determine the Purpose

Determining how writing will ultimately be used and why a topic is being researched enables writers to convey the information in ways that are practical and useful. For example, if the writing is to be used in preparation for a trial, it will be written persuasively; whereas if the writing is to be used to advise a client, it will be written objectively and informatively. The following examples of audiences and purposes of writing indicate how the audience and purpose affect writing:

Types of Writing, Audiences, and Purposes				
	Poetry	**Exams**	**Legal Memo**	**Opinion Letter**
Audience	Public	Professor	Lawyer	Client
Purpose	Inspire	Assess	Inform	Advise

Each purpose requires a different type of writing in terms of content, form, and organization.

Although readers of legal writing will often be other lawyers, it is advisable not to assume that these lawyers are knowledgeable about the research topic. As you delve into the law, you become somewhat of an expert. Therefore, it is good practice to always introduce the subject at a basic level and work towards the more complicated, as if you were giving instruction about the law. There is some skill involved in deciding in how much detail of the basics should be discussed.

Step 3: Gather, Analyze and Organize the Information

After identifying the purpose of the writing and the readers, researchers should gather together the law, read it, and attempt to make sense of it.

At this stage, relevant statutes and cases should be briefed and important concepts and quotations should be noted. The cases should be organized in terms of importance and relevance. This step is described in detail in Chapter 9.

Step 4: Prepare an Outline

The use of an outline cannot be overemphasized.

Researchers who develop comprehensive outlines spend significantly less time later at the writing stage. Although it is often difficult to hold back from writing, the benefits of doing so are numerous. Without an outline, your thoughts are less organized and it is difficult to be objective about them. Using an outline will encourage you to be more critical of your words and ideas. Outlines have other advantages. Drafting an outline:

- Highlights gaps and overlaps in information and discussion;
- Indicates where each case and statute will be discussed and the connections between each;
- Shows logical inconsistencies; and
- Forces you to stay on track and to be systematic and logical.

An outline should include all issues, ideas, and law in tabulated form. It should, ideally, fit onto one page and refer to cases and statutes in support of each proposition.

Stage 2: Writing

Writing involves describing the law and its application to the facts in a comprehensive and concise way. If you prepare a solid outline, you will know prior to writing what you generally want to say and how it will be organized. Therefore, the focus at the writing stage is on putting thoughts into words and connecting the thoughts together into a whole.

The first attempt at writing should be a fast, rough draft and should not take as much time as either planning or revising. Lawyers often dictate a first draft. This enables them to quickly get thoughts down and recite quotes from the actual text of cases without rewriting entire quotations. It is recommended that the entire first draft be written in one sitting — even if in point form — so that there is some flow to thoughts.

It is not necessary to wait until your analysis of the law is perfect before beginning your writing. Often thoughts become clearer as they are put into writing. It is important not to get caught up in words at this particular stage. Instead, focus on content and organization. Put everything you want to say in writing and edit it later.

Content

What you decide to include in your writing will obviously depend on a number of factors, such as time, complexity of the law, and the nature of the problem. For example, if a researcher has only one hour to find an answer to a legal problem, the written response may be only one page. However, if a researcher has a week and the law is particularly complex, it is likely that a comprehensive analysis will be more than just a few pages.

How Many Cases to Include

One of the most common questions of the novice researcher is: How many cases should I include and how much should I say about each case?

You should include as many cases as are necessary to describe the law in a clear and concise manner. Although this may sound elusive, once you begin your research you will begin to recognize cases that are critical and those which are subsidiary.

Try not to include cases that say almost the same thing. At a point in your research, certain cases begin to be repeatedly referred to in other cases. This is one of the first clues that your research is beginning to gain focus. Another key turning point in research is when you find a case that refers to a number of other key cases related to your topic. These cases are particularly helpful because they often summarize the law from the other cases. To ensure brevity, legal researchers should refer to the most recent cases and only mention cases separately if they are foundation cases, are critical to the analysis, or have particularly relevant facts.

Deciding on the number of cases to include is always a balancing act. Often novice researchers, in a desire to include all of the research, include cases that are not necessary. One of the most difficult tasks of legal writing is paring down the law so that just enough, but not too much, information is included. It is said that a famous writer once wrote, "I would have written you a shorter letter but I didn't have time."

You can be sure that judges are bombarded with cases in trials, yet their decisions include only those that are important to the outcome of the case.

How Much Information to Include about Each Case

There should be enough said about each case to indicate to the reader why the case is important to your situation. In other words, what does the case add to the analysis?

When including cases, researchers must make decisions about whether to include the following components of each case:

- Name of case and citation;
- How the case fits into the analysis;
- Brief outline of facts;
- Issues; and
- Holding or reasoning.

There is no "right" amount of information to include. The amount and type will be different in each situation, but there are some general patterns. For example, typically a discussion of the law begins with a general overview of the law and moves towards a more detailed description of particularly relevant cases. In other words, the discussion usually moves from the general to the specific, like a funnel:

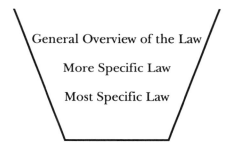

General Overview of the Law

More Specific Law

Most Specific Law

The general overview is a broad statement of the law. It often includes the principles of a few foundation cases and includes only a few facts from each of those cases. In some areas of the law, in which the law is relatively settled, there may be no need to include the facts of a well-known case. Providing the rule of law or the principle resulting from this case may be sufficient.

As researchers begin to go into more detail about particularly relevant cases, the discussion of the cases expands. At this stage, the facts and issues of each case are important for purposes of distinguishing cases and, therefore, should be included in the discussion. At the same time, the writer should try to link each case to both the prior case and the following case, so that the reader is able to see how the law developed.

Organization

Organization is critical to legal writing and the successful communication of thoughts. Lack of organization is the most frequent cause of miscommunication in legal writing. Organization means putting thoughts in an order that permits ideas to flow smoothly from the beginning of the writing through to the conclusion. The reader should be led from one idea to the next and never stumble over ideas. Keep the following rule in mind: "State where you are going; go there; and then state where you have been."

Always provide introductions to new thoughts and conclusions at the end of these thoughts. It is the writer's responsibility to lead the reader through the discussion.

The order of your discussion will depend on the area of law discussed, the particular set of facts, the audience, and your personal style. There is no single, right way to organize, but here are a few tips.

Discuss Each Legal Issue Separately

The most important organizational tip in legal writing is: discuss each legal issue separately. For each issue there should be a discussion of:

- The law pertaining to that issue;
- How that law applies to the particular facts; and
- A conclusion.

This method of organization is not always as simple as it looks. Most cases include several issues, so one of the more difficult tasks in legal writing is deciding how to divide the issues and where and how often to mention a case. This is discussed further below under The Legal Memorandum heading.

Organize Issues Logically

Dividing the law into separate issues requires deciding how to divide the issues clearly and logically.

Many legal problems have natural divisions. For example, in criminal law, two necessary components to a criminal offence are the *actus rea* and the *mens rea*. Therefore, the first issue may be: Was there a criminal act? And the second issue may be: Was there intent? Researchers should avoid falling into the trap of categorizing legal matters in the same way that legal textbooks do. Textbook writers often divide legal issues into those categories that are easiest to teach. These divisions are not always applicable to real-life situations. Some sense of how to organize legal issues can be elicited from the cases being researched.

Theoretically, there may be a different way to organize the legal issues in every new legal problem. Your task is to search for the one that explains the law to the reader in the clearest fashion.

Select a Specific Order for Statutes and Cases

You must make a decision not only about what cases and statutes to include, but also how you will include them and where. Regardless of how you decide to order the cases and statutes, there must be some logic to the order. It should never be random.

For example, it may be desirable to discuss the statute first and the cases second. It may also be preferable to mention the oldest cases first and work forward, or mention the most recent case first and work backwards. Each decision about organization must be rational. Some logical legal patterns are chronological, historical, or general to specific.

When drafting an outline, some of the questions you might ask yourself are:

- Why did I put the cases in that order?
- Do the cases flow logically from one to the next?
- Why did I put the statute where I did?

Your decisions should be driven not only by the subject matter, but also by the expectations of your readers and the rules of good communication.

Stage 3: Revising

Revising involves ensuring that the content, organization, paragraphs, sentences, words, and style are effective at conveying thoughts and information.

Revision is a long and sometimes tedious process. A significant amount of time should be spent on revision. It is recommended that the original draft be revised up to five times — each time for a different purpose. Revising requires the writer to amend what has already been written and then walk away and come back later for further revisions. The writer must be particularly rigorous at this particular stage and be prepared to seriously edit. The recommended way to revise legal work is in the following order:

1. Content
2. Organization
3. Paragraphs
4. Sentences
5. Words
6. Style
7. Form

A writing checklist is included in Appendix C to this chapter, which summarizes the things to look for when editing and revising.

Content

Revising content primarily involves scaling the work down to that which is relevant. This first edit should focus on the bigger concepts and not on the words. Some questions you might ask yourself are:

- Have I covered all the main legal issues?
- Have I included the key statutes and cases for each issue?
- Did I include any cases that basically say the same thing?
- Is there a reason why each case is included?
- What does each case add?

Organization

Revising organization involves ensuring that the facts, brief answers, issues, analysis, and conclusion are in an order that best conveys and expresses your ideas. You should ask yourself the following questions after you have completed your memorandum to ensure that your organization is appropriate:

- Have I explained my organization to my reader?
- Have I told my reader where I am going?
- Is the organization I have selected easy to follow? Does it flow?
- Is there a reason why I have put these issues in this particular order?

Paragraphs

Revising paragraphs involves ensuring that your thoughts flow logically from paragraph to paragraph. Recall that the main rule of organization is to state where you are going; go there; and state where you have been. In order to do this, the writer must provide the reader with "sign posts." Often, new legal writers do not articulate each of the steps in their analysis because they are so immersed in the subject that they forget that the reader needs to know each step that led to the analysis. To assist the reader, it is a good idea to make use of transitions between paragraphs and to tell the reader in the first sentence of each paragraph what that paragraph will include. Transitions provide the reader with directions. They state where the writer has come from and where the writer is going.

The following are examples of transitions. Select the one you like the best.

Examples of Transitions Between Paragraphs

1. In *Brooks v. Goet* a purchaser of a doll sued a toy manufacturer after her child swallowed one of the doll's eyes.
2. Another case involving liability of a manufacturer was *Brooks v. Goet*. In that case, the purchaser of a doll sued ...
3. Several other cases held toy manufacturers liable for faulty construction of dolls. One of theses cases was *Brooks v. Goet*. In that case ...
4. The issue of liability for faulty toys was considered most recently in the case of *Brooks v. Goet*. That case involved ...

You should ask yourself the following questions to ensure your paragraphs are appropriate:

- Have I provided "sign posts" for the reader?
- Would a lay person who knows nothing about the law be able to pick up my writing and understand it?
- Does the first sentence in each paragraph tell what the paragraph will be about?
- Does the last sentence in each paragraph tell what the next paragraph will likely include?

Sentences

Revising sentences involves eliminating excess words, ensuring sentences are short, and using an active rather than passive voice. Although variation in sentence structure keeps the writing interesting, too much variation can be unsettling to a reader.

Words

Revising words involves selecting words that are clear and understandable to the reader. This means using plain English, avoiding Latin, using gender-neutral language, and avoiding jargon. Correct spelling and punctuation are also very important.

Style and Form

The last edit involves revising the style and form of writing. Revising style involves detecting tones that may emerge in your writing. The most important rule with regard to style is to remain objective. The purpose of a legal memorandum is to provide a summary of the law in an impartial manner. While the tone of a memorandum should be objective, there is another style of legal writing besides the informative — the persuasive style.

To achieve objectivity, it is important to avoid identifying too closely with a particular client's concerns. It is better to try to anticipate the other party's position. Even if required to answer to one party in a dispute, researchers should avoid the compulsion to argue in their favour, or the temptation to make their case sound better than it is. Phrasing a letter or memorandum in terms of an argument can unnecessarily split the law into pros and cons and often does not describe the law as a whole. Students who use an argumentative style tend to find it difficult to come to a final decision because the argument necessarily fragments the law and the discussion.

Generally, it is improper in informative writing to include personal opinions about the law. For example, words such as "promising" or "unfortunately" should be saved for persuasive writing. Your writing, even if friendly, should always have a professional tone. For example, you should not use slang and you should never be flippant.

Form and presentation are also very important. The look of the print and the use of divisions and subheadings should invite the reader to read on.

Format

Most legal writing, including judgments, case briefs, letters to clients, and legal memoranda, tends to follow a particular format. This is not the only way law can be communicated, but this particular format has become an acceptable and commonly used means of discourse in the law.

Many readers of law, such as lawyers and judges, expect legal writing to follow a particular format. The format allows them to read the law much more effectively because they know ahead of time where the information they are looking for will be located in the text. It is therefore important to recognize the format when reading and writing about the law.

Other types of writing follow their own particular formats as well. For example, newspaper articles tend to follow a pyramid format: providing the most important information in the first paragraph and expanding on this information in sequential paragraphs. The pyramid format allows readers to move quickly through newspapers selecting the information needed. Newspaper readers have come to expect this type of format and can become frustrated if the format is not followed.

The format used most frequently in legal writing is called FILAC (Facts, Issues, Law, Application, and Conclusion). You will note that the FILAC format of writing is similar to the five-step process recommended for researching the law. In legal writing, however, it looks like this:

> **F**acts — State the legally relevant facts
> **I**ssues — State the legal issues
> **L**aw — Describe the law (cases and statutes)
> **A**pplication — Describe how the law applies to the facts
> **C**onclusion — Conclude and state the likely outcome

There are several benefits to dividing the discussion into these five components. First, the reader can quickly select what to read. Second, the reader can see the separation between the law and the application of the law. This is important because the description of the law is totally objective. The application of the law, on the other hand, necessarily includes the opinions of the writer, since it is an estimation of how a judge will apply the law to a particular circumstance. If the reader does not agree with the application, he or she can still benefit from the objective description of the law and attempt an alternative application.

FILAC is not the only format of legal discourse. Legal writers should understand why it is an effective format and strive to improve it by adding their own particular style and creative touches.

The Legal Memorandum

A legal memorandum is a written document that expresses the results of legal research. It is a summary of the law and the application of the law as it applies to a particular situation. It is used as a basis for advice to a client. Although clients rarely see legal memoranda, the memoranda are used to assist lawyers throughout the entire life of the file. Decisions such as whether to proceed, settle, or abandon a claim will be made on the basis of the information and analysis provided in the memorandum. Based on a memorandum, lawyers will often write letters to clients providing opinions about the merits of a case and the likelihood of success.

Before describing how best to put a legal memorandum together, imagine the following situation:

Situation

You are a judge. The two lawyers in the case before you have provided you with about 60 cases and one statute, which they suggest is the law pertaining to the case before you. You have heard the witnesses in the case and have a good idea of the facts involved. Your task is now to write a decision. This means you must restate the facts as you see them, summarize the law as you read it, and tell the parties how the law applies in this particular case. You must then come up with a decision that makes some sense and is clear and concise. How will you do this?

A judge's job is very similar to a legal researcher's, except that, instead of coming to a decision, researchers predict the likely outcome of the case. A legal memorandum, if properly written, will look very similar to a well-written judgment. Although each judge has a particular style, readers can quickly detect which judgments are easiest to follow and get to the point quickly. The same qualities you appreciate as a reader of cases should be incorporated into your own legal writing.

Format of a Legal Memorandum

There is no required format for a legal memorandum. Since memoranda are usually law office documents, the format will usually be dictated by the particular law firm or legal department. The format recommended here is one used in a number of law firms. It is designed to communicate the law in the most useful way for a busy lawyer. Researchers, however, should remain flexible with the format and be as creative as a particular situation may require. The recommended format is as follows:

1. Facts
2. Issues
3. Brief answers
4. Analysis (law and application)
5. Conclusion

You will note that this format follows both the research process and the common discourse in law, which was described earlier. Each component is discussed below.

Facts

The facts in a legal memorandum are the legally relevant facts of the problem presented. A recital of the facts in a legal memorandum should look much like those facts found in judgments. Although the way in which facts can be articulated is unlimited, the goal is to include only relevant facts. This is discussed in more detail in Chapter 2.

Often a first attempt at summarizing the facts is incomplete. As researchers become more familiar with the law pertaining to their case, they begin to recognize the importance of the facts that have been taken into consideration in other cases. Therefore, the facts should be reviewed periodically as research progresses. Any necessary assumptions should also be stated.

Issues

The issues are the legal questions to be answered. Proper drafting of issues enables a reader to know exactly where the writer is headed. Drafting issues is discussed in more detail in Chapter 3.

Drafting issues is not a one-time task. Ideally, the issues should be redrafted as the research and writing progress. It is always good practice to review the legal issues at the very end of writing to ensure that these are the specific questions that have been answered in the legal memorandum.

Some tips when drafting issues are as follows. Legal issues should:

- Be drafted as a single question;
- Include both facts and law;
- Use the actual names or roles of the parties in the issue (*e.g.*, not "plaintiff" or "defendant"); and
- Be divided into sub-issues where possible.

Brief Answers

The brief answers in the memorandum are the likely outcome of the case supported by reasoning. A sample brief answer is as follows:

> It is likely there is no contract between Mr. Job and Type Company because there was no consideration flowing from Mr. Job when Type Company forwarded merchandise that was not included under the original contract.

It is advisable to use words such as "likely" or "probably" in the brief answers since there is rarely a situation where the outcome of a case is guaranteed. It is also good practice not to include references to specific statutes or cases in the brief answer unless they are critical to the outcome of a case.

Analysis

The analysis part of the memorandum is the bulk of the memorandum. It includes an analysis of the law and a determination of how the law applies to the facts.

Organization is critical to the analysis. As indicated above, it is important to keep each legal issue separate. It is also important to keep the description of the law separate from a description of how the law applies to the facts. For each issue state the relevant law first (*i.e.*, cases and statutes), synthesize this law into a paragraph or two, and then apply this law to your particular facts. This is discussed in more detail in Chapter 10.

Any discussion of policy should appear at the end of the analysis.

Conclusion

The conclusion in a legal memorandum summarizes the information contained in the memorandum. It essentially gathers all of the conclusions reached under each of the issues into one or two concise paragraphs. It is important not to include any new information in the conclusion. Nothing in the conclusion should surprise the reader, since it is simply a brief restatement of what has already been said. Often a reader will only read the issues, the brief answer, and the conclusion of a memorandum. Therefore, the conclusion should include the likely outcome of the case and the reasoning.

It is rare to include case names in the conclusion unless they are very important to the analysis. Mention of policy for the first time in the conclusion should be avoided.

The Opinion Letter

An opinion letter is a letter to a client advising about the state of the law and how it applies to a situation.

Opinion letters are usually written on the basis of legal memoranda and include the same components as the legal memorandum: the facts, the law, the application of the law to the facts, and a conclusion. However, the format is much more flexible. The ultimate aim is to answer the client's question.

Both the format and the language used should enhance understanding. If the law does not support the client's position, this should be made clear and alternatives should be briefly considered. To test the clarity and conciseness of a letter it is a good idea to ask a layperson to provide feedback. A layperson should be able to understand what you have written.

The suggested format of an opinion letter is as follows:

Part 1: Introduce yourself (if necessary) and define your task. State where you are going and what you are going to say. Sometimes it is good to state the conclusion right up front.

Part 2: Introduce the subject at hand generally and give a simple overview of the relevant area of law. Then describe the law in more detail by focusing on the specific wording of statutes or the factors that the courts have taken into consideration in determining past cases. You may want to refer to a specific case if it is very similar to your client's situation.

Part 3: Apply the law to the client's situation and describe the likely outcome of the case if it were to go to trial.

Part 4: Conclude and describe the next steps to be taken.

Self Test

The answers to these questions are found at the end of the book in the "Answers to Self Tests" section.

1. Name a few basic rules of good writing.
2. List the three stages in the legal writing process.
3. Name the four steps involved in planning.
4. What are five parts of a legal memorandum?
5. In what order should you revise your writing?
6. What is the form of a typical opinion letter?

Appendix A: Sample Memorandum of Law

The following memorandum of law was prepared by a first-year law student. It is only an example and should be critiqued by students.

To: M.F. Fitzgerald
From: Michael Lee
Re: Ravi and May — Liability of Partners
Date: November 24, 2000

Statement of Facts

Ravi, May, and Jan formed the law partnership of "JMR Legal Services" to provide traditional legal and mediation services. Their partnership agreement stated that all profits from the law practice were to be shared and the firm's name and facilities were only to be used for activities related to the law practice.

In building their practice, Ravi and May regularly referred clients requiring mediation work to Jan. However, Jan eventually decided that since her mediation work was separate from the traditional law practice she would keep the profits generated from this work. Consequently, she started "Jan's Mediation Services" (JMS), set up her own bookkeeping, banking, and advertising, and met her mediation clients at home. Although Jan tried to keep the two areas of her practice separate, she occasionally asked the secretary at JMR to type correspondence relating to her mediation work. It is assumed that the secretary did not use JMR letterhead.

Viewing the mediation services as integral to the firm's practice, Ravi and May wrote a protest letter to Jan stating that the mediation profits should be shared. However, before this dispute was resolved, Jan was charged with theft for misappropriating $30,000 from the Regal Bank, which had retained Jan to provide mediation services. During the mediation process, Jan had held the money in a trust account under the JMS name. Since Jan had no assets, the bank sued Ravi and May as partners in JMR. It is assumed that there was no previous relationship between Regal Bank and JMR and that the bank did not know that Jan was a lawyer.

Issues

The main issue of whether Ravi and May are liable for Jan's misappropriation of funds may be divided into two issues: (1) Was Jan's provision of mediation services to Regal Bank and subsequent misappropriation of funds within the ordinary course of the business of the firm? (2) Was Jan acting within the scope of her apparent authority when she provided mediation services to Regal Bank and misappropriated the funds?

Brief Answer

Under the *Partnership Act* of B.C., a partner is liable for the wrongful act of another partner if he or she was acting in the ordinary course of the firm's business, or within the scope of his or her apparent authority. Case law identifies the following factors as acting in the ordinary course of business where: (1) there is no agreement excluding the activity from the firm's business; (2) the firm's staff and facilities are used; and (3) the profits from the activity are shared. Acting in the scope of apparent authority can be defined as when: (1) a partner uses the firm's name and its facilities to hold himself or herself out as acting with the approval of the other partners; and (2) a client is under the impression that the individual is acting within his or her authority as a partner in the firm. Most of these factors were not present in this case, so it is unlikely that Jan could be viewed as having acted either in the ordinary course of the firm's business, or within the scope of her apparent authority. Consequently, Ravi and May likely will not be found liable.

Analysis

Issue 1: Ordinary Course of the Firm's Business

The Law

The applicable statute law is s. 12 of the *Partnership Act*[1] *of B.C. which states*:

> Where by any wrongful act or omission of any partner acting in the ordinary course of the business of the firm, or with the authority of his co-partners, loss or injury is caused to any person not being a partner in the firm, or any penalty is incurred, the firm is liable for that loss, injury or penalty to the same extent as the partner so acting or omitting to act.

In *Patchett v. Oliver*,[2] the Supreme Court of B.C. applied the *Partnership Act* to find Oliver's law partner liable for Oliver's wrongful

---

[1] *Partnership Act*, R.S.B.C. 1979, c. 312.
[2] [1977] 5 W.W.R. 299 (B.C.S.C.).

acts, because he was acting within the ordinary course of the business of the firm and within the scope of his apparent authority. From the case it may be inferred that the important factors in making this determination were Oliver's acting as a solicitor and using the firm's bookkeeper and accounts to carry out his wrongful acts.

In *Public Trustee v. Mortimer* ("*Mortimer*"),[3] the Ontario High Court of Justice applied the *Partnership Act* of Ontario, which is similar in language to the B.C. Act. The defendant, Mortimer, a solicitor in a law firm, acted as an executor and trustee of an estate. Using the staff and facilities of his law firm to administer the estate, Mortimer stole money from the estate. The court found the defendant partners liable for Mortimer's wrongful acts because he was acting within the ordinary course of the firm's business. To reach this decision, the court outlined several *indicia* as possible ways to separate a partner's activities as an executor of an estate from the ordinary course of the firm's business [p. 413]:

> There would probably be an agreement between the partners to that effect, and one might expect to find that the partner would not charge the estate on an account issued in the firm's name, would personally keep any fees and compensation paid, rather than treat them as revenues of the firm, would keep the funds of the estate in an account separate from his firm's trust account, and would keep a set of accounting records from the estate separate from those of his firm. If he wanted to be careful to make it clear that his work as an executor was not part of the firm's business, he would not use the firm letterhead when writing as an executor.[4]

None of these *indicia* were met by Mortimer and his firm. In addition, Mortimer used a junior solicitor and the firm's management company for the typing and bookkeeping work on the estate. The executor's fees were also directed into the firm's revenues. Consequently, the court concluded that Mortimer's activities as an executor were within the ordinary course of the business of the firm.

In *Tomiyama v. Riley* ("*Tomiyama*"),[5] the defendant, Riley, asked his client, Mrs. Tomiyama, for a personal loan in exchange for a mortgage on three residential lots owned by Riley. He asked her to make separate diskharges of the mortgage, then sold the lots, but failed to repay her. The Supreme Court of B.C., in applying the *Partnership Act* of B.C., found that Riley's firm was liable for Riley's wrongful act, because he was acting within the ordinary course of the business of the firm. This finding was based on Riley's use of his secretary, the firm's facilities, and his position as a partner in the firm to carry out these transactions. For example, the court cites that Riley applied for the releases of the mortgage as a member of the firm and used his firm's business address.

---

[3]   (1985), 16 D.L.R. (4th) 404 (Ont. H.C.).
[4]   *Ibid.*, at 43.
[5]   [1978] B.C.J. No. 1942 (B.C.S.C.).

In not separating his activities from the firm, the court inferred that
these releases were secured in the ordinary course of the business of the
firm.

In *Korz v. St. Pierre et al.* ("*Korz*"),[6] Korz, a solicitor in a law firm,
entered into a business agreement with two clients to form a company
and serve as its directors. He did not contribute his share of the
financing, nor did he help his two clients settle the debts when the
company went bankrupt. The Ontario Court of Appeal, applying the
Partnership Act of Ontario, found Korz's partner liable for Korz's
wrongful acts because he was acting in the ordinary course of the
business of the firm. This finding was based on Korz acting as the
solicitor to the company and, by extension, the directors, and on his long
record of solicitor work for both clients prior to the company's
formation. In addition, all meetings of the company's directors were held
in Korz's law offices.

Synthesis

From these cases, the factors defining when a partner is acting in the
ordinary course of business of a law firm are where: (1) there is no
agreement excluding the activity from the firm's business; (2) the firm's
staff (including lawyers, secretaries, and bookkeepers), facilities (including accounts and offices), and name (including letterhead) are used; and
(3) the profits from the activity are shared.

Application of Law to Our Situation

These factors must now be applied to determine whether Jan's
activities were in the ordinary course of the business of the firm. As in
Mortimer, there was no agreement excluding mediation work from the
firm's business. Rather, the partners had an understanding, reaffirmed
in Ravi and May's protest letter, that the practice was to include
mediation work.

However, Jan separated her mediation activities from the business of
the firm. Meeting several of the key *indicia* laid out in *Mortimer*, Jan kept
separate accounting records and bank accounts and did not share the
profits from her mediation work. Although Jan occasionally used the
firm's secretary for correspondence related to her mediation activities,
this use of the firm's staff was minor compared to Mortimer's use. Jan
did not use a junior solicitor of the firm or employees of the firm's
management company for bookkeeping. In addition, unlike the *Korz*
case, Jan did not use the offices of the firm to conduct meetings with
clients regarding mediation services. Jan also did not conduct her

---

6   (1988), 43 D.L.R. (4th) 528 (Ont. C.A.); leave to appeal refused (1988), 62 O.R. (2d) ix
     (S.C.C.).

mediation activities under the firm's name, as opposed to the *Tomiyama* case. As a result, it is unlikely that her activities would be found as having taken place within the ordinary course of the business of the firm.

Issue 2: Apparent Authority

The Law

The applicable statute law is s. 13(*a*) of the *Partnership Act* of B.C. which states:

> where one partner acting within the scope of his apparent authority receives money or property of a third person and misapplies it ... the firm is to make good the loss.

In *Mortimer*, the Ontario High Court of Justice, in considering the claim of the managing partner that Mortimer's activities were not in the course of the firm's business, also reviewed the use of apparent authority. Despite the managing partner's claim, Mortimer was allowed to use the facilities of the firm to carry out his activities as an executor. The court held that the firm: "by permitting Mortimer to use the stationery, accounts, staff and other facilities of the firm in connection with his activities as executor and trustee, had vested Mortimer with apparent authority to receive the money or property of the estate which he subsequently misapplied."[7] In this way, through his use of the firm's accounts, letterhead, and staff, Mortimer's activities appeared to be authorized by the partners in his firm.

In *Tomiyama*, the Supreme Court of B.C. applied the decision from the *Mortimer* case regarding apparent authority to suggest that Riley's use of the "trappings of the firm" to carry out his fraud was analogous to Mortimer's activities. The court found that Tomiyama was under the impression that Riley was acting within his authority as a senior partner in the firm. This impression was in part based on her long history of dealings with Riley in a solicitor-client relationship. Tomiyama was also under this impression because Riley carried out these activities using the firm's facilities and staff, such as his secretary. The court summed up Riley's use of his apparent authority: "[w]ithout the aid of his secretary and the trappings of the firm Riley could not have accomplished fraud upon her in the manner that he did. Theoretically perhaps he could have perfected the fraud personally and outside the scope of his firm, but he did not."[8] In this way, Riley by using the firm's name and facilities took advantage of his apparent authority.

---

[7] *Supra* note 3 at 414.

[8] *Supra* note 5 at 5.

Synthesis

From case law, the factors defining acting within the scope of apparent authority are: (1) when a partner uses the firm's name and its facilities to hold himself or herself out as acting with the authority of the other partners; and (2) when the client is under the impression that the individual is acting within his or her authority as a partner in the firm.

Application of Law to Our Situation

These factors must now be applied to determine whether Jan was acting within the scope of her apparent authority. Jan had the authority of her partners to carry out her mediation work, because of the partners' understanding that their practice was to include mediation work. She also did not sever her partnership with JMR. In addition, like the *Mortimer* case, her partners permitted her to use the firm's facilities to carry out her mediation work.

However, in forming JMS, Jan separated her activities from the firm and did not use her authority as a partner in JMR. Unlike both *Mortimer* and *Tomiyama*, Jan did not use the facilities of the firm to give the appearance that her activities were authorized by her partners. In using her own promotional materials and facilities, Jan carried out her mediation activities under a separate business name — unlike Riley, who acted as a partner of his firm. Consequently, it is unlikely that Jan will be found to have been acting within the scope of her apparent authority.

Conclusion

It is likely that Ravi and May will not be held liable for Jan's misappropriation of funds from the Regal Bank because Jan was not "acting in the ordinary course of the business" of the firm and not likely acting within the scope of her apparent authority. She had effectively separated her mediation work from the firm's practice. She did not use the firm's facilities or her position as a partner in the firm to give the impression to the bank that she was acting with the authority of her partners. In short, the action against Ravi and May is likely to fail. A recurrent policy theme in case law is holding partners responsible for their partners' wrongful acts where there is a sharing of profits. Should this policy consideration be given more weight, the argument in Ravi and May's favour would not be weakened because Jan kept her mediation work profits separate from those of JMR.

Appendix B: Sample Opinion Letter

The following is a sample opinion letter written by a first-year law student. It is only an example and should be critiqued by students.

November 14, 2000

Ravi and May
JMR Legal Services
Victoria, B.C.

Dear Ravi and May:

Re: Liability in Jan's Misappropriation of Funds

I have been assigned your case by Ms. Fitzgerald, and am responding regarding your potential liability in Jan's misappropriation of funds from the Regal Bank. Ms. Fitzgerald gave me the facts of your case and, based on this information, the following letter outlines the issues, case law, and application of the law to your situation.

Under the *Partnership Act* of B.C., you would be liable for Jan's wrongful acts if she was either acting in the ordinary course of the business of the firm, or within the scope of her apparent authority.

The factors used by the courts to define acting in the ordinary course of the firm's business are: (1) there is no agreement excluding the activity from the firm's business; (2) the firm's staff and facilities are used; and (3) the profits from the activity are shared. The factors defining acting in the scope of apparent authority are: (1) a partner uses the firm's name and its facilities to hold himself or herself out as acting with the authority of the other partners; and (2) a client is under the impression that the partner is acting within his or her authority as a partner of the firm.

In applying these factors to your case, it is likely that, although there was an understanding that the firm's practice included mediation work, Jan effectively separated her mediation activities from the law practice. She informed JMR, made arrangements for separate bookkeeping, banking, and advertising, and kept the profits separate from JMR. Although Jan may have had your authority to do mediation work as part of the firm's practice, she did not use the firm's staff, facilities, or name to make it appear as though her activities were authorized by you, her two partners. Rather, Jan used her own facilities and conducted her mediation activities under her own company name.

Therefore, it is likely that the court will find that Jan was neither acting in the ordinary course of the firm's business, nor acting within the scope of her apparent authority. In our opinion, it is unlikely that a court would find you liable for Jan's wrongful act.

Should you wish to discuss this opinion further, please contact me.

Yours sincerely,

Student

Appendix C: Legal Writing Checklist

The following checklist summarizes many of the tips provided in Chapter 10. It can be used as a guide for legal writing or as a checklist on completion of your writing to ensure that you have written in an accurate and concise manner.

Content

❑ The purpose is clearly stated.

❑ All relevant facts are identified and necessary assumptions are stated.

❑ The main issues and sub-issues are identified and worded as questions.

❑ The probable outcome is briefly summarized.

❑ The law is synthesized and applied to the facts.

❑ The analysis reconciles or distinguishes conflicting case law.

❑ The conclusion briefly summarizes the law and states the probable outcome.

❑ The text is consistent with the stated purpose.

Organization

❑ The information is presented in logical order.

❑ Topics are discussed in a logical sequence.

❑ There are smooth transitions.

❑ The conclusion summarizes the discussion.

❑ Issues are discussed separately.

Paragraphs

- ❏ Each paragraph explains no more than one main idea.

- ❏ The main idea is stated at the beginning of the paragraph.

- ❏ Each paragraph flows logically from one to the next.

Sentences

- ❏ Sentences are short, accurate, and clear.

- ❏ Each sentence is connected to the surrounding sentences.

- ❏ Complex sentence structure is avoided.

- ❏ Active rather than passive voice is used.

- ❏ Sentence structure varies.

Words

- ❏ Language is concise (*e.g.*, no repetition or wordiness).

- ❏ Language is precise, and concrete words are used (*e.g.*, no ambiguity or vagueness).

- ❏ Language is consistent and objective.

- ❏ Language and tone are suitable for the purpose of writing and the reader.

- ❏ Legal jargon is avoided.

- ❏ Legal terms are explained where necessary.

- ❏ Gender-neutral language is used.

- ❏ Correct punctuation and spelling is used.

Style and Form

❏ Headings and definitions are used effectively.

❏ A suitable format is adopted.

This Legal Writing Checklist is adapted from: Modern Writing for Lawyers (Continuing Legal Education Society of British Columbia, 1992) Writing Guide, p. 3. Used and adapted with permission.

American Legal Research Basics 12

Canadian researchers often look to the United States for legal sources. The recent "internationalization" of legal subjects and the opening of international doors to free trade has led Canadian researchers to look more and more to American sources.

Canadians usually turn to American legal sources in areas where the law in Canada has not yet evolved, such as product liability law and environmental law. Canadian courts considering issues that are new to Canadian law often rely fairly heavily on other jurisdictions' jurisprudence. Although foreign law is not binding on Canadian courts, it is persuasive. For example, the Supreme Court of Canada often refers to cases from other jurisdictions, since many cases that are elevated to the Supreme Court of Canada involve legal issues that require clarification in Canadian law.

With the recent introduction of electronic research tools, access to American law has become easier. This is discussed further below.

This chapter provides a simple, step-by-step approach to American legal sources. It describes how American law is made, where it is found, and the research aids used to assist in locating and interpreting the law. However, this chapter is merely an introduction to those American sources that are most useful to Canadian researchers.

Learning Objectives

At the end of this chapter you will be able to:

- Explain two key differences between Canadian and American law-making powers
- Name two American commercial legal publishers
- Name the highest level court in the United States and two reports in which these cases are published
- Name two American legal encyclopedias
- Describe what "Shepardizing" means
- Name two American computerized legal research information systems

American versus Canadian Legal Research

Researching American law is very similar to researching Canadian law primarily because both countries' legal systems have their roots in the common law. Both the United States and Canada have systems of law that are developed through decisions of the courts, which form the common law. This common law is heavily supplemented by statutory and administrative law.

The process of American legal research is the same as described previously in this book: analyzing the facts of a problem, determining the legal issues, finding the law, analyzing the law, and communicating the results. As in Canada, when locating the law, the researcher usually refers first to secondary sources and then to primary sources.

Although there are 50 states and hundreds of courts in the United States, American legal research is fairly straightforward. This is primarily because publishers of American sources have developed comprehensive indexing systems that link both primary and secondary sources.

West Group, the most comprehensive publisher of legal materials in the United States, has greatly simplified American legal research by developing a comprehensive "Key Number System" or subject index to case law. Under this system, key numbers are assigned to points of law. Headnotes are written for each case and classified to the Key Number System. Therefore, once a researcher finds the key numbers relating to the subject being researched, case law can be located through this number.

Another exceptional American research tool is *Shepard's Citation*. It is an exhaustive citation system for American cases, which enables researchers to easily update cases. American lawyers often refer to the task of updating cases as "Shepardizing." *Shepard's Citation* is now available online and is much more current than the paper version.

Canadian researchers should be cautious, however, because the terminology used in the United States is different from that used in Canada. This is one reason why it is best to begin research in the secondary sources, such as encyclopedias or textbooks. The three main texts used for locating U.S. law are:

Berring and Edinger, *Finding the Law*[1]
Jacobstein, Mersky, and Dunn, *Fundamentals of Legal Research*[2]
Kunz, *The Process of Legal Research*[3]

---

[1] R.C. Berring & E.A. Edinger, *Finding the Law*, 11th ed. (St. Paul, Minn.: West Group, 1999).

[2] J.M. Jacobstein, R.M. Mersky & D.J. Dunn, *Fundamentals of Legal Research*, 7th ed. (New York: Foundation Press, 1998).

[3] C.L. Kunz, *The Process of Legal Research: Successful Strategies*, 3rd ed. (Boston: Little, Brown, 1992).

Statutes

How Statutes Are Made and Reported

The division of law-making powers between American federal and state governments is similar to that in Canada, with two key differences: in the United States criminal law is primarily state law (as opposed to federal law), and residual law-making power goes to the states (as opposed to the federal government).

As in Canada, the federal government legislates such things as patents, copyright, and admiralty law. State governments legislate activities within state borders. The federal government's powers are defined in the Constitution of the United States. All other matters are reserved for the states.

State Laws

Each American state except one has two houses that pass legislation or "session laws" by obtaining the consent of both houses. Statutes are typically published at the end of each session.

Every state has an annotated "code." These codes are similar to Canadian statute citators and include the text of the statutes, as well as amendments and short summaries of cases that interpret the statutes.

Federal Laws

The United States federal legislature, like Canada, has two houses: the House of Representatives and the Senate. The House and the Senate are often jointly referred to as Congress.

Bills can be introduced by either house, and all federal legislation must be passed by both houses and signed by the president. Once signed, statutes are officially published as "slip law" but called public laws. Each session of Congress lasts two years and at the end of each session the slip laws are bound in chronological order and published in the *United States Statutes at Large*. These are the official texts of the statutes. Each sessional set of statutes contains an index for that session. The *Statutes at Large* are difficult to use because the statutes are published chronologically.

An aid which is published by the United States government to assist researchers in using the *Statutes at Large* is the *United States Code* (U.S.C.) or "codification." In this code, all public statutes and revisions are collated into subject titles. Similar to Canadian statute consolidations, American federal statutes are consolidated in a new edition every six years.

Because Congressional sessions last two years and the government does not formally publish statutes until the end of each session or later, commercial publishers publish federal and state statutes as soon as they are available. Commercial publishers' versions of statutes or codes are published more quickly and tend to be easier to use than the government publications. These commercial publications include annotations or summaries of cases, which interpret the statutes and provide references to other secondary legal materials. Each code has a table of contents, similar to Canadian tables of public statutes, which include a list of all statutes by title. These tables refer researchers to the specific statute and list amendments. Amendments to the statutes are typically included in "pocket parts" or pamphlet supplements to the publication.

The following schedule indicates the main publishers of statutes and the titles of their publications.

Publisher	Title of Statute Publications
U.S. Government	*United States Statutes at Large*
U.S. Government	*United States Code* (U.S.C.)
West Group	*United States Code Annotated* (U.S.C.A.)
LEXIS	*United States Code Service* (U.S.C.S.)

West Group: United States Code Annotated

West Group publishes the *United States Code Annotated* (U.S.C.A.), which is based on the official text of United States statutes, as well as amendments and references to cases that have considered statutes. This set of statutes includes a paperback general index, which is published annually. This code is available on CD-ROM and online.

LEXIS: United States Code Service

LEXIS publishes the *United States Code Service* (U.S.C.S.), which is very similar to the annotated code published by West Group. It includes amendments, refers to cases judicially considered, and includes a general index, which is published annually, to assist researchers. This code is also available on CD-ROM and online.

How to Find Statutes

Most American statutory research begins with a review of secondary materials to determine whether the legislation to be located is federal or state legislation. Secondary sources, such as law reviews, often provide citations to statutes that lead researchers to the next step: annotated federal or state codes.

Since most jurisdictions have annotated codes with comprehensive subject indexes, once the controlling jurisdiction is determined researchers can usually look up a topic in the relevant state's code index and be directed to a statute. These annotated codes greatly assist research by including the history of statutes, cases that considered statutes, secondary sources that discuss statutes, and references to West's Key Number System (discussed below).

Case Law

In order to research American case law, it is necessary to understand the American court system and how cases are reported. Researchers should also be familiar with American research aids, including encyclopedias and digests.

The American Court System

The biggest difference between the Canadian and American court systems is that in the United States there are two distinct court systems. The federal courts deal with matters within federal jurisdiction, and the state courts deal with matters not reserved for federal courts, all the way up to final appeal.

Federal courts can hear cases involving state law in some situations, such as when the litigants are from different states or when a case involves both federal and state law. Most federal courts are not bound by state court decisions unless the federal court is interpreting state law. But state courts may be bound by federal court decisions. The United States Supreme Court, which is a federal court, will not deal with matters arising from state law except in situations involving constitutional issues.

Within each of these two systems, there are three levels of court: trial, appeal, and a court of final appeal.

Federal Courts

Trial Courts: District Courts

Each state has at least one federal judicial district each with a trial level federal court. These are called United States District Courts. There are 89 district courts in the 50 states. The federal system also includes specialized trial courts such as the Court of International Trade and the United States Tax Court.

Appeal Courts: Circuit Courts

The federal appeal courts are called the Federal Courts of Appeal, or Circuit Courts. Not every state has a federal appeal court; there is one federal court of appeal for each of 13 geographically defined "circuits." Eleven of these circuits are numbered consecutively (*e.g.*, 1st circuit, 2nd circuit). The two remaining circuits are the District of Columbia and the federal circuit.

Court of Final Appeal

The court of final appeal in the federal court system is the United States Supreme Court. This court hears cases from the federal circuit, district courts, and the state courts of final appeal (or last resort), if a constitutional or federal question is at issue. The United States Supreme Court has discretionary jurisdiction and selects the 150 to 170 cases they decide each year from over 5,000 petitions.

State Courts

Most states have three levels of courts, although a few have only two. Each state refers to its courts by a variety of names. For example, a highest level court may be called a Court of Appeal or a Supreme Court. The trial level courts are sometimes called Circuit or District Courts, which should not be confused with the federal circuit or district courts.

Appeals from the highest state courts may be heard by the highest federal court, the United States Supreme Court, at the court's discretion.

Illustration 12.1
American Court System

Typical Court Structure	Federal Example	State Example
Final Appellate Court	U.S. Supreme Court	Wisconsin Supreme Court
↑	↑	↑
Intermediate Appellate Court	U.S. Court of Appeals (for the 9th Circuit)	Wisconsin Court of Appeals
↑	↑	↑
Trial Court	U.S. District Court (for the Central District of California)	Dane County Circuit Court

Reproduced with permission from C.G. Wren & J.R. Wren, The Legal Research Manual (2d ed). Copyright 1986 by the authors. Further reproduction prohibited without written permission of the authors, c/o the publisher (Legal Education Publishing, a division of the State Bar of Wisconsin, P.O. Box 7158, Madison, WI 53707-7158; tel. 800/957-4670; e-mail info@legaledpub.com).

Illustration 12.1: This is an example of the structure of the American federal and state court system.

How Cases Are Reported

Decisions of state and federal courts are published both in official and unofficial reports. Trial Court decisions are rarely published in the United States because they are not considered to be precedent-setting. Many courts have rules about what cases should be published. Each year an estimated 60,000 court decisions are not published in regular print sources but may be found by way of computer search.

Although many states publish official reports of cases, virtually all cases are also reported in what is a called the *National Reporter System*, which is published by West Group. This comprehensive reporter system includes cases from all federal courts and all 50 states (divided into geographic regions). It is available through WESTLAW (an online service provider).

West publishes most cases only once, but other publishers may publish these cases elsewhere. West's *National Reporter System* publishes two state court reports, seven original court reports, and three federal court reports.

State Court Reports	
California Reporter (Cal.Rep.)	*New York Supplement* (N.Y.S.)
California	New York

Regional Court Reports			
Atlantic Reporter (A., A.2d.)	*North Eastern Reporter* (N.E., N.E.2d)	*North Western Reporter* (N.W., N.W.2d)	*South Eastern Reporter* (S.E., S.E.2d)
Connecticut Delaware Maine Maryland New Hampshire New Jersey Pennsylvania Rhode Island Vermont Dist. of Columbia	Illinois Indiana Massachusetts New York Ohio	Iowa Michigan Minnesota Nebraska North Dakota South Dakota Wisconsin	Georgia North Carolina South Carolina Virginia West Virginia
Pacific Reporter (P., P.2d)		*Southern Reporter* (So., So.2d)	*South Western Reporter* (S.W., S.W.2d)
Alaska Arizona California Colorado Hawaii Idaho Kansas Montana	Nevada New Mexico Oklahoma Oregon Utah Washington Wyoming	Alabama Florida Louisiana Mississippi	Arkansas Kentucky Missouri Tennessee Texas

Federal Court Reports		
Supreme Court Reporter (S.Ct., Sup. Ct.)	*Federal Reporter* (F., Fed.)	*Federal Supplement* (F. Supp.)
Includes all decisions of the United States Supreme Court	Includes reported federal appeal court decisions	Includes federal district court decisions and other special court decisions

Canadian researchers are usually most interested in the United States Supreme Court and Courts of Appeal decisions. Rarely will research extend to the state courts.

The *United States Supreme Court Reports* (abbreviated U.S.) is the official version of the United States Supreme Court decisions and is published by the government of the United States. The two unofficial versions of Supreme Court decisions are *West's Supreme Court Reporter* (above) and the *United States Supreme Court Reports, Lawyers' Edition* (abbreviated L.Ed. and L.Ed. 2d) published by LEXIS. U.S. Reports are also available free on the Internet. For a useful start into federal materials on the Internet go to the University of Washington website at http://lib.law.washington.edu/research/research.html.

The following schedule describes the three levels of federal courts and describes where these federal cases are published.

The Publication of U.S. Federal Cases			
	Official Report: Gov't Printing Office	*Unofficial 1: Lawyers Coop. Publishing*	*Unofficial 2: West Publishing*
Supreme Court	*United States Reports*	*U.S. Supreme Court Reports, Lawyers' Ed.* (L.Ed. & L.Ed. 2d)	*Supreme Court Reporter* (S.Ct. or Sup. Ct.)
Courts of Appeal	N/A	N/A	Federal Reporter (3 series)
District Courts	N/A	N/A	Federal Supplement

The Form of the National Reporter System

There are a few differences in the way in which Canadian and American cases are reported. The headnotes in the *National Reporter System* contain very different information from Canadian headnotes. For example, cases reported in the *National Reporter System* include a prefatory statement or summary of the case and a headnote with assigned key numbers. The prefatory statement or synopsis is similar to a Canadian headnote and is very useful. *National Reporter* headnotes summarize the legal issues raised, and are also very useful.

Illustration 12.2
Sample Headnote

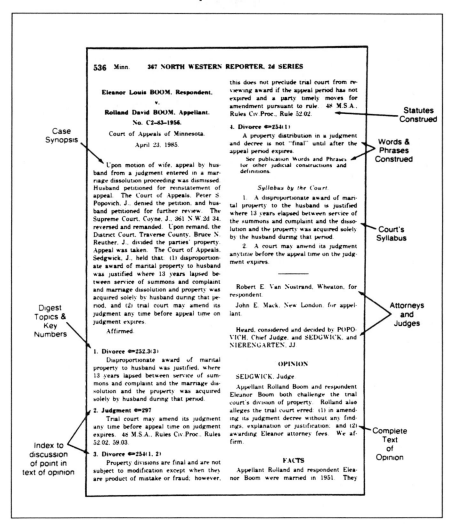

North Western Reporter, 2d. Series, in West's Law Finder, 1991. Reprinted with the permission of West Publishing Company.

Illustration 12.2: This is a sample headnote from a case published in West's *National Reporter System.*

American Law Reports Annotated

Another case reporter is the *American Law Reports Annotated* (ALR). It includes cases of interest and essays on specific points of law (called annotations). Because the coverage of the ALR is not as comprehensive as the *National Reporter System*, it is not usually used to locate cases. However, researchers often refer to the annotations since they summarize and discuss very specific areas of law. These annotations are a very useful starting point for legal research but they primarily refer to case law. The ALR consists of six series: ALR 1st through 5th and ALR Fed.

Through the use of computers, Canadian lawyers can access most American law through WESTLAW and LEXIS, the two main online service providers in the United States. As well, cases can be found on the Internet through government and courthouse websites.

How to Find American Cases

The most important tool for American research is perhaps West's *Key Number System*. It is a classification system which helps researchers find legal sources by subject.

West's Key Number System

In Canada, the editors of the *Canadian Encyclopedic Digest* (Carswell) divided the law of Canada into about 170 subject areas. In the United States, West Group set up an indexing system which divides the law of the United States into the following seven main divisions:

- Persons
- Property
- Contracts
- Torts
- Crimes
- Remedies
- Government

These topics are further divided into approximately 400 subjects and individual points of law identified by West's editors and written in headnotes are assigned a numerical classification or "key number."

The key system is very useful because cases with the same key number and presumably the same subject can be located quickly — even those from other jurisdictions. It is particularly useful when conducting searches on WESTLAW.

Finding Cases By Subject

As stated at the beginning of this chapter, locating American case law is very similar to locating Canadian case law. The first step usually involves referring to secondary sources such as encyclopedias, texts, or law reviews. This is necessary to help researchers understand the areas of law, learn new terminology, and the like.

The main difference between Canadian and American case law research is that American researchers often refer to case digests, whereas Canadian researchers do not. This is primarily because the American system of indexing case digests is very well designed and easy to use. Canadian case digests are primarily found in the *Canadian Abridgment*, which, although comprehensive, can be difficult to use.

It is important to recall the difference between encyclopedias and digests when searching American sources. Digests are summaries of points of law in cases, whereas encyclopedias are explanations of the law. Digests are organized by subject matter and key number so that researchers can locate a number of points of law with citations to cases pertaining to a particular subject area.

Encyclopedias and Other Secondary Sources

As with Canadian research, American legal research often begins in the legal encyclopedias. There are two American encyclopedias that cover American case law, much in the same way as the *Canadian Encyclopedic Digest* covers Canadian law. The first is called the *Corpus Juris Secundum* and the second is *American Jurisprudence* (2d). Some researchers also use the *American Law Reports Annotated* (described above) if they know the general subject area of the search.

Corpus Juris Secundum

The *Corpus Juris Secundum* (CJS) is the more comprehensive of the two encyclopedias, consisting of over 150 volumes summarizing American case law. It is published by West Group. This set claims to summarize all American decisions since 1658. Like the *Canadian Encyclopedic Digest*, the CJS divides all of the law of the United States into a number of subject areas and allocates one chapter to each subject title. For example, there are chapters on negligence and on divorce.

The main research tool to the CJS is the three-volume index called The *General Index*. It is a comprehensive subject index and refers the researcher to the title and section number in the encyclopedia. The *General Index* is published annually.

If a researcher knows about the subject area generally, he or she could also go directly to the volume of the encyclopedia that contains the relevant subject title. Each title has a *Title Index* at the end, which is very useful.

Like the *Canadian Encyclopedic Digest*, the CJS has extensive footnotes. These footnotes are arranged by state and refer researchers to reported cases in the *National Reporter System*, the *American Law Reports Annotated*, and other reporters.

American Jurisprudence (2d)

The *American Jurisprudence* (2d) (Am. Jur. (2d)) is another encyclopedia of American law. It is published by LEXIS. Like the CJS, it consists of many volumes summarizing American law. This set consists of about 83 volumes plus a five-volume index. It, like CJS, divides the law into a number of subject areas. *American Jurisprudence* (2d) summarizes the law and references only selected published decisions, as opposed to all decisions. This is often beneficial, since researchers do not always need to know every single case on a specific subject.

Like CJS, *American Jurisprudence* (2d) refers to cases found in the *National Reporter System*, the ALR, and other court reports in its footnotes. It has a general index and individual subject title indexes, which are good starting points for most research. *American Jurisprudence* (2d) tends to focus more on statutes and Supreme Court decisions than CJS does. The encyclopedias provide researchers with a summary of the law and citations primarily to cases. One of the most valuable pieces of information to take from an encyclopedia is the West key number. Because points of law from cases are indexed according to West key number, this number may assist you later.

Digests

Digests are a particularly useful secondary source for American research. Digests of American cases are created by West Group. West publishes digests for:

- Each state (except Delaware, Nevada, and Utah);
- All federal courts;
- Some of the West Regional Reporters; and
- All reported state and federal decisions (in the *American Digest System*).

The most comprehensive set of digests and the one most useful for Canadian researchers is the *American Digest System*. The volumes in this system are called the *Decennial Digests*. This series indexes or digests points of law from most appellate court decisions (federal and state) since 1897. The following is a list of the volumes in the *American Digest System*.

The American Digest System

Century Edition	1658–1896
First Decennial Edition	1897–1906
Second Decennial Edition	1907–1916
Third Decennial Digest	1917–1926
Fourth Decennial Digest	1927–1936
Fifth Decennial Digest	1937–1946
Sixth Decennial Digest	1947–1956
Seventh Decennial Digest	1957–1966
Eighth Decennial Digest	1967–1976
Ninth Decennial Digest, Part I	1977–1981
Ninth Decennial Digest, Part II	1982–1986
Tenth Decennial Digest, Part I	1987–1991
Tenth Decennial Digest, Part II	1991–1996
General Digest	current

Several times a year, West digests cases from all federal and state jurisdictions in the *General Digest*. Every five years, these *General Digest*s are cumulated into a new *Decennial Digest*. Because the *Decennial Digest*s are now published every five years, the title can be misleading.

The master index is called a *Descriptive Word Index*. This index is the primary access tool for the digests. This *Index* lists words that indicate either facts or legal concepts and links these to West's Key Number Classification System.

Illustration 12.3
Descriptive Word Index

ASSUMPTION OF RISKS—Cont'd
Automobiles—
    Burden of proof in action for injuries from operation or use of highways. **Autos 242(8)**
    Evidence of assumption of risk by occupant. **Autos 244(56)**
    Guest passenger, host's failure to look. **Autos 224(1)**
Hockey spectator. **Theaters 6**
Hunting party members. **Weap 18(1)**
Motorboat race, voluntary entry. **Collision 15**
Operation of doctrine. **Neglig 105**
Passengers. **Carr 323**
Patron of amusement device. **Theaters 6**

Swimming pool patron. **Theaters 6**
Tenant. **Land & Ten 168(1)**
Tenant's injuries, evidence. **Land & Ten 169(6)**
Tractor operator voluntarily assisting truck driver. **Autos 202**
Willful and wanton conduct of defendant. **Neglig 100**
Workmen's compensation—
    Abrogation or modification of defense. **Work Comp 772, 2110**
    Failure of employee to elect to come under act. **Work Comp 2114**
Wrestling match spectator injured by referee thrown from ring. **Theaters 6**

ASSUMPTION OF SKILL
Master as chargeable with knowledge

From West's Law Finder, 1991. Reprinted with the permission of West Publishing Company.

In addition to the *Decennial Digest*, there are also regional, state, and court digests. These digests are helpful for researching cases from particular jurisdictions or a particular court, allowing you to avoid the laborious task of going through all the cases in the *Decennial Digest*. For example, four of West's regional reporters have their own digests, such as the *Atlantic Digest* and the *North Western Digest*. United States Supreme Court cases are indexed in the *United States Supreme Court Digest*.

It is not a good idea to start research in the digests — they are best used to find further relevant cases after preliminary research has been completed.

Using the Digest

All digests in the West system are organized by topic and key number. The digests are grouped in volumes according to topic. Under each topic and key number the digested points of law are grouped alphabetically by state, with federal cases listed first. A topic and key number can be obtained in the following two ways.

Method 1: Corpus Juris Secundum or Headnote of Cases

As mentioned, both legal encyclopedias include references to West's key numbers. Key numbers are also found in the headnotes of cases reported in West's *National Reporter System*.

Method 2: Descriptive Word Index

A key number can also be found by using the *Descriptive Word Index* of any of the digests. As mentioned above, this index contains descriptive words and refers the researcher to a topic and a key number. This is a very good way to locate relevant topics. A researcher should look in each of the *Decennial Digests* under the same key number for all of the relevant digests.

Other Secondary Sources

Other secondary sources can be helpful for specific types of legal research.

The *American Jurisprudence Proof of Facts* 2d (*Proof of Facts*) is an encyclopedia used primarily by litigators. It explains how facts can be proved at trial. It consists of several volumes and is organized alphabetically by subject area.

Restatements are like textbooks in that they summarize or restate the law in a text format. They are designed to be authoritative statements of the common law or a codification of the common law and are published by the American Law Institute. There are restatements in several areas of law including agency, conflict of laws, contracts, foreign relations law, judgments, property, restitution, securities, torts, and trusts. Because restatements are organized by subject, researchers must know the subject they are looking for in order to use them. However, each restatement has an index to aid in use of the contents.

Finding Cases by Case Name

The easiest and quickest way to locate the citation to an American case if you have only the case name is by way of an electronic search either of public access Internet sites or through an online service provider such as WESTLAW or LEXIS. Another method is using the table of cases in any West digest.

The digests include tables of cases, which list all cases digested, their citation, and West's topic and key numbers. These tables are helpful for finding the citation of a case or finding key numbers.

**Illustration 12.4
Table of Cases**

TABLE OF CASES

ABBREVIATIONS

aff	affirmed	mod	modified
am	amended	rearg	reargument
cert	certiorari	reh	rehearing
den	denied	rev	reversed
dism	dismissed	transf	transferred
foll	followed	vac	vacated
gr	granted		

References are to Digest Topics and Key Numbers

A

A A Augustus, The (DCNY) 2 FSupp 494—Ship 177(1), 184.
Aab v. French, MoApp, 279 SW 435 —Banks 63½, 135; Bills & N 357; Pigs 6, 30(1, 2), 58(3).
Aab v. Schonlau 184 Minn 225, 238 N W 480, 77 ALR 423—Lim of Act 28 (1), 49(1).
Aachen & Munich Fire Ins Co v. Guaranty Trust Co of New York, DCNY, 24 F2d 465, rev, CCA, 27 F 2d 674, cert den Guaranty Trust Co of New York v. Aachen & Munich Fire Ins Co, 278 US 648, 49 SCt 83, 73 LEd 560—Banks 188½; Courts 99(1); Lim of Act 46(2); War 12.

Aachen & Munich Fire Ins Co v. Sutherland 56 AppDC 314, 13 F2d 286—War 12.
A A Davis & Co v. Young 154 Okl 144, 7 P2d 459—Work Comp 2005, 2030.
A A Gambill & Co v. First Nat Bank 222 Ala 490, 132 So 725—Ven & Pur 214(1), 275.
Aagard v. Juab County 75 Utah 6, 281 P 728—Counties 213.
Aaker v. Quissell 60 SD 513, 244 NW 889—Autos 150, 244(2); Neglig 93 (1); Trial 251(1, 8), 260(8).

From West's Law Finder, 1991. Reprinted with the permission of West Publishing Company.

How to Update American Cases

The final step in locating American cases is to check cases to be sure they are still good law. This can be done by using *Shepard's Citations* or by using the electronic citators available through WESTLAW or LEXIS.

Shepard's Citations is a comprehensive citator service which updates cases and statutes. Because of the importance of this service to American legal research, the updating of cases is often called "Shepardizing." Shepard's citators for cases include the following information in the following order:

1. Parallel citation in parentheses;
2. Case history (under "History of Case");

3. Citations of cases from the same jurisdiction that considered the case (under "Treatment of Case");
4. Citations of cases from other American jurisdictions that considered the case (federal first, then in alphabetical state groupings);
5. Citations to journal articles;
6. Citations to ALR and L.Ed. annotations; and
7. Citations to other annotations.

Just as there are regional case reporters and regional case digests, there are also regional *Shepards*. For example, cases from the Atlantic Region can be found in *West's Atlantic Reporter*. Digests of these cases' points of law can be found in *Atlantic Reporters Digests*; these cases are updated in *Shepard's Atlantic Reporters*.

Each set of *Shepard's Citations* consists of a few bound volumes, a cumulative annual supplement, and further supplements. Research in *Shepard's*, therefore, involves looking at the bound volume and at least two supplements.

How to Use Shepard's Citations

Although at first glance *Shepard's Citations* looks overwhelming to a Canadian researcher because of the strange numbers and letters, it is extremely useful. The steps in using *Shepard's Citations* are as follows:

Step 1: Find the Citation of the Case to Be Updated. Shepard's citators refer to cases by volume and page number of the case in the *National Reporter System*, as opposed to the name of the case. There-fore, the first step in using *Shepard's* is to find the citation of the case you wish to update and make note of the relevant volume and page number.

Illustration 12.5
National Reporter System — Sample Case

910 Mo.	666 SOUTH WESTERN REPORTER, 2d SERIES	
dated in the sense that the amount due is to be measured and determined by the standard of reasonable value of the services *** If the defendant is liable for the reasonable value of services he is under a legal duty to liquidate the sum due and interest should be allowed from the time he should have paid *** This principle has been applied often in actions for the reasonable value of work and labor.		F.W.H., Petitioner-Respondent v. R.J.H., Respondent-Appellant,
		No. 46701.
		Missouri Court of Appeals, Eastern District, Division One.
[12-14] Defendant contends that the plaintiff is precluded from recovering interest because he failed to request it in his petition. Plaintiff did request the court to grant "such other relief as may be proper under the premises." In *Hayes v. Allen*, 482 S.W.2d 85, 89 (Mo.App.1972), this court stated that such a similar prayer authorizes ...		Feb. 7, 1984.
		Rehearing Denied March 8, 1984.
		Action was instituted for dissolution of marriage. The Circuit Court, St. Louis County, Robert Lee Campbell, J., entered a ...

Southwestern Reporter, 2d. Series. Reprinted with permission of West Publishing Company.

Illustration 12.5: This example shows that the case of *F.W.H. v. R.J.H* is found in the *South Western Reporter*, 2nd series, in volume 666, at page 910.

Step 2: Find the *Shepard's Citator* for the particular reporter series.
Since there are numerous Shepard's citators, the next step is to locate
the volume that covers the relevant region (*e.g.*, *Shepard's Atlantic Reporter
Citations*).

**Step 3: Find the entry for the volume and page of the case you are
updating and review the entries.** Within each volume (bound and
supplements), information is grouped according to the volume and page
number of the original case. Therefore, once the proper volume is
located, you can search by page number (citation) of your case.

The entries under each case are grouped into two types: history of the
case and treatment of the case. Following this are references to the ALRs
and other secondary sources.

Illustration 12.6
Shepard's Abbreviations

History of Case

a	(affirmed)	Same case affirmed on appeal.
cc	(connected case)	Different case from case cited but arising out of same subject matter or intimately connected therewith.
D	(dismissed)	Appeal from same case dismissed.
m	(modified)	Same case modified on appeal.
r	(reversed)	Same case reversed on appeal.
s	(same case)	Same case as case cited.
S	(superseded)	Substitution for former opinion.
v	(vacated)	Same case vacated.
US	cert den	Certiorari denied by U. S. Supreme Court.
US	cert dis	Certiorari dismissed by U. S. Supreme Court.
US	reh den	Rehearing denied by U. S. Supreme Court.
US	reh dis	Rehearing dismissed by U. S. Supreme Court.
*	(writ of error)	Writ of error adjudicated.

Treatment of Case

c	(criticized)	Soundness of decision or reasoning in cited case criticized for reasons given.
d	(distinguished)	Case at bar different either in law or fact from case cited for reasons given.
e	(explained)	Statement of import of decision in cited case. Not merely a restatement of the facts.
f	(followed)	Cited as controlling.
h	(harmonized)	Apparent inconsistency explained and shown not to exist.
j	(dissenting opinion)	Citation in dissenting opinion.
L	(limited)	Refusal to extend decision of cited case beyond precise issues involved.
o	(overruled)	Ruling in cited case expressly overruled.
p	(parallel)	Citing case substantially alike or on all fours with cited case in its law or facts.
q	(questioned)	Soundness of decision or reasoning in cited case questioned.

Illustration 12.6: This is a sample showing the terminology and symbols used in *Shepard's Citations*.

To update your case, you should carefully check any case that has symbols indicating a reference to the history of your case (*e.g.*, a = affirmed; r = reversed; D = dismissed). In addition, you may also want to look at cases that criticized (c), distinguished (d), limited (L), or overruled (o) the case being Shepardized.

Shepard's citators are also available in WESTLAW and LEXIS.

Periodicals

There are hundreds of legal periodicals published in the United States. The most frequently used periodical indexes are the *Index to Legal Periodicals*, the *Current Index to Legal Periodicals*, and the *Legal Resources Index*. All three index articles contained in major legal journals from the United States, Canada, the United Kingdom, Ireland, Australia, and New Zealand, and other legal periodicals. These indexes are available on CD-ROM and on either LEXIS or WESTLAW.

Self Test

The answers to these questions are found in the back of the book in the "Answers to Self Tests" section.

1. What are the two key differences between Canadian and American law-making powers?
2. What are the names of two American commercial legal publishers?
3. What is the highest court level in the United States?
4. Name two case reporters in which the United States Supreme Court decisions are published.
5. What is the *National Reporter System*?
6. What is West's Key Number System?
7. What does "Shepardizing" mean?

Appendix A: Summary: How to Find and Update American Cases

Step 1: Locating Cases by Title

If you know the title of the case look in:

- Tables of Cases in the various West digests (e.g., *Decennial Digest*);
- WESTLAW or LEXIS; and
- *Shepard's Citations*.

Step 2: Locating Cases by Subject

If you do not know the title of the case, you will need to do a search by subject area. This requires analyzing the situation, eliciting descriptive words, and going to encyclopedias, textbooks, digests, or law reviews as follows:

- Encyclopedias (CJS or Am. Jur. 2d.) or textbooks. Look in the indexes of the encyclopedias or textbooks to gain a general understanding of the law. Citations to relevant cases, statutes, West key numbers, and ALRs are provided in these sources.
- *American Digest System*. Refer to the *Descriptive Word Index* in the *Decennial Digests* to locate the subject classification relating to your situation (*e.g.*, topic and key number). Find the digest volumes that cover that topic and key number, and you will find points of law from digested cases.

Step 3: Updating Cases

Once you have located relevant cases, they must be updated or "shepardized." This means you must ensure that they have not been overturned by a higher court (*i.e.*, history) or considered adversely in another case (*i.e.*, judicial treatment). Cases can also be updated most quickly through online service provider such as WESTLAW or LEXIS.

Cases can also be updated through *Shepard's* as follows:

1. Find the citation of the case you wish to update in the *National Reporter System* and note the reporter name, the volume, and the page number;
2. Find the volume of *Shepard's* for that specific reporter *(e.g., Atlantic Reporter*, 2d series); and
3. In that volume, look up the volume number and page number of the original case and review the information underneath.

A Research Plan

13

Legal research should be done as quickly and inexpensively as possible. This means that researchers should devise ways to conduct research effectively and efficiently.

There are many ways to conduct legal research. There is no single, best way. The research method used will depend on a number of factors, such as the nature of the problem and the researcher's abilities. Because legal research is as much an art as a science, the ability to research the law will develop with practise. As lawyers become more familiar with legal sources and more proficient with the research process, they learn shortcuts. Solving legal problems effectively and efficiently, however, should be done in a systematic way. Irrespective of ability and knowledge, researchers are continually confronted with new problems and issues. In these situations, it is advisable to go "back to the basics" of research.

Regardless of the approach taken, each researcher must have a plan prior to beginning the research process. Before heading to the library, researchers should plan where they intend to look and what they hope to find. This gives some direction to the research and keeps researchers from sinking in the myriad of books. Developing a plan eliminates wasting effort in looking at irrelevant sources and provides a checklist indicating steps taken.

This chapter explains what a research plan is, describes some practical considerations, lists some research tips, and describes how to develop a research plan. Appended to this chapter is a sample research plan.

Learning Objectives

At the end of this chapter you will be able to:

- Explain what a research plan is
- Explain why a research plan is necessary
- Name a few practical considerations in preparing a research plan
- Describe the basic parts of a research plan
- Describe some advantages to note-taking

What Is a Research Plan?

A research plan is a written plan describing how research will be conducted. As soon as a problem is presented, a researcher will begin to think about possible ways to solve the problem. Some problems will be easy to solve and require little research, whereas others will require extensive research. Each legal problem requires a unique research plan.

At a minimum, a research plan should consist of the five broad steps of the legal research process: **F**actual analysis, **I**ssue determination, finding the **L**aw, **A**nalyzing the law, and **C**ommunicating the law (FILAC). However, the details of how each of these steps are accomplished will vary from problem to problem.

Although there is no magic plan, all research plans should indicate, in as specific terms as possible, where the researcher intends to go and what she or he hopes to find. A research plan evolves as the research progresses and, thus, should remain fairly flexible.

Practical Considerations

When devising a research plan, some practical factors must be taken into consideration.

Before diving into the research process, researchers must know something about the persons requesting the research (audience), why the research is necessary (purpose), and limitations on the research, such as time and cost. All legal research depends on these factors.

The audience and the purpose of the research are very important considerations when defining the ambit of the research. The most typical purpose of research is to advise a client, in preparation for trial or in preparation for negotiation. Although the research process will be similar in either case, the purpose of the research will define exactly how deeply a researcher may delve into a particular area. For example, if the research is being done for a knowledgeable client or a lawyer, the researcher may decide not to include some very basic information on a particular area. However, if the research is being prepared directly for a less sophisticated client, then the researcher may want to include more general or basic information about the particular legal subject.

There will almost always be constraints placed on researchers. Typically, there are time or financial constraints. If, for example, a client is disputing a contract with a value of $100, it would not be practical or proper to spend days researching the issue.

Researchers are also often limited by availability of information. Many libraries do not carry information that could be useful. A researcher must be aware of what information is available and at what cost.

Research Tips

The following are some tips for legal researchers. The first group of tips deals with the legal research process. The second group deals with note-taking, and the third deals with knowing when to stop.

The Legal Research Process

These tips will assist legal researchers during the legal research process.

- *Think through the whole research process.* It is very important to thoroughly think through the entire research process before beginning research. Although this may seem like a tedious task, it will save you time and effort in the long run.

- *Move from broad to specific.* Researchers should almost always move from the broad to the specific when conducting research. This means that research should begin at the general level and move towards research of more specific legal issues. It is important not to get trapped into a narrow category of law early in the research. For example, when perusing indexes for a legal topic, do not consider your search complete if you find one relevant topic. Often legal subjects span a number of legal areas.

- *Try not to jump back and forth between sources.* It is usually not efficient to interrupt your review of one source and immediately go to another source. It is best to use one source completely so that you do not have to go back to it and wonder how far you have read in that particular source. If you feel compelled to jump ahead, make detailed notes about where you are so that you can return to the source without retracing steps.

- *Look for "meaty" quotes.* Often court cases are well-written and include excellent summaries of the law. Therefore, when reading cases, researchers should be on the lookout for "meaty quotes," which can ultimately be included in the final written product. A good habit is to photocopy important quotations. Handwritten quotations leave room for error when transcribed. Photocopies can also be used to proof the final product.

- *Stay flexible.* Perhaps the most important tip is to stay flexible. If you find yourself off on a tangent, be prepared to abandon what you have done and start again. Try not to be narrow in focus, and continually ask yourself whether the route you are taking is the most effective and efficient. Remain open to new ideas as they present themselves.

Note-Taking

Since legal research can often take weeks or months and uncover vast
quantities of information, researchers must be organized and devise
systems to record research steps taken. Some of the suggestions made
below should assist researchers in doing this.

- *Summarize the facts and issues on one page.* It is a good idea to summarize the facts and legal issues on a separate page. This page can
  be carried into the library and referred to as necessary and revised
  as the research progresses.

- *List the key words that you search.* Listing the words or phrases that are
  searched is particularly important because these words are often
  forgotten later. It is helpful to dedicate a specific page for a list of
  descriptive words that could be searched. This way the list can be
  lengthened or shortened. This list is particularly helpful when
  narrowing down the legal issues and later in the research process
  when computer searches are conducted.

- *Devote a separate page to each legal issue.* It is recommended that a
  separate page be devoted to each legal issue. This ensures that the
  legal issues are dealt with separately and thoroughly. If the
  information on legal issues is combined, it is very difficult to
  separate the legal issues later.

- *Record citations as you conduct your research.* It is always a good idea to
  record the full citations of cases, statutes, and secondary sources as
  you are conducting your research. This cannot be over emphasized.
  Many researchers know how frustrating it is to have to search for a
  citation of a source later, when only a scrawl has been recorded.

- *Photocopy statutes.* When referring to statutes it is critical that the
  exact format of the statute be maintained. Therefore it is best to
  photocopy the relevant sections of the statute.

- *Record particular insights.* Often as research progresses, researchers
  are struck by particular insights. It is a good idea to jot down the
  ideas you may have, although they need not be researched at that
  particular moment. These insights often provide the basis for policy
  discussions later in the analysis.

- *Photocopy key cases.* It is recommended that very important cases that
  are referred to repeatedly be photocopied. This is to enable researchers to re-read cases a number of times and highlight the
  important parts. These cases often include citations and summaries
  of other relevant cases.

- *Devote a separate page to a list of sources referred to.* It is a good idea to keep a separate page listing authorities referred to. This will be your bibliography. Sometimes researchers will be asked to produce this list to ensure that the research is complete and that all relevant sources have been canvassed. It is recommended that a specific coloured page be devoted to the bibliography because of the importance of keeping a record of the sources referred to.

- *Date every page.* Often, dating pages of notes serves as a reminder of the series of steps taken. It can also trigger a researcher's memory so that tracks can be retraced if necessary.

Knowing When to Stop

There is no simple way to know when to stop. If you are consistent and thorough, you will begin to see your research coming into focus. The most obvious clue that research is narrowing is when the sources you are referring to refer you back to ones you have already examined. If you are getting no new leads or no new references to new legal sources, the research is nearing completion. When you get the sense that you are repeating steps or that the sources are becoming exhausted, you can stop your research.

Developing a Research Plan

Although a research plan will constantly evolve, the framework of each plan should ideally remain constant. In other words, the five-step process (FILAC) should remain the same, although the steps taken within each of those steps might vary.

In earlier chapters, a number of other steps are recommended within this five-step process. These steps are summarized in a sample research plan and are appended to this chapter.

The step that requires significant advance planning is finding the law in the law library. There are two fundamental steps in finding the law: refer to secondary materials, and then refer to primary sources. The way in which secondary materials and primary sources are found and used will vary. However, each researcher should have an idea about which secondary materials will be reviewed and which primary sources he or she hopes to find in the library.

Self Test

The answers to these questions are found in the back of the book in the "Answers to Self Tests" section.

1. What is a research plan?
2. Why is a research plan necessary?
3. Name a few practical factors to consider when preparing a research plan.
4. Describe the basic parts of a research plan.
5. Describe some advantages to note-taking.

Appendix A: Sample Research Plan

The exact steps taken to research a legal problem depend on a number of factors. The following plan is a guideline consisting of the basic steps in the process of legal research. It should be adjusted to the particular needs of the research and researcher.

Name of Researcher:_____   Date Assigned:_____

Research For: _____   Date Due: _____

Preliminary Step: Identify Audience, Purpose, and Limitations

❑ Determine the purpose of the research, who the research is for, and any limitations on the research, such as time and cost. At this stage, you should estimate how much time should be spent on the total research. A record should be kept of all steps taken.

Step 1: Analyze the Facts

❑ Gather and organize the facts (*e.g.*, identify the parties, events, and possible claims).

❑ Identify the legally relevant facts by reading generally about the law in secondary materials such as textbooks or the *Canadian Encyclopedic Digest*.

❑ Summarize and formulate the relevant facts.

❑ Reformulate the facts later in the research process as the legally relevant facts become clearer.

Step 2: Determine the Legal Issues

❑ Determine applicable areas of law by brainstorming, word association, and/or using the subjects of law courses.

❑ Identify the general legal issues by consulting secondary materials such as the *Canadian Encyclopedic Digest* or textbooks and reading about the law generally. When reading about the law, move from general to specific.

❏ Formulate the specific legal issues by reading about the law in more detail. Articulate the issues as questions of law and fact.

❏ Reformulate the legal issues later in the research process as they become clearer.

Step 3: Find the Law

Refer to Secondary Materials

❏ Locate and read secondary materials to gain an overview of the law.

❏ Record references to specific cases, statutes, and other secondary materials. This includes the following:

- *Canadian Encyclopedic Digest (Western or Ontario version)*: Locate the *Key* volume and look in the indexes for relevant subject areas or titles. Go to the alphabetical volumes and read generally at first. After you have focused your research, record cases and statutes that are referenced. If you have access to an electronic version, scan the table of contents first then read the text.

- *Textbooks*: Look in a computer catalogue to locate textbooks or go to library shelves and browse. Scan the textbook's table of contents or index first. After you have focused your research, go back and record the relevant cases and statutes that are referenced. Some researchers photocopy relevant pages from textbooks for future reference. If you have access to electronic textbooks, scan the table of contents or index before conducting a word search.

- *Legal Periodical Indexes*: Look in a couple of the legal periodical indexes to confirm or narrow your choice of subject area for research. All journal articles include references to statutes and cases. Periodical indexes are available on CD-ROM, through online service providers, and more recently on public access Internet sites, searchable by a word query.

Refer to Primary Sources: Statutes and Cases

Statutes: Find and Update Relevant Statutes

If you know the **title** of the statute, look in any of the following:

❑ electronic collection of statutes such as

  • CD-ROM
  • Online service providers such as *e*Carswell, Quicklaw, or LEXIS
  • Internet on government websites

❑ printed federal or provincial tables of statutes. Statutes are listed alphabetically and direct you to the printed source.

If you are researching by **subject,** you can locate statutes in the following sources:

❑ Secondary materials, such as the *Canadian Encyclopedic Digest*, textbooks, and periodicals (above). Those sources refer to relevant statutes.

❑ Federal or provincial subject indexes of statutes. Search these indexes for descriptive words.

❑ Ensure the statute is effective by determining whether it has a delayed effective date. If there is a commencement clause (*i.e.*, it is brought into effect at a later time), you must determine the effective date of the statute.

❑ Determine whether a statute has been amended by looking in the federal or provincial tables of statutes or tables of legislative changes. Statutes can also be updated unofficially by looking in statute citators, which include not only amendments to the statutes but also cases that have considered statutes.

❑ To further update a statute and its amendments, look in the most recent publications from the various legislatures.

❑ Look for cases that have considered statutes by looking in statute citators.

❑ If necessary, search for regulations pertaining to the relevant statutes.

Cases: Find and Update Relevant Cases

If you know the **title** of a case look in either:

- ❏ Electronic collections of cases:

  - CD-ROM
  - Online service providers such as *e*Carswell, Quicklaw, or LEXIS
  - Internet on court house websites

- ❏ *Canadian Abridgment, Consolidated Table of Cases*, which lists all cases alphabetically and their citations.

If you are researching by **subject**, the most direct way to locate cases is through secondary materials. The following sources could be referenced:

- ❏ *Canadian Encyclopedic Digest*, textbooks, and periodicals (above). Locate and read those cases cited and note other cases that are referred to in those cases.

- ❏ Case digests in the *Canadian Abridgment, Case Law Digests*. Look at the *Key & Research Guide* and figure out how your subject is categorized in the "key classification scheme." Find the volumes of case digests on that subject. Read the digests and record the citations of relevant cases.

Check if the relevant cases have been appealed or considered in other cases (i.e., note up the cases) through the following sources:

- ❏ Electronic citators through online service providers such as *e*Carswell, Quicklaw, or LEXIS

- ❏ *Canadian Abridgment, Consolidated Table of Cases*, which lists all cases alphabetically and the history of each case.

- ❏ *Canadian Abridgment, Canadian Case Citations*, which lists all cases alphabetically, the history of each case, and judicial consideration of each case.

Step 4: Analyze the Law

- ❏ Read the secondary materials and primary sources.

- ❏ Analyze and brief cases and identify whether the cases are similar, binding, or persuasive.

❑ Analyze the relevant statutes.

❑ Synthesize the law (distinguish and analogize cases and merge with statute law).

❑ Apply the law to the legal problem.

Step 5: Communicate the Law

❑ Consider options or ways to communicate the results of the research (*e.g.*, legal memorandum or opinion letter).

❑ Plan your writing:

1. Identify the reader;
2. Determine the purpose;
3. Gather, analyze, and organize the information; and
4. Prepare an outline.

❑ Write a first draft focusing on content and organization.

❑ Revise your writing in the following order:

1. Content;
2. Organization;
3. Paragraphs;
4. Sentences;
5. Words; and
6. Style and form.

Answers to Self Tests

Chapter 1

1. The five steps of legal research are:

    *   Facts — Analyze the facts
    *   Issues — Determine the legal issues
    *   Law — Find the relevant law
    *   Analysis — Analyze the law and apply it to the facts
    *   Communication — Communicate the results of the research

2. Factual analysis involves gathering the facts and determining which facts are legally relevant.
3. Issue determination involves determining what the legal issues or questions are.
4. Legal analysis involves three tasks: reading the law, synthesizing the law, and applying the law to the facts.

Chapter 2

1. The three steps of factual analysis are:

    *   Gather and organize the facts
    *   Identify the legally relevant facts
    *   Formulate the facts

2. PEC stands for Parties, Events and Claims.

Chapter 3

1. The three steps in determining legal issues are:

    Step 1: Determine applicable area of law
    Step 2: Identify the general legal issues
    Step 3: Formulate the specific legal issues

2. Some methods that might assist you in thinking about applicable areas of law are: first-year law courses; brainstorming or word association; or using library sources such as the *Canadian Encyclopedic Digest* and textbooks.
3. Library sources that might assist in determining legal issues are the *Canadian Encyclopedic Digest*, textbooks, and legal periodical indexes.
4. Correctly formulated legal issues include both facts and law.
5. Yes, legal issues should be drafted as questions.

Chapter 4

1. The two types of law are legislation or government-made law, and case law or judge-made law.
2. The term "common law" originates from the travelling courts in England.
3. Legislation is law made by federal and provincial legislatures and municipalities. It includes statutes, regulations, and municipal by-laws.
4. The law-making process consists of governments making laws (legislative powers), governments enforcing laws (executive powers), and courts interpreting the laws through specific cases (judicial powers).
5. Primary sources are the law. Secondary materials are aids in understanding and locating the law.

Chapter 5

1. Door 1: general materials such as textbooks; door 2: journals and periodical indexes; door 3: legislation; and door 4: cases.
2. Two benefits of using computers are speed and access to unreported cases. Three limitations of using computers are that sometimes databases are not complete; searches can be costly; and the search is only as effective as the researcher.
3. The largest computer service providers in Canada are Quicklaw, which provides Quicklaw; Carswell, which provides *e*Carswell; and Butterworths, which provides LEXIS.
4. The four steps of computer research are:

   - Plan the research;
   - Select a data source;
   - Select a database; and
   - Formulate a word search.

5. A literal search means that a computer will search for the exact words that you have requested.

Chapter 6

1. A textbook can be located by using a library computer catalogue and searching by author, title, or subject.
2. To locate journal articles by subject, look in a periodical index in the subject index or do a word search on CD-ROM.
3. The *Canadian Encyclopedic Digest* is an encyclopedia of all of the law in Canada, arranged by subject.
4. A book of words and phrases includes alphabetical lists of words and phrases that have been considered by the courts.
5. A case digest is a brief summary of a case. These digests are compiled in periodic publications and sorted by subject area.
6. A citator is an annotation of the law. There are case and statute annotators. They include information about whether the law is still current and accurate.

Chapter 7

1. Statutes can be located on the Internet on provincial government websites and university websites.
2. Statutes are located in one area in a law library, sorted by jurisdiction.
3. A table of statutes is an alphabetic listing of statutes. There is usually one for each set of statutes published and they are usually consolidated.
4. Companies that provide access to statutes on their data base include Quicklaw, Carswell, and LEXIS.
5. The most recent amendments to a statute can be found by calling the provincial or federal legislative library.
6. A statute citator is a book that lists statutes, their revisions, and any cases that have considered these statutes.

Chapter 8

1. A regulation is law that is created through delegated authority. It is also called subordinate legislation and is made pursuant to a statute.
2. Regulations become law by order-in-council.

3. A consolidation of regulations contains all of the regulations in place up to a particular point in time. It consolidates prior regulations so you need not look "behind" a consolidation.
4. A regulation can be found through use of consolidated indexes of regulations either by title of the statute that empowered it or the title of the regulation.
5. A statute will not become effective on royal assent if there is a commencement clause in the statute that delays or makes retroactive its effect.

Chapter 9

1. A case report is a series of books that contain decided cases.
2. A few case reports are: *Supreme Court of Canada Reports* (S.C.R.), *Dominion Law Reports* (D.L.R), and *British Columbia Law Reports* (B.C.L.R.).
3. To locate a case by name, go to the *Canadian Abridgment, Consolidated Table of Cases* or the tables of cases in individual case reports.
4. To locate a case by subject, use the *Canadian Encyclopedic Digest*, a textbook, or the *Canadian Abridgment, Case Digests*.
5. Updating a case means ensuring that the case is "good law." This involves finding its history and any judicial considerations.
6. To update a case you can use the *Canadian Abridgment, Canadian Case Citations*, or individual case report research aids.

Chapter 10

1. The doctrine of precedent means that courts use precedents or prior decisions as examples or authorities to assist in deciding cases. The doctrine of precedent is designed to promote consistency in law and provide a tool to predict the likely outcome of a case.
2. The doctrine of *stare decisis* means "to stand by the decision." This doctrine means that courts must follow prior decisions of certain other courts.
3. The three basic levels of court in Canada are trial, appeal, and court of last resort.
4. The three steps in case analysis are: determining relevance of cases, reading cases, and synthesizing cases.
5. "Synthesizing the law" means merging all the law from the relevant cases and statutes into one general statement of law.
6. The "Golden Rule" of statutory interpretation means that the plain meaning of the words in a statute are to be applied unless it leads to

some absurdity or inconsistency. If so, the statute should be inter-preted to avoid this.

Chapter 11

1. A few rules of good writing are: omit surplus words, use short sen-tences, use the active voice, arrange words with care, and avoid lan-guage quirks.
2. The three stages of the legal writing process are: planning, writing, and revising.
3. The four steps of the planning process are: identify the reader; de-termine the purpose; gather, analyze, and organize the information; and prepare an outline.
4. The parts of a legal memorandum are: facts, issues, brief answer, analysis, and conclusion.
5. Revisions should take place in the following order: (1) content, (2) organization, (3) paragraphs, (4) sentences, (5) words and style, and (6) form.
6. A typical opinion letter has four parts: introduction, description of the law, application of the law to the facts, and conclusion.

Chapter 12

1. The two key differences between Canadian and American law-making powers are: in the United States, criminal law is state law and resid-ual law-making power goes to the states.
2. The names of two American commercial legal publishers are: West Group and LEXIS.
3. The highest court level in the United States is the United States Su-preme Court.
4. Two reporters that publish United States Supreme Court decisions are:

   • *U.S. Supreme Court Reports, Lawyers' Ed.* (LEXIS); and
   • *Supreme Court Reporter* (West Group).

5. The *National Reporter System* is West Group's system of reporting fed-eral and state cases. It consists of hundreds of volumes of cases or-ganized by region and courts.
6. West's Key Number System is the system used by West to index cases and includes digests of points of law in cases.
7. "Shepardizing" means using *Shepard's Citations* to update cases.

Chapter 13

1. A research plan is a written plan of how research will be conducted. Each legal problem requires a unique research plan.
2. A research plan is necessary to give some direction to the research and keep researchers from sinking in the myriad of books. Developing a plan eliminates wasted effort and provides a checklist indicating steps taken.
3. A few practical factors to take into consideration are audience, purpose, cost, and time.
4. The basic parts of a research plan are FILAC: factual analysis, issue determination, finding the law, legal analysis, and communicating the results.
5. The main advantage of note-taking is that it provides a record of steps taken. This enables researchers to interrupt research without losing position and provides a reminder of what has been done to avoid gaps and repetition.

INDEX